Best Wishes,
Irene Vosbikian
2014

Bedros

Irene Vosbikian

For Peter and his father, on whose life this true story was based.

Der Zor is a small province near Aleppo, Syria. In Der Zor there is a mass gravesite where hundreds of thousands of Armenians were buried – some alive – at the culmination of a Turkish 'death march'. One need only scratch the surface of this site to unearth thousands of bones. Peter Vosbikian, and many like him, rose from these bones in defiance of tyranny everywhere.

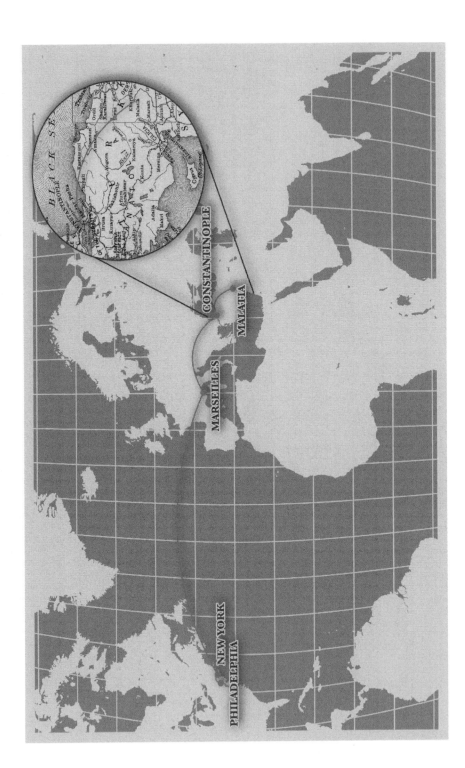

"Who, after all, speaks today of the annihilation of the Armenians?"
-Adolf Hitler, August 22, 1939, in a speech given to his commanders a week before the German invasion of Poland.

PROLOGUE

The room was filled with them—the aspiring salesmen, the hapless hopefuls with their *attaché* cases, crisp, white shirts and pseudo grins. They waited, lined up in a row, their dark business suits casting sharp contrast against the long, red vinyl bench on which they sat. They were all neat and polished and desperate. Some things about them were different. They wore different shades of the same suit; different styles of short, slick hair; different colors of printed ties. Different, but the same. All of them, except for one.

He sat defiantly by himself in a corner, looking amusingly unique. He had on an old gray suit and shoes that were shabby but nevertheless, well polished. His hair was an unruly mass of violent, swept-back waves of salt-and-pepper. His nose was strong and prominent, and thrust itself forward like a monument to his thick-skinned, well-chiseled face. And his eyes—they were unlike most human ones. They danced about in their sockets like ebony marbles in fleshy cups of a bright, translucent liquid. They spun around the dismal room cantankerously and acted like separate, seething entities from the body in which they lived. But the cardinal intrigue of this fascinating man was the sound he was making. He was humming—humming rather loudly, with no inhibition. He had a gravelly sort of voice, which gave his murmurings less the sound of a tune and more the sound of a motor running somewhere deep within him.

He had time. He had come in from Philadelphia the evening before on the Broadway Limited. It had been a luxurious trip, one he could barely afford. But it was an investment that had to be made. Now there was little else to do but sit and wait his turn. He looked out the window at the swirling snowflakes being whipped about by the merciless Chicago wind. He thought about how similarly life had whipped him about, and he smiled proudly that he had made it this far.

It was 1945, and he had turned fifty-three only a few months before, and now half of his life was just beginning. The first half had been more pregnant than two lifetimes for most men. This day, this meeting, was to be only another in a series of crucial turning points. His life's graph had dropped down momentarily from its seesawing over the past half century. He had to make the upswing happen. Today, in a few short minutes with a man named Whitticomb, he would have to make the sale of his life—the sale that would determine his very future.

He wasn't afraid. He never had been. The man in the worn, gray suit hummed a little louder, and the others waiting turned to eye him curiously. He didn't care. He smiled at them in unabashed self-esteem. Then for a moment he closed his eyes. But the moment became a memory, and the magnificent man drifted off to the time when it had all begun...

Chapter 1

MALATIA

The beautiful, young boy squatted, his legs bent awkwardly beneath him, by the damp shore of the bubbly, bright water. The Armenians called it "Babulchdi Chur," the lucid, crystal-like river that slithered through the small village of Malatia. The innocents, like this child, believed Malatia was in a country called Armenia. But, like a hundred other towns inhabited by large numbers of Armenians, Malatia was a possession of the Ottoman Empire, which was Turkey. In the world of political reality, Armenia didn't exist.

The dark, little man tossed his pebbles playfully into the churning stream. The ripples from each tiny splash radiated out, growing larger and more separated from the tiny plunk that had borne them. A mammoth, double-peaked mountain formed a majestic backdrop to the artist's scene. The blue sky was flawless in its presence. But what the sky and river and mountains knew, the precious, young child couldn't foresee. A terror was imminent, a terror that would turn the translucent waters blood red and the air thick with the stench of death.

The year was 1895, and the swarthy child was called Bedros. Bedros Sahag Vartanian. He was three years old, he thought...wasn't sure. They made little of such things. His body was a child's. His face was a man's. It was as though he had always been a man.

Bedros had no desire to go home that day. His mother had been cranky of late. She brooded. She had been giving him tedious chores, chores better reserved for his older brothers. But more than the work, Bedros hated the dismal mood that had overcome his normally pleasant household.

1

His infant eyes detected pain and fear in his parents' faces. The morbid whisperings of his mother and her neighbors made him uncomfortable. Then, when this fanciful child could bear it all no longer, he would run away, fleeing down the long path to the frivolity of his river.

"Bedo!" The harsh voice of his brother Ara shattered his daydreams. "What's the matter?"

He spoke fluent Armenian for his three years, and his precociousness was a source of some envy among his brothers, all of them except Ara. His seven-year-old brother had always been Bedros's favorite. In three years Bedros and Ara had formed an unusual bond the other brothers didn't share.

Khatchadour was twelve and already involved in the wanderings of older boys. Hovsep was a baby, just under a year, and knew little of what went on around him. That he was clothed, however modestly, and had a full stomach—that was all the infant understood. And Garo, strange Garo, the oldest at sixteen, was markedly worn and weary—a man of the world. He had become a stranger to his family, an occasional drop-in guest.

Ara, his younger brother's keeper, was breathless after the mile run from his home to Babulchdi. He was angry with Bedros.

"Mother has been looking all over for you! Why do you disappear like this? Come, we must hurry home right now!"

Bedros frowned at the seriousness in his brother's tone. He didn't like serious things.

"What's wrong, Brother? Why does *Mayrig* worry about me so much? I can take care of myself."

"I don't know for sure, Bedo, but she has a reason. There is danger from the Turks. That is all I know."

Ara gently pushed the wet, curly, black hair off his baby brother's face. He was placid and serious, and at seven he was mature enough to meet his world. Ara was slighter than Bedros, and his complexion was less dark. His smooth, fair face made him appear timid, but inside he was a young bull.

He took his brother's tiny hand and pulled him up impatiently. The two skipped home quickly, while Bedros performed to make his brother laugh. He conjured up stories, deftly displayed acrobatics, and dawdled, creating time-consuming snags in their journey. The two formed a fanciful, double-dancing silhouette against an aging sky and impoverished surroundings that portrayed dismal nothingness.

The home of Sahag and Yughaper Vartanian was a modest one, like most in the village of Malatia. The adobe, one-story dwelling was one large room. The kitchen, bedroom, and living area were not defined but were recognizable by nature of the furnishings alone. In the kitchen were a clay fireplace and a large kettle. The living room held only wooden benches and primitive tables. Slabs of thin wood lay out over earthen floors and covered with natural sheepskins, were their beds. The bathroom was an outhouse located several feet beyond a tiny, fenced-in garden.

All the homes in the Armenian sector had these backyard gardens. From the poorest little patch to acres of lush greenery, the land gave forth and multiplied. In their farming the Armenians of Malatia shared the greatest comradeship. So abundant were the apple orchards, some travelers would remark that when reaching the outskirts of the village the aroma of apples would virtually permeate the air. One always knew when he was close to the town by the arrival of that sweet, wet smell. It was commonplace to see men leaning over their fences, displaying three-foot-long cucumbers and four-pound tomatoes. Such meetings inevitably ended in shouting disagreements over whose prized produce was the best.

Ara and Bedros at last reached the path to their home. They procrastinated, impishly kicking over stones in the dusty sand and pausing to pick wild poppies. Bedros ran into the garden and jostled the cucumber leaves in search of a fresh, new fruit. Finding one, he thrust it hastily into his mouth. He chomped with exaggerated jaw contortions, while his brother pushed him toward the door. In their concern over their mother's disposition, the two boys failed to notice that the normally bustling village was unusually quiet and deserted. Doors commonly flung open in welcome to all were securely shut. Malatia was frightened.

Yughaper Vartanian was waiting. She was a strikingly attractive woman but so tiny that it was often embarrassing to her to stand among other women. She would sometimes jump up on a chair when meeting someone for the first time so as not to startle them with her minute stature. But tiny as her body was, her features were large and strong, incongruously so. She was infinitely proud and courageous, and the lines in her face wrote her life's story.

Yughaper, like her mother before her, was an accomplished healer, the doctor of Malatia. From childhood she had learned the uses of various herbs and roots, all of which she grew in her gardens, and the lush greens flourished. Her mother had taught her how to deliver a baby. She could cure the common cold. She knew mysterious methods of successfully treating wounds and rashes. In Malatia she was a respected woman who had saved the lives of the most common peasants to the father of the Turkish vali himself. She had delivered hundreds of babies of all nationalities.

One of her most cherished plants was an aloe, which she called "The Medicine Plant." She would break off one of its prickly branches and extract from it a clear, alcohol-like serum she used as a healing balm for skin rashes and cuts. She had thought of collecting the serum and somehow selling it. But life was too busy, and feminine ingenuity in business was unheard of at the time.

Lately, though, this seemingly indestructible woman appeared haggard, and her personality had lost some of its spark. She seemed weakened somehow, sad and somber. Those who knew and loved her didn't like this change. The gusto with which she had performed her normal chores was gone. Everything had become tedious and tiresome. She answered calls for her medical assistance begrudgingly or often not at all. It was as though some inner voice told her that all her labors in raising a healthy family and curing the sick were in vain.

Impatiently she glanced out the window for her delinquent sons. Seeing them, she threw open the wooden door and grabbed each by the arm, tugging them into the house.

"Where have you been, Bedros?" she scolded. "I have told you, haven't I, not to wander away from home again! There is trouble, big trouble. We must all stay together at all times until it passes." She pleadingly glanced up to heaven.

Little Bedros hugged his mother heartily about her knees. That was his way when he had been naughty. He would squeeze with all his might, wrapping himself parasitically around her so that she couldn't move. A dimple would appear, one eyebrow would arch high above the other, and a sad tear would run down one cheek.

"I am sorry, *Mayrig.* I am sorry. I was having fun, and I forgot."

It was all he needed to say. Yughaper melted like butter resting in an urn under a hot afternoon sun.

She bent down on tired knees and enveloped her young son. There was something about him—she couldn't admit to the others—something special about Bedros. It was as though all her hopes, her dreams, were in him. Privately she believed this tiny child would one day be her savior. From his birth on Christmas Day and the three years that followed, he had shown vitality and brilliance. By seven months he had toddled around the house. In one year he had spoken not only words but complete, meaningful sentences. He possessed a rare talent, a talent for handling people, reading them, calculating them, making them do his bidding.

"Bedo," she began, barely able to speak for the lump swelling in her throat. She looked haplessly over at Ara, who stood silently by, hoping somehow her explanation would allay his fears as well. "You are so young, so innocent. I don't know how to explain to you. I have seen many bad things in my life. I have a way of knowing when trouble is about to happen. I'm afraid that—" She stopped herself. Did she hope to find solace in the frightened eyes of a child? How would she tell a three-year-old child of death and destruction? How would she tell him that a seemingly gentle gendarme on the street could suddenly turn and cut him down in cold blood? She would not.

"Dearest child, I didn't mean to frighten you. It is just me. I have been very tired, and your father has been very busy making many guns to sell so that we can buy food to eat. I have been feeling sorry for myself, and that is selfish. I know I make you work too hard for one so young. Forgive me, Bedo. I will try to bring back joy to this household. I know—please, God—this little trouble will pass soon."

It was enough. It was a lie, one of many a mother must tell in her lifetime. Satisfied, Bedo darted outside toward the outhouse, and Ara stole quietly away to his bed, nestled in a remote corner of the house. He called out the window to his little brother.

"Hey, Bedo, hurry up out there. You and I will play together and tell stories until dinner."

"What are we having?" the muffled little voice called out from the wooden, outdoor closet.

"Dolma!" Ara answered with glee.

"How do you know?" the little boy persisted.

"Because I can smell it," Ara responded.

"I surely can't smell it out here!" exclaimed the naughty comic.

Ara laughed, and it felt good. Bedo always made him feel good, especially in these days when he often felt so bad.

Soon the two brothers were wrapped together in their tiny bed—whispering, giggling, and wrestling—and then fast asleep.

It was the three youngest sons who spent most of their time in the house. Khatchadour was gone most of the day. He was learning the gunsmith trade from his father and spent a good deal of time at the foundry. Though the foundry was just a few yards from the house, Khatchadour didn't come home during the day, not even for lunch as her husband, Sahag, usually did. At twelve, Khatchadour was a hard worker. He had never been outgoing in any way. He was the silent son, always well behaved. He was also a good student, though he was permitted to leave the foundry only for a day or two of schooling. Soon he would be a talented gunsmith like his father. And even though he lacked something of the fire of Bedros and the sensibility of Ara, Yughaper and Sahag were proud of his goodness. Also lately his skilled hands had been indispensable in helping Sahag keep up with the mounting orders for guns.

During most days Bedros and Ara would play and do their chores while baby Hovsep spent his time toddling around the tiny home, using the wooden floors, benches, and tables for crawling under and climbing over. If he was permitted outdoors at all, it was only within the confines of the family's fenced-in garden. In the warmer weather he would play with the old goat, which gave the Vartanians their milk. His chubby, little legs would continually attempt climbing the wiry animal, and after a few gentle kicks, the forlorn goat would give in to him.

On very hot days, Hovsep and Bedros would play naked in the fountain in the center of the garden. It was actually a tiny pool, which spouted out water fed to it from an underground stream. All the homes in Malatia had these fountains. They were connected to the wells in the garden area and served to refresh livestock or provide laundry and cleaning water. Theirs was an impoverished suburbia.

Caring for Hovsep was laborious for Yughaper. It took hours to make by hand the smelly, brown soap and boil the water for bathing and washing clothes. For this reason diapers were simply out of the question. During waking hours infants relieved themselves wherever they willed. At night for sleeping, a hole was dug in a quiet corner of the house. The hole was filled with very soft, absorbent sand. These were the cribs of old Armenia. Baby Hovsep spent one-third of his day in this tiny, human litter box. Yet he was a contented, well-cared-for child.

Yughaper was thankful that most of her sons stayed within the family. There was only Garo, the brooder, who was never home. Garo spent most of his time in the local Armenian school, which was not common among sixteen year-olds of that time. He had always been bright and eager to learn. Still, clouds of mystery surrounded Garo's every action. He was a stepbrother to the other sons. Yughaper had been married before she met Sahag. The family knew little about Garo's real father, and Yughaper preferred it that way.

It had been said that Garo's real father, Krikor, dabbled in the occult. In time his reputation had gained him a respectful fear from his townsmen. He was a heretic. He despised the priests and the chanting of the congregation in the church. He was reddish in color, bristly, often scowling. They said he could make objects move about the room with merely a thought. They said once in his early years, when Turkish attacks were less expected, he had performed a mystical act.

The Turks had set fire to his home. Krikor and his mother and father were huddled on the floor, surrounded by smoke, waiting to die. The mud and straw walls were slowly caving in on the family. Suddenly the young Krikor went into an eerie trance. He began to rock back and forth, babbling in an unknown tongue. He rose slowly, lifted up his arms and spread them apart in prophet-like form. The walls went back into place; the fire ceased. When they opened the door, the Turks had gone.

Though he wasn't so much the genie his real father was, Garo had gained a somewhat different reputation. He was a rogue. He gambled heavily, drank older men well under the table in sleazy cafés, and had begun a wave of petty thefts. He stole what he could when he could, mostly guns and hardware.

It was also hinted that Garo was the head of a secret resistance to Turkish oppression. That was probably why he stole the kinds of equipment he did. To some of the younger boys, Garo was a Robin Hood-like savior. But Malatia wasn't Sherwood Forest. There was no place to hide in its barren openness. Garo was playing a deadly game with his life, and so far he was winning. For safety Garo had taken to sleeping in various homes. If he came home, it was usually for a meal or some money. He spoke little and left quickly. Yughaper and Garo's stepfather, Sahag, had resigned themselves to this. Perhaps they felt more comfortable and safe in his absence.

The tangy aroma of the simmering dolma began to fill the air in the tiny Vartanian home. Her experienced nose told Yughaper the dish was nearly done. Dolma was one of the few dishes cooked in Armenian homes that were traditionally Turkish. Armenians had created so many delicacies out of talent and plentiful crops that they needed few Turkish foods to adopt as their own. Dolma, like shish kebab and pilaf, was one of them.

Like most Armenian women, Yughaper was precise and dedicated in her cooking. The tiny, meat-and-rice-filled grape leaf rolls had been meticulously lined up, like miniature soldiers, in their pan. Row after row and then up and up in pile after pile, they rested, soon to be drowned in a bubbling broth of tomatoes and lemon juice. The dish simmered in a huge pot over the fireplace. Shortly the dolmas had absorbed all the broth and lay patiently plump, waiting to be devoured.

Yughaper had also made *parag hatz*, thin, round, cracker-like bread that took a full day to prepare. The family loved it. There would be soft, white cheese and sliced fresh vegetables from the garden—cucumbers, tomatoes, bell peppers, and parsley. Yughaper was satisfied that her meal would be delicious, ample, and frugal—the indelible characteristics of Armenian cuisine.

While her two sons slept and Hovsep was toying with an old wooden spoon, Yughaper prepared the table her husband had made by hand. She placed five stone platters, clay cups for water, and then added the flatware. The forks and spoons were pure, hand-wrought silver. This incongruously lavish silverware was one commodity the Vartanian family understandably cherished. It was kept carefully hidden, it was rarely used, and its hiding place changed periodically. Often it was buried in a wooden box under the floorboards or out in the garden.

Yughaper's family had been wealthy landowners in their time. Her father owned a silver mine and employed many Armenians. It was a bustling, productive mine, of which her family was deeply proud. Yughaper tried to control the depression that overcame her each time she looked at the precious silver items and remembered her family's short reign of prosperity. Tears rolled down her cheeks as she held up one spoon, perusing its delicate lines and fine sparkle. She recalled the day their silver domain ended so cruelly.

Her father had been a wise and cautious man. In his rising productivity and profit, he worried about the ever-suspicious Turks, who frowned upon Armenians succeeding in almost any endeavor. His concern was that the *mutessarif*, the Turkish mayor, would come charging in with his band of political bullies and shut him down. Worse, he had continual nightmares that hordes of gendarmes would swoop down on his home and slaughter his family in their beds. He made it a point to give gifts to various Turkish officials whenever he could. Soon the soldiers—*valis, califs*, all of them—knew where to come when they needed a special gift. To pay for such items was, of course, out of the question.

As it happened one day, a Turkish soldier wasn't satisfied with a particular piece of silver Yughaper's father had given him. The diabolical gendarme decided to call attention to the silver mine among the bureaucrats in the area. Abdul Hamid was supreme ruler of the Ottoman Empire at the time and was just beginning to feel secure and ruthless in his power. When his messenger came to the mine to observe its workings, Yughaper's father welcomed him meekly and offered him many pieces of fine silver and even some platinum necklaces he had personally made. His gifts had tremendous effect on the sardonic pasha but not as the miner had hoped.

When Abdul Hamid received the expensive and beautifully crafted gifts, he became infuriated. That mere Armenians should possess a mine of such productivity, that mere Armenians could create giftware of such elegance, was intolerable to him. He was considered mad, even by his Turkish followers. He resented foreign meddling and above all was determined that no nationality other than the Turks should achieve positions of wealth or power in his domain. He immediately summoned a force of soldiers who, in the name of the empire, fired all employees of the mine, confiscated whatever silver had been mined, and destroyed all its equipment. The mine was ordered to be shut down, and any trespassers were threatened with death. The ignorance of Abdul Hamid showed itself not only in his decree but also in the fact that it never occurred to him that the Turks could have taken over the mine and utilized it for the benefit of his empire.

Yughaper collected her thoughts and went on with her dinner preparations. She had chores to do. She would soon find her satisfaction in feeding these hungry bellies. Lamenting over the past wasn't her style. This was the present, and these days might turn into a tragedy far worse than the mere shutting down of a business. There could be no luxury so frivolous as to dote on her own worth. That she was physically needed was fulfillment enough.

Sahag Vartanian returned home with Khatchadour just as the clear Malatia skies were turning from blazing pink to cool purple. They walked together just a few steps when the savory smell of dolma enticed them on. In those ominous days he and Yughaper were especially grateful that the foundry was so close to their home.

Sahag Vartanian was a large man, a little over six feet tall. He was burly and tanned with graying, thick, black hair. Like most Armenian men, he was handsome and virile, and at forty he looked not much over his age. His craft wasn't a physically strenuous one. It required the work of gifted hands and ingenuity, both of which he amply possessed. Only the deep lines in his face, the growing dark shadows under his black, olive eyes, showed the burden with which he lived, the fear that grew like a cancer within him. It had been one of a series of endless days.

The Turkish gendarmes had been ordering more and more guns from the highly skilled gun maker, and now the Armenians were secretly buying them too. These transactions were done as little as possible and always at odd hours or through go-betweens. Many of the guns were ordered especially small so that they could be easily concealed. He had been busier than he would have liked to be, and he didn't like what it all meant.

Yughaper welcomed her husband with a modest hug. It was improper to show affection in the kitchen. She gently ran her finger down his pale cheek. It felt cold, and she shuddered. Teasingly she placed two fingers on either side of his mouth and pulled it upward to form a smile. Her jest had little effect on his somber stare.

She quickly snatched his favorite silver chalice and filled it abundantly with homemade grape wine, made from their vines.

"Sit awhile; tell me what has happened to make you look so ill." She gently pushed him down into a chair by the table as she spoke. "What could be so awful to make such a handsome face turn so sullen?"

Sahag looked over at Khatchadour and gave his wife an annoyed glance. She shouldn't have begun such a conversation in front of the child. Embarrassed at her mistake, she smiled a little girl's smile and called her family together for dinner. Ara and Bedros came instantly.

Seeing that he had hurt her, Sahag took his wife aside. He whispered weakly into her ear.

"Let us enjoy this beautiful meal and settle the children. After dinner I will tell you what, up until now, I have dared not."

They sat without a word and ate quickly. Yughaper held Hovsep on her knee and spoon-fed him. She couldn't eat. Sahag and the boys ate with appreciative gusto.

After dinner, while Yughaper began the difficult task of cleaning up, Sahag and his three sons sat for a while together. Hovsep, his belly well filled with dolma, lulled around on the floor with little energy. Bedros sat at his father's feet silently. His eyes stared up, mesmerized by the massive man who was his father. After dinner was the only time of day Bedros would be seen sitting still. His fullness and the romping of long days always put him in peaceful moods during the night. Sahag enjoyed being able to look at his three-year-old son in this still position. It was a blessed chance for perceiving and appreciating.

Khatchadour kneeled by Sahag with a new gun in his hand. The two discussed the intricacies of the mechanism with great pride. They had made the gun together. It wasn't for sale. Sahag gave Khatchadour a few instructions for finishing touches, and proudly the twelve-year-old walked over to a secluded corner and began diligently working on his masterpiece.

Ara wanted to speak but patiently waited, never intruding. Finally he asked his father questions about the new gun, not understanding many of the answers. He had just begun a two-days-a-week attendance at the Armenian school in Malatia. Excitedly he told his father about his strict teacher and the chaos in the classroom. Ara Vartanian was a hard-working boy. He possessed an inventive mind, which made him indispensable around the house. Most of his days were spent fixing or remaking things for Yughaper. Otherwise he was tending the goat and the crops or chopping wood from one of the few trees near his home. With Hovsep as yet an active infant and Bedros always chattering and running helter-skelter, Ara was a settling, secure child for his parents to have around.

Bedros soon began jostling around on his father's lap. First he was a pony, then a camel, then a baby squirrel nuzzling and tickling the warm, muscular arms of his father. Sahag looked deeply into the hazel, sometimes-brown eyes of his young son. Those eyes! —How they would change from color to color with the vastly changing moods of the tiny man. This one is different, Sahag thought, almost ashamed at his inward favoritism. But Sahag had always felt that way, even from the day Yughaper bravely gave birth to him in the small bed, surrounded by rough sheepskins and pails of boiling water. Perhaps it was written in his eyes, limpid pools—no, more like torrents, sometimes seething, sometimes calm and still like a lake. They were the eyes of a leader.

They reached out, grasped you, pulled you in, and commanded that you do their bidding.

Sahag found himself praying a silent prayer. He grabbed the young boy about the waist and sacrificially lifted him up to the ceiling. Bedros giggled and wiggled at what he thought to be a fine game.

"May this child, Lord, survive all that I dread is to come. May this baby, Bedros Vartanian, carry my name, my family, into a new life, a new world."

And then the giant man, who dared show no weakness, wept, pulling his child close to his bosom so that the little one couldn't see. But Bedros perceived even those things he couldn't see. He sharply ended his wriggling pranks and threw his tiny arms around his father's neck.

"Why do you cry, Poppy? Did I hurt you?"

"Hurt me? You? You are my life. You could never hurt me." Sahag quickly cleared his throat and forced a smile. "Now, my son," he said, gently patting the boy on his behind, "off to bed; it is late."

Bedros obeyed. He never went to bed at first command, but tonight was different, and at three years old, he understood.

Yughaper at last finished with the tedious workings of boiling water, brown soap, and dirty dishes. She sat by the kitchen table and rested. She was almost nine months pregnant, but except for her husband, no one knew. It wasn't considered proper for a woman to draw attention to her pregnancy. Larger, heavier women had no trouble concealing their condition under the massive layers of fabric that fell loosely from their shoulders. But Yughaper, being tiny, took special care to wear very full, soft garments. It seemed that her stomach began protruding from the very moment of conception.

After regaining her strength, she picked up Hovsep, dunked him in fresh, sudsy water, which she had prepared earlier. The baby splashed with glee. Bracing an aching back with her hand, his mother wrestled with him, at last pulling him up into her arms. She wrapped him in a coarse towel. Hovsep cried at the scratchy feeling on his tender baby skin. Finally Yughaper pulled a tiny, homemade nightshirt over his head. She laid the infant in his sandy box bed and crouched next to him, soothing the thin hair on his head. Softly she sang a lullaby.

It didn't take very long before Hovsep slipped a tiny thumb into a tiny mouth and went into a peaceful sleep. Yughaper always knew by the sound of his breathing when he couldn't be awakened. If it was short and light, he was only pretending. But when it was deep and raspy, he was settled in for the night.

One by one the mother counted her sons, covered little bodies bent in embryo-like positions. She wished she could have prolonged this task, one she normally hurried through after the exhaustion of a full day. But the story Sahag had to tell her was something she wasn't anxious to hear. When she came back to the small grouping of tables and chairs, which was their living room, Yughaper found that Sahag had dozed off in his chair. She had taken a little too long with her after-dinner routines. She was sorry now. She knew terror could exhaust one more than the most arduous of physical labors.

Quietly she took her place next to him and thoughtfully perused this strong and gentle man, whom she so loved. *Love* wasn't a common word between husband and wife during these times, but Yughaper had felt it for Sahag from the moment she met him. He had brought her true devotion, the feeling of worth. Unlike her first husband, Krikor, Sahag was a churchgoing, deeply religious man. He was kind and sought only the good in people. He was moral in every aspect of his life.

When she had met Krikor, her first husband, she disliked him instinctively. He was sullen, moody, and frightening to her. Their marriage was arranged out of convenience and family ties, as were most marriages at the time. What was desired by mother and father was faithfully accepted by their children, even the choosing of a mate. So Yughaper married Krikor Gortian without a priest, without a celebration, without love. She was fifteen years old. And without knowing how or why, in nine months she bore him a son.

They named him Antranik. Yughaper remembered how she wrapped him in a goatskin, pretending she carried a pile of hides for marketing, then smuggled the infant into the Armenian church to be baptized. Krikor would have scolded her if he had known. She laughed whimsically at her youthful daring. Then her smile was taken over by a frown, and a look of confusion came over her face. For from the moment he was born, Antranik was a stranger to her. It was as though he wasn't of this world.

In her pervasive wanderings, bits and pieces came back. Even when the child wasn't much older than Hovsep, he appeared lazy to her. Walking never seemed to matter to him. One day Yughaper discovered why the young baby had no need to walk.

He had been lying in his sandy crib, cooing in a strange fashion. He had spotted his favorite toy, a small, stuffed goatskin doll his father had made for him. The doll had a diabolical face painted on it. Yughaper had always felt it looked like Satan. Antranik went into a frenzy showing his mother that he wanted his doll. The memory of what had happened next was still spine tingling to her. She had often thought herself insane, but she knew what she had seen. The infant began to babble to the doll, commanding it in a special tongue. Incredibly the doll began to move swiftly from its place into Antranik's baby hand. It seemed to float on a cushion of air. From that moment on, Yughaper questioned little of what her firstborn did or said. She wanted no explanations and dared not ask for any.

Through the years of his early life, Antranik continued to perform such mystical acts that several doctors and priests asked Yughaper's permission to examine him. She always refused. When Antranik was just over three, Krikor and Yughaper received their second son and named him Garo. Yughaper thrust herself into caring for her second son, who seemed far more normal and much easier to manage. Still Krikor and Antranik held each other closest, often going off together for days, not telling Yughaper a thing about their whereabouts. Slowly she began to alienate herself from the devil's twosome.

Only once she found herself bound to defend Antranik. The child was seven at the time, and Yughaper had sent him to the butcher shop for one pound of lamb meat. Quantity wasn't the point; she had only enough money for that amount. In a half hour she was startled to see her son at the door in tears. Holding onto the young child's ear and nearly twisting it off was the butcher.

"He has stolen meat from me!" shouted the irate businessman.

"How can this be?" Yughaper asked, astounded.

"I sold him one pound as he asked. Then I busied myself in the shop. When I glanced out the window, I saw him looking into the bag, and it seemed much fuller than it should."

"You are crazy," Yughaper insisted, grabbing her son from his hold and embracing him.

"Crazy, *ayo,* so I thought. But I took him back into the store and weighed the bag of meat. It totaled over three pounds!"

"Antranik," she gently begged him, "how do you explain this thing?"

"*Mayrig,*" the young child sobbed, "I did it for you."

"You stole!" she screeched, grabbing him by the back of his neck.

"No, *Mayrig*!" the terrified child insisted. "Not stole! It just happened. I make it happen. I wish it to happen. For you, *Mayrig*, for you!"

With great pain, Yughaper remembered the tormented look on her child's face, the sarcastic snickers of the butcher, who believed it all a lie. She calmed the young boy, gently sent him to his bed for a nap, and then assured the butcher he would be reimbursed for his two pounds of meat. It was months before she was to know without question that Antranik hadn't lied to her that day. Tears poured from her eyes as she relived the day she'd learned so pathetically of his powers.

It was a bleak Sunday morning, just one week before Antranik was to reach eight years of age. The humidity was intensely heavy that day. There wasn't a flurry of breeze to bring relief. Garo and his father had gone off together for a change. As usual, Krikor didn't bother to tell his wife where they would be. Yughaper busied herself as she did every day but suddenly noticed Antranik hadn't yet come to her for his breakfast. She had baked fresh *choeregg* that morning, and it was almost cooled.

She went to his bed and found the child lying deathlike, staring in melancholia. His hands were cupped under his head as a perch, his legs stiff and straight. Yughaper immediately felt the child's head. With a shudder she swiftly withdrew her hand. Years of medicine had taught her how to know instinctively what ailed most people, especially children. But her son was clammy and cold and his eyes had lost virtually all their color.

"What hurts you, *daghas*?" she asked him gently. Then, kissing his brow, she bent down low to hear his whispered response.

Antranik looked at his mother. The peace on his face turned to sorrow as he considered her. Lifeless eyes brought forth thin, scanty tears.

"I shall die today, *Mayrig*. At last I shall die."

She remembered how she had scolded him, shaken him, and run to the kitchen to prepare a tea of special herbs, which often cured cases of delirium due to high fevers. She remembered bringing the bubbling brew over to the still body of her seven-year-old son, who lay dead with a smile on his face.

After that, until the day she met Sahag Vartanian, she cared for little. Garo and Krikor had naturally become inseparable, but Krikor never seemed to have the mystical partner in Garo that he had had in Antranik. Krikor had died of pneumonia less than one year after Antranik. Yughaper believed they had it planned that way. And so the widow with the difficult young son became fair game for the bachelors of Malatia. It took the attractive young woman little time to decide. Sahag Vartanian was everything Krikor hadn't been. There was no question that he was the man she would marry.

She sat patiently waiting for her husband to wake up. His eyes had fluttered open several times during her voyage into the past, and now he sat up before her. She squatted at his feet and looked up, childlike. She smiled through her anxiety. Sahag Vartanian was in anguish, and she ached for him.

"Are the children well asleep?" he asked, looking around uncomfortably.

She answered with a reassuring nod.

He looked deeply into her frightened eyes. Always before he could handle anything, any problem, domestic or business related. He had been her pillar, her protector. But tonight he felt so weak, so inadequate. Perhaps in telling her his fears, he could regain his strength. He drew a long breath and grasped her hands tightly as he began.

"Today a young friend of Garo's came by for a gun he had ordered. His name was Tavit. I don't recall his family name. I remembered him from before; he was a violent-looking boy with a fire in his eyes. I suppose he is Garo's age, though like Garo he spoke and acted more in his twenties." He paused absent-mindedly.

Yughaper interrupted impatiently. "So, go on!"

17

"This Tavit began to tell me that I must be proud of my son, Garo. He called him a leader of the young Armenian revolutionaries. I told him I know of no revolution. I tried to make him stop right there—I was afraid for him to continue. But he was excited, overwhelmed with Garo and his plans."

"Garo is a bull, Baron Vartanian. He will lead us out of bondage. He will end the killing, he and all of us who follow him!"

"So Tavit went on and on, telling me of how Garo has stolen, lied, fought—even murdered for the Armenian cause. At last I understood why he is gone for so many days at a time and why he is so secretive."

Yughaper shook her head in disbelief.

"I have tried to spare you this, my wife, but now you must know Garo must not come back into this house. His obsession to save the lives of his Armenian friends shall be our death warrant."

Yughaper was shocked at her husband's strong words. He had never treated Garo as anything less than his own son. She believed he had grown to love him.

She placed her hand gently over his mouth.

"Garo is at that age, Sahag. He is impetuous, emotional. It is all boyish pranks, wild dreams. I—"

Sahag quickly stopped her.

"Do not be fooled, my wife. You know me well enough. I do not speak of things unless they are serious matters."

Indeed she did. "I am sorry. Go on."

"Yughaper, what is more tragic than Garo's involvement is that he is right. The death of our people is at hand."

Yughaper gasped. She couldn't speak; she only stared as he morosely went on.

"I am in business. I hear the stories again and again. At first they were scattered and came from questionable sources. But of late they are more frequent and told by those who cannot be disbelieved."

"What stories?" she begged.

"A week ago a student came to the shop. He told me he had received a letter. This letter told of his uncle, a professor and highly respected Armenian scholar, who had been kidnapped right on the steps of the university. There has been no word of him, only that a few bystanders observed two Turkish gendarmes carrying him off on horseback. No one dared go to his aid. No one questioned the incident. The family just waits for some news."

"What does it mean?" Yughaper questioned, not yet sure of the seriousness or the connection in all this.

"Until today, Yughaper, I might have put this all aside. Such things are not foreign to our people. We have lived with oppression from our days of grandeur, when all that is the Ottoman Empire was Armenia. Until today, my wife, I would have ignored the other stories, stories of stoning, beatings, house searches, and more that I have dared not tell you."

Sahag stopped abruptly, as though he hadn't the strength to speak another word.

"And today?" Yughaper begged. "What of today, my husband?"

Sahag Vartanian glared a crazed stare at his waiting wife. His eyes rolled up into his head, and he slumped back as if in a coma. Yughaper shook him, crying bitterly; he had begun; he had to go on.

"Yughaper, my life, how can I tell you? Shant is dead."

The words choked as they came out, and Yughaper wept, throwing her head forward into his lap. Shant Gureghian had been Sahag's friend since childhood. It was Shant who had told him of Yughaper's availability after the loss of her first husband. The two had grown from boys into men together. Sahag had chosen his craft, staying in Malatia and creating his gun foundry. Shant, ever serious and ever wise, had gone on to become a respected scientist and philosopher. He had earned a coveted position at the university in Sivas, just north of Malatia.

Through gulps and thick swallows, Yughaper urged her husband on.

"How did this happen to one so young, so gifted?"

Sahag answered quickly as though her words had given him the reason.

"They killed him because he was gifted."."

"What does that mean?" she asked.

19

"It happens the way it always happens. The Turks have to keep us in our places. If we remain ignorant farmers and keep our Christianity to ourselves, then we are tolerated. But the Turkish leaders grow suspicious when too many of us gain high positions in intellectual circles. It is the same when any of us excel in business."

"Yes, it was that way when they took over my father's mine and shut us down."

"Now it happens again. How far will it go? Who will it affect? Only God knows."

"But I must ask you, Sahag, how did he die? What happened?"

"I received the letter from his cousin today. It is a hideous tale, not for a woman's ears."

Yughaper was offended. She had never been weak. Sahag knew that. In all her years as a doctor, she had seen unspeakable things, gruesome diseases, and endless death. In endurance she was on a par with most men. Her haughty frown convinced him he should tell her everything. He had hoped that retelling the story might also relieve him of the gnawing pain that had persisted in his gut since he had read the letter from Shant's cousin.

"Shant had gone to church by himself after a class at the university. He had begun the practice of lighting a candle every day on his way home. I suppose he was already aware of some impending horror, and so he felt the need for special prayer.

"After lighting the candle, he walked to the center of the altar and knelt. Suddenly the doors at the front entrance were kicked open, and there stood a Turk, his gun pointing precisely at Shant. In seconds the gendarme shot Shant in the back of the head. He seemed to die instantly. Praise God for that anyway."

Yughaper wept bitterly. "*Asdvadz heru bahe*," she begged, asking God to keep such things from them. "How do you know this is the way it happened?"

"It seems the priest from the church was in the sacristy, sorting some vestments, when he heard the door burst open. He ran out just as Shant fell. He was bleeding profusely from the back of the head."

"As the letter described, the poor priest was so terrified, he just froze. He quickly hid behind a side altar because the Turk was bounding down the aisle toward Shant."

"Yes, yes, and go on, Sahag." Yughaper was horrified but hungry for more knowledge in the whole affair.

Sahag again paused, frowning. He cleared his throat and went on, supporting his heavy forehead with a quivering hand.

"As the priest tells it, the Turk was laughing hysterically. He made his way to the candles and picked up the one Shant had just lit. He put the candle to Shant's hair and set it ablaze! For a while he stood, howling with enjoyment, and then looked around wildly and marched out. He turned before leaving the church and hollered to the dead man, 'So, Armenian scholar! Let's see if your God puts out the fire! Let's see how your Christian God raises you from the dead.'"

"Did he just lay there and burn?" Yughaper asked pitifully.

"No, the *der hayr* ran out and threw a chapel cloth around Shant's head and extinguished the fire. The old man grew sick at the sight. He told Shant's cousin that his hair and part of his scalp were completely gone. The priest and a deacon he called to the scene quickly buried the body. They wanted no one to know. It was hideous."

Yughaper remembered how she had often teased Shant about marrying and having many scholarly children. She thanked God now that he hadn't.

"Though they tried to keep the whole thing a secret, word quickly spread among the local Armenians. There were protestors, but the mutessarif's office has denied the whole charge. They claim Shant was an eccentric professor. They say he just left town without telling anyone."

"Who in Malatia knows of this?"

"No one but us and so it must remain."

He knew he needn't have said that. Yughaper Vartanian wasn't a gossip. In telling her of these horrors, his pain was somewhat relieved. His quaking legs ceased their shivering. Now his only sorrow was that his beloved wife need bear the fear he had been carrying with him for so long. However, now she would be more careful, trust no one, and carefully account for the whereabouts of the children. Yes, he consoled himself. It was good that she knew.

Yughaper embraced her husband and kissed his cheek. Some of his color had already returned. She lifted his tired body and coaxed him to bed. In less than a moment he snored in an uneasy sleep, but now she would remain awake for the rest of the night.

As the blackness of midnight fell ominously over Malatia, all her citizens—Armenians, Turks, Greeks, Russians—slept in uncanny unison. But one remained awake and alone. In the tiny kitchen surrounded by the hushed snores and deep breathings of her family sat Yughaper Vartanian. If she allowed herself to think about what she had been told a few hours before, her stomach would turn. If she tried to send her thoughts into different channels, the waters there would be bloody with human suffering.

For a moment it occurred to her that if indeed the Turks were on a new rampage under Abdul Hamid, then no one was safe. But if Garo was involved in crimes against the empire, then her family was in particularly severe danger. It was odd, she thought, that Sahag and his family might suffer for a son who wasn't his, a son who'd come from a lesser man, a man she sometimes believed was worthy of whatever fate Satan might have in store. But then she would allay her fears, assuring herself that Garo was too sly to ever be suspected; and even if he were, surely everyone in Malatia knew he wasn't the son of Sahag, that Sahag had nothing to do with Garo's comings and goings. Still the thought wouldn't leave her, nor would any of the things she had heard earlier. There was only one thing to do. She would cook. She would prepare *mander yapragh.* It would be tedious enough to get her through the night and tomorrow they would delight in its lusciousness.

She began by preparing the filling- a mixture of water, fine ground *bulghur* and stone-ground wheat. As she kneaded the mixture into dough her hands ached from the pain. Then she tore tiny grape leaves into even tinier pieces, which she would fill one by one with the doughy mixture. She hoped it would take all night, and it did.

The large pot rested on the wooden table. It was filled with hundreds of tiny grape leaf envelopes painstakingly filled by hand. Tomorrow they would be boiled in a broth of tomatoes, plums, sugar, and lemon juice. Gloriously they would be tossed with pounds of softly sautéed onions mixed with *matzoon*, her homemade yogurt. The results would be called *mander yapragh*. The words meant "small leaves." The recipe was made only in Malatia. The women through the years had traded recipes until this final version was agreed upon. It was the fare of kings made and eaten by paupers; the glories of being poor, the delicious taste of ingenuity. Huddled beside the creation was the creator. She slumped, hands and arms wrapped around a weary head, nestled on a table. Yughaper Vartanian at last fell asleep.

• • •

As most of Malatia slept soundly, life seethed in the smoke-filled Armenian café located in the center of town. Voices were muffled, heads bent over in drunkenness and secret whispers. A young, moustached man with long, greasy-looking hair blared out a sultry melody on a *doodoog*, a sort of primitive horn. An old man slouched in a corner, singing to himself, oblivious to those around him. Now and then someone would jump up and shout, then look cautiously about, settling back into a secret conversation again. The smashing of backgammon chips would periodically break the eerie mumblings in the café.

The place was called Vahak's. There was always whiskey, *choeregg*, and some olives. Once in a while the proprietor would put out some fresh cheese and homemade brandy. The place was where the Armenians came for entertainment, only the Armenians. Each of the nationalities had their own cafés, their own churches, and their own schools—all within this one small city.

Over the past few months, Vahak's had become less of a café for good times and more of a discreet meeting place. Since the beginning of Abdul Hamid's reign over the empire, the Armenians found themselves living more and more under the shadow of death. The monarch had conceded that these fools claiming to be the first nationality to adopt Christianity could keep their ridiculous faith. But it wasn't unusual for him to close a church for security reasons. He excelled in surprise visits, when his men would enter an Armenian home, search it, and seize its books, valuables, and occasionally a family member for random questioning.

Such practices had never been unusual in Turkey, but they were becoming more frequent under the new leaders of 1895. Turkish oppression went back centuries. The valleys and plateaus of this arid vastness, surrounded by the looming peaks of Ararat and the Caucasus, had been incessant battlegrounds. Invaders came and went. What had been the real Armenia was an area as large as Turkey and part of Russia today. It was a delectably sprawled-out meal for the ravenous wolves of the times.

It was in 1514, when the Ottoman Turks attacked Persia, that the unarmed, unorganized Armenians suddenly found themselves to be a part of the ever-expanding Ottoman Empire. From then on they were the oppressed. They were the ruled. They lived as *dhimmis*, tolerated infidels. By law, *dhimmis* could be killed, and no case would be brought before the *qadi*, the empire's court of law. The encroaching Muslims begrudgingly allowed them their Christianity. Strict laws forbade the building of new churches, with few exceptions. Armenians were forced to open their doors to any Turkish official. Food and lodging could be taken from Armenian homes at will. If an Armenian settlement grew too heavily populated, the Ottomans encouraged nomadic Kurdish tribes to displace them with barbaric attacks.

It had become clear that the Armenians must organize—if not in military fashion, at least politically. Several groups of young men joined together for this purpose. The *Hunchakist* was one. It was a group made up of older men. Then the *Tashnaktsutiun* party formed. These were the young Armenians, the strong, proud bulls who wouldn't sit back and be spat upon, as did their ancestors. As yet they had done no political wrong, but the very fact that they existed made Abdul Hamid anxious.

The *Tashnaktsutiun* was gaining power, and each village boasted of its own active group. Most of the older Armenians frowned upon them. They feared that the very existence of such a radical group would one day cause the total extermination of the Armenian people. Ironically that was the very holocaust the *Tashnaks* hoped to prevent. Furthermore, there was turmoil within the Tashnaktsutiun. Most of these young men were content to keep a watchful eye, make ready a meager arsenal, and attack only if all-out genocide should begin. The others argued they wouldn't wait for such a massacre. They were assured it was going to happen. They proposed all-out attack. They favored organized revolt to regain full political and religious power over the vast lands that had once been Armenia. They were foolhardy and reckless in their beliefs.

The Tashnaks were exceptionally powerful in Malatia. Most young men from fourteen years of age on were actively involved. They had to be very careful. Meeting places were continually changed. Messages were never written but sent by word of mouth. Small boxes of rifles and handguns were hidden in scattered locations throughout the town. Their leader had to be uncompromising, courageous, and intelligent. He had to have access to guns of all kinds. He had to live for the Tashnaktsutiun alone and be willing to die for it. It took a unique, perhaps slightly mad, human being.

In Vahak's café, around a small table, huddled a group of young Tashnaks—the saviors of Malatia. Captivated, they listened to the profound proclamations of their leader. He was a darkly handsome young man with an unyielding countenance. He was Garo Vartanian.

The young men were tipsy from liquor and high on emotion. Tears flowed; fists banged down angrily on the shaky table. Threats flew wildly. But Garo, knowing that Turkish spies were everywhere, continually calmed them. By his side sat Tavit, engrossed in his leader's words. The plan this night was to steal money from the Turkish merchants in the grand bazaar, which was to take place in a few days. The money would be dispersed to various members, and they would buy guns and ammunition. Tavit would take the items and hide them in a place he alone would know.

Soon Vahak's café began to empty out. The exhausted war hawks slowly dispersed. Tavit and Garo stayed on; discussing last-minute plans they didn't wish the others to hear. The two had vowed that if any Armenian were killed in Malatia, they would be self-appointed executioners. They would bring a reign of terror down on the Turks in retaliation. This was their promise to each other. The two embraced to seal their pact. They left, going in opposite directions, not acknowledging each other as they walked through the door and out into the dusty, black night.

Vahak's was empty now except for the old man, who was singing to himself in the corner. Garo and his friends hadn't noticed, but the man had stopped his melodious murmurs a few hours back. The old, wrinkled man had been listening, absorbing with ears that weren't as old as they seemed. The drunken, stupid stare he had displayed all evening had left his face, and as he emerged from Vahak's he had a different expression on his face. It was one of sardonic knowledge, shifty and sly. The old man looked cautiously around, and proceeded confidently toward the office of the *kaimakam*, the commander of the Turkish gendarmes in Malatia.

• • •

Yughaper was startled and embarrassed to find herself awakening, slouched over the pot which was filled to the brim with the *mander yapragh*. She hadn't realized how exhausted she must have been. Quickly she splashed her face with some water, which had cooled in a jug outdoors overnight. It refreshed her. She hastily removed her soiled dress and placed it in a pile of other dirty garments. She would have to fetch water from the well that day and begin boiling it to do a wash for the family. Quickly she put on a long, full muslin dress, which she had made. She marveled at the tremendous size of her stomach. She pondered whether the baby had already dropped into position. Then busying herself over breakfast preparations, she chuckled; amazed that she had been able to conceal her pregnancy so skillfully.

She set the fire to boil water for *surj*, the rich, black coffee Sahag so loved early in the morning. There was fresh *choeregg* in the crock and freshly formed goat's milk cheese. She would slice a prized Malatia tomato and cucumber. It would be a fine breakfast.

Hovsep began to gurgle and she went to him. Fastidiously she attended to his needs and sifted the wet sand which was his tiny bed.

Bedros walked in, his eyes especially round and wide open for so early in the morning. Yughaper laughed when she saw him. His innocent, chubby-cheeked face and dancing eyes always made her laugh. It was his way. He made people laugh.

Khatchadour and Ara lumbered to the table in sleepy unison and sat down, still unaware that the other was awake. Soon around the breakfast table sat the Vartanian sons. Yughaper stood back for a moment and boastfully admired those she had created. They were a beautiful lot, worth her every labor.

Sahag awoke to the sounds of his family chatting and joking. It was a pleasant way to wake up. He believed it would be a good day. There stood his fine wife, about to give him another fine child. There sat his sons, each different, each handsome, each a harbinger of his great pride. What then could he fear? What dread could he hold with so much life and joy around him? None, he convinced himself as he freshened his face from the crock. He was very hungry and decided he would hold off dressing until after breakfast. Right at this moment, he had but one desire—to sit with his family in peaceful contentment.

Sahag sat at his regular place and was served quickly, as was the way in Armenian households. The boys jabbered incessantly about school, about the gun shop, and about their plans for the day. Everyone, it seemed, was speaking at the same time. Little Hovsep sat precariously on a bench, chomping on a piece of *choeregg*. The crumbs encircled his face like a premature beard. Yughaper and Sahag gave each other the kind of father-mother glance parents often do. They smiled in amusement at it all. It was a heavenly moment.

An impatient pounding at the door shattered the scene. Sahag jumped up, signaling to his wife that he would open it. He glanced back at Yughaper with a questioning look in his eyes. The entire family stood together around their mother, who had scooped Hovsep up into her arms. They all stood frozen as Sahag walked toward the door.

There came a second pounding, which nearly broke down the door. Sahag opened it. Five Turkish gendarmes stood menacingly before them. They were fully armed.

"Sahag Vartanian?" questioned the largest and ugliest of the five.

"Yes," replied Sahag, trying hard not to let his fear show.

"You are the father of Garo Vartanian?" the wild gendarme demanded.

"Yes."

"Come out now, into the road. Keep your hands up!"

The children began to scream, hanging on to Yughaper in fright. Absent-mindedly the Turk motioned the whole family out of the house. Sahag weakly protested.

"What have I done? What is the meaning of this?"

"We have been informed that you harbor criminals against the state. You are a gunsmith. You are giving guns to Armenians for revolt. You are the father of a revolutionary against the state."

"It is not true!" Sahag pleaded. "I—"

His words were cut off as hundreds of shots poured out. Sahag's raised hands fell to his sides. Some inner longing made him turn half-way to look into the horrified eyes of his family. His look cried good-bye, and he fell into the dusty sand. The ground turned red beneath him.

Screaming, nearly insane, Yughaper and her wailing children ran and fell over their father. Neighbors had gathered, staring in terrified disbelief. The gendarmes glanced defiantly at the crowd.

"Learn from this man, Armenian dogs. Such is the fate of any person who threatens Abdul Hamid's empire!"

The soldiers raced away. Yughaper sobbed, gathering up her children. A neighbor led her back into the house. Friends would take up the body and plan the funeral for her. Such was their way.

The following day Sahag Vartanian was buried. The Armenian church was crowded. Sobs and hymns permeated the walls of the modest building. Yughaper only stared. Another woman catered to Hovsep. Khatchadour stood with tears streaming down his face. His father wouldn't have approved. Ara watched the costumed priest dumbly, wondering what possible good all this ceremony could do for his family or his beloved father. Bedros looked about inquisitively. He didn't fully understand what had happened until this moment. First he cried; then he stopped himself and formed his little hand into a fist. Defiantly he glared up to heaven. It wasn't clear whether the young boy was furious with the Turks or with God himself. Yughaper glanced at him, not liking what she saw. She tugged at his sleeve and went back into her mournful prayers. Her stomach had been aching since the killing, and she knew her time was at hand.

When the family returned home, they found their grandmother, Yester, busily preparing dinner and straightening up the house. She had been staying with a sick friend in town and was called home immediately upon Sahag's death. She was desperately needed, and her wisdom and strength helped to somehow soothe the void of the powerful man who had left them all.

Yester was Yughaper's mother. She may have been eighty; no one knew. But for her age and her thin frame, she was a wiry woman. She had seen it all. This kind of madness was all too familiar to her. Her sober attitude helped everyone bear the horror of what they had just experienced. Yughaper was grateful for the presence of her mother, though she wished to spare her the work and worry to come. Yester embraced her poor daughter and immediately forced her into bed. Everything would now be under control.

The next morning Yughaper went into labor. An experienced midwife herself, she knew the symptoms. Yester came immediately to her bed. The water, the knife, and the piles of coarse muslins were ready. Yester had been an accomplished doctor for half of her life and had proudly bestowed her talents upon her daughter. Now the two self-made physicians would bring a tiny life into a world that wasn't worth living in. Quietly and quickly the baby emerged. It was once again a boy. Sahag would have been overjoyed. The baby gave out a burst of healthy yelps.

"Enter Sahag Vartanian once again!" cried Yughaper. And so he was named.

In her aged wisdom Yester knew her family would now need assistance. Yughaper was weak, with an infant at her breast and another still in infancy. Bedros was young and energetic. Even Ara in all his maturity was too young to completely fend for himself. Khatchadour couldn't yet make a living. The wage earner was gone. To Yester, self-assurance was one thing, but good common sense was quite another. This ageless, little lady with the leathery skin had an abundance of both. As she valiantly went about her household duties, a plan came to her. She would go to town alone the next morning. Let them kill her if they cared to. She would go directly to the *mutessarif*, the mayor himself. She would boldly plead her case. Insanity was her privilege in these senior years, but she had another reason to believe the Turkish official would hear her case and comply.

It was a brisk morning, with autumn frolicking in the air. Yester had gotten Ara and Khatchadour off to school. She had decided that until a decision was reached regarding their futures, they would spend as much time in the Armenian school as possible. Hovsep was safely at home, playing in the fenced-in yard with Bedros. Yester had warned Bedros that he must stay with his baby brother and dare not leave the yard. After the horror of his father's death, the little man was less impetuous and far more willing to stay near his mother and grandmother.

She cast a long, thin shadow as she bounded down the sandy road toward the center of town. It was astonishing that one so frail and elderly could walk with such agility. Pausing only to greet an occasional neighbor and tell them about her plan, the old woman hastened on. Heads turned, children giggled, neighbors whispered. The people of Malatia had always questioned Yester's sanity and now they feared the years had finally taken their toll. The closer Yester came to the looming stone-and-mortar building, which housed the murderers of her son-in-law, the more she questioned it herself.

Turkish guards were everywhere now, watching her with cold stares and warning frowns. They followed the tiny figure with amazement. As she made her way through the courtyard and up the path toward the mayor's quarters, two gendarmes quickly stood together in front of the door to block her entry.

"What business do you have here, old lady?" blurted a gruff voice from one.

Yester put out a skinny arm to push him aside, but then caught herself before touching him. She scowled like a matriarch about to scold a little boy.

"I must see the *mutessarif!*" she exclaimed with authority in her shaking voice.

"He is busy. Be gone, old fool!"

"You will have to kill me then, in front of all Malatia." She asserted herself with some incorrigible inner strength, and then went on with sly sarcasm in her tone. "But that would not be difficult for you, to gun down an old lady in cold blood!"

The two guards looked at each other, puzzled. She knew she was getting somewhere and wisely softened.

"Young men, you have mothers and grandmothers. Please let an old lady through. My business is urgent, and surely you can see that the likes of me could cause the mutessarif no harm."

It worked. The two men nodded and let her pass through the huge, hand-carved, wooden doors. The soldiers explained the situation to the string of guards in the alcove of the building, and tiny Yester was escorted to the large office of the Turkish mutessarif.

He was a young man for such a high position. Yester thought him handsome as Turks went. He frowned up at her from a mass of paperwork. A pistol lay resting on its side on top of an endless pile of reports.

"You have business with me, old woman?"

"Sir, I am Yester, mother of Yughaper Vartanian." Her voice was strong and unfaltering. She had gotten this far, and nothing was going to stop her.

"And should that mean something to me?" he questioned.

The man looked troubled. Yester sensed it immediately. The human suffering and hatred over which he reigned were weighing heavily on him. Her small presence was nothing compared to the troubles he dealt with every day—the troubles yet to come. She was angry with herself for feeling any pity for this murderer.

"You know of me and my daughter, sir," she continued. "Yughaper is the midwife of Malatia as I was for many years before her. We both have done much to help, not just Armenians but all people in our *vilayet.*"

"I thought I noticed an Armenian accent to your Turkish."

"So you did," she continued, ignoring his remark about her accent, though it did bother her. She prided herself in speaking fluent Turkish along with her mother tongue.

"Three days ago, five of your men burst into my daughter's home and murdered her husband before the very eyes of his entire family." She fought back the tears as she recounted the story.

"I know that," he responded quickly. Yester sensed a touch 'of sorrow in his voice.

"Did you order such a hideous thing?" She stood firm, glaring squarely into the man's eyes. "If so, what could have been your mad reasoning?"

The mutessarif paced the room, trying not to let his eyes reach Yester's. He glanced out the window at his city, Malatia, which he loved. He had been born here. He had had many Armenian friends here. Fate had put him in this unwanted position.

"It is not my authority that orders such killings, woman. The military handle all executions. The *kaimakam* ordered Sahag Vartanian's execution." Yester was furious with his matter-of-fact answer. She wasn't about to let go of him yet. Not until he, or someone, made retribution.

"So just like that, a man is killed! And what if I tell you he was innocent of the charges? If I tell you he was a good person who did no harm to any man, Armenian or Turk?"

"It means nothing!" the mutessarif went on. "He was accused of treason. Garo, the criminal, is his son."

"Fools!" Yester screamed, surprised at the volume in her old voice. "Garo is not Sahag Vartanian's son at all! He was the son of another man, Krikor, a devil of a man." Yester was breathless now. The thought of hideous irony made her ill. "My son-in-law paid with his life for taking in and nurturing another man's son! That boy had nothing to do with Sahag Vartanian. Believe me when I tell you that Garo hasn't even lived at home for over one year."

The mutessarif was astounded by her story and shocked at the madness that had overcome Malatia and the empire.

"Then I can only say I am sorry." He suddenly grew stern, clearing his throat gruffly. "But you Armenians have been getting out of hand, I am told. And such things can happen, even under the veil of suspicion."

"So then." The grandmother composed herself. "What are we to do? My daughter has just had a baby. There are young mouths to feed, then myself and my daughter. There is no money. Your animals have killed the father, the wage earner of our family."

"And what would you have me do, old lady?" he asked.

"You must go to the *vali* and request assistance for us. A small weekly pension so that we might survive." She was firm and demanding.

"Is that all?" chuckled the Turk, amused at the audacity of this amazing woman.

"Yes, young man, that is all. Then the children may go to an orphanage, and we, left at home, can at least eat and maintain our existences."

"I see, and just tell me why—why I should do this for you, with so many of your fellow Armenians out there with the same need?"

"I will tell you. You are how old?" She squinted at him inquisitively.

"Thirty-one," he exclaimed. "And what in Allah's name has that to do with all of this, old woman?"

"I thought so. And your mother? She still lives here in Malatia?"

"Yes," he answered, now becoming annoyed with this inquisition.

"So," Yester smiled, sizing up the young man with a grandmother's critical eye. "Thirty-one years ago, sir, I delivered a baby to a young Turkish nobleman's wife. I have been told that the child had grown into one of great power in Malatia."

"Indeed, and what position might that be?"

"They say," smirked the wise old lady, "that he is now the mutessarif of all citizens of Malatia."

The Turk stood stunned, his mouth gaping open. He couldn't speak. In embarrassment he turned away. He stood silently for a moment. At last he spoke to the proud woman standing defiantly before him.

"I shall speak to the vali tomorrow."

"And if he refuses?" she persisted.

"Fear not, old lady. He will not refuse."

•   •   •

Not far from the Vartanian household lived the family of Hovnan Hamparian. Their house was similar to others in Malatia. It did, however, have a few differences. The house had been built craftily out of a cave. It was the kind of cave that appeared everywhere throughout the vast wilderness of Turkey. Outside, Hovnan, a farmer by trade, had an immense plot of land that was resplendent with vegetables and fruits of all kinds. The lavish mass of emerald appeared like an incongruous carpet amid the blankness of sand around it. In the center of the front courtyard of the Hamparian home was a large fountain, which was nearly three times the size of others in the area. Adjoining the fountain was the largest and deepest well in Malatia.

Hovnan and his invalid wife, Arpine, had only one child. His name was Garabed. Most of the Malatia Armenians considered the small family to be eccentric. The huge farm, with its ostentatious fountain and sprawling greenery, simply didn't merge comfortably with the peasant-like existence of its neighbors. But to Hovnan, his farm was his life. He cared little about interaction with others. Arpine had been immobile since giving birth to the now ten-year-old Garabed. The child clung continually to his ailing mother, much to his father's dismay. It was only in the warmth of the sandy soil and the overgrown garden that Hovnan Hamparian found his passion in life. What others misunderstood didn't matter to him. All that mattered was the farm, the land, his homestead. It was his birthright. It was all God, in His strange system of rationing, had seen fit to grant him.

In all his lifetime in Malatia, Hovnan Hamparian had but one friend, and that was Sahag Vartanian. Being the kind of level-headed, tolerant man he was, Sahag saw the reasons for Hovnan's oddly introverted ways. The two saw little of each other, but each had helped the other during hard times. Yughaper had assisted in Garabed's difficult birth, and periodically the two families would socialize.

But if Hovnan Hamparian had been odd before, the brutal murder of his friend thrust the man into hopelessness. He couldn't sleep at night. He would lie awake staring, imagining hoards of Turks bearing down on his beloved farm, and then stealing into the house and murdering Arpine and Garabed as they slept.

As he labored through the lingering heat of September, he would visualize himself single-handedly slaughtering Turks, ten and twenty at a time. As his grief for his lost friend grew, paranoia overcame him. Hovnan slowly began planning a real attack on the unsuspecting Turks. Day and night the orderly plan materialized.

Hovnan Hamparian's suspicions were well founded. He was a prosperous farmer, more so than most men at the time. His home and surroundings were lavish for this area. Perhaps for these reasons he posed a threat to the watchful Turks. But with or without valid reason, Hovnan proceeded with his calculated plan. He ate it for dinner and relished it through wakeful nights. His heart throbbed in anticipation, and his mind spun with the bold threads of his desire.

Hovnan made his way to the kaimakam's office one Sunday morning after long hours of prayer and meditation. He explained to the high commander of the Turkish gendarmes that his farm had overproduced its usual bounty. So plentiful were his crops that he wished to make a gift to the soldiers of hundreds of tomatoes, squash, cucumbers, eggplants, apples, and pears. The kaimakam was most impressed. Hovnan explained that the produce would be placed in seven large crates and that it would take as many men to transport them from his home back to the kaimakam's headquarters. Even with a donkey cart, he insisted, transportation would take at least seven men.

Hovnan Hamparian would soon become a legend. His story would epitomize the horror of Armenian existence in Ottoman Turkey at the time. His was the kind of tale many Armenians would wish to forget. His was the kind of sad glory most Armenians wouldn't want to bestow upon their children. But it was Hovnan and men like him whose legends would haunt the valiant glory of the Armenian past. Because of the fiendishness of those times, a people who should have been remembered as brilliant scholars, skilled craftsmen, devout Christians, and proud patriarchs are instead remembered as an unlucky race of slaughtered outcasts. Hovnan Hamparian thought nothing of his place in these bloodstained pages of history. He thought only of the demon chewing up his insides—a demon who wouldn't cease—not until he had killed his Turks.

He calmly went to Garabed and asked the child to stay with his mother in her private bedroom area with the door closed. He didn't want the Turks to know of his son's presence. The boy obeyed. Hovnan brought his wife some fresh goat's milk and a piece of thin bread, and then told her about the visiting Turks. It was better, he told her, that she and Garabed remain inconspicuous.

At last the stage was set. Hovnan walked out to his beautiful garden and bade his crisp, dewy friends a fond farewell. He then selected the largest shovel he owned, the one with the massive iron head. He glanced around at the tranquility of unsuspecting Malatia. He absorbed her vastness, sparse trees, and distant mountains. He bade her good-bye, sorry that she hadn't loved him as he had her. Finally, determined and prepared, he entered his home, closed the door, and squatted behind it...waiting for his guests.

He heard the rolling of the donkey cart wheels on the sandy road. He heard the laughs of the Turkish soldiers as they came for their bounty. Inside he seethed. In his mind, these seven men were the Turkish nation. These were the dogs who had murdered his dearest friend. They would never stop, this much he knew. For himself, he would slaughter the pigs. For Sahag, for Armenia, he would slice them down one by one as they entered for the promised fruits. Hovnan would see to it that they received the fruits of their own labors.

As he expected, the fools didn't bother to knock on his door. He was already on his feet, well concealed behind the large wooden door. Hovnan's demon then encouraged him, gave him the swiftness, the superhuman strength, the determination to club seven Turkish heads so precisely and powerfully that one by one the unsuspecting gendarmes fell to the floor like a pile of bloody garbage. Though all seven were quite dead, the pathetic man continued hacking and slicing with his farmer's tool, the one he had used so gently and lovingly all his life. At last, the demon inside him flew away. Hovnan stood over his harvest, exhausted from the most laborious task he had ever performed. He didn't know, didn't care, that there was one more Turk who had remained outside to tend to the donkey and prepare the cart.

The gendarme, upon hearing the suspicious sounds from inside the home, decided to investigate. He entered the home and stood dumbfounded. He stared aghast at the old man who was slumped down before him. Hovnan's head was down. He was still grasping the bloody shovel. The soldier was seized with fury. The Turk grabbed Hovnan by the neck and began to choke him. The old man didn't resist. Looking at the pile of bodies of his compatriots, the enraged Turk felt that mere strangulation wasn't enough for this Armenian pig. He dragged Hovnan out into his garden, bound his hands and feet, and forced him into a kneeling position. Then he grasped a huge ax resting on its side by a host of other tools. Beside himself with rage and before a horrified gathering of neighbors, the gendarme chopped Hovnan Hamparian into pieces.

The Turk was salivating and grunting like a wild boar; he wasn't yet satisfied. He strutted over to the cart as the horrified neighbors ran in all directions. He pulled out a large sheet of muslin on which he had planned to lay the crates of vegetables the dead man had promised. He thrust the heavy cloth on the ground, and with his bare hands he picked up the bloody parts of bones and flesh that had been Hovnan Hamparian and threw them onto the muslin. He then wrapped up the sickening package and ran around the house with it flung over his shoulder. At last, his war dance completed, the soldier took his booty and thrust it down the huge well, of which Hovnan had been so proud. Unknowingly the mad Turk had granted Hovnan Hamparian a fitting grave site.

A frightened hush fell over Malatia that day. It was as though the whole town had disappeared. Nothing could be heard—nothing—except the faint sobbing of a young boy, who stood staring out the window of his mother's room. While his mother blissfully slept, Garabed Hamparian had witnessed the brutal murder of his father.

• • •

In a few hours another group of gendarmes arrived to clean up the mess, which hatred and intolerance had left. It was officially decided that Arpine Hamparian would be sent to a government asylum in Constantinople. Garabed would be sent to Saint Mary's Orphanage, which was run by the friars, a few miles north of Malatia. This would all be done at government expense to show the Armenians the deep regard the Ottoman Turks had for human rights.

That same day a messenger came to the Vartanian home with news from Garo. The young revolutionary was overcome with grief at the loss of his stepfather and rightfully blamed himself. The message said that he had fled to Aleppo, where supposedly the Armenians were higher in number and more organized. There he would continue his work with the Tashnaks.

Yester and Yughaper had begun to receive their meager pension. They knew it was time for Ara and Bedros to go to the orphanage. Yughaper was physically very weak, and emotionally she was virtually lifeless. She had taken to smoking an endless string of harsh Turkish cigarettes. She ate barely enough to sustain her life and drank only enough liquid to create the milk upon which tiny Sahag existed.

In her old age Yester struggled to keep up with the energetic Hovsep, prepare the meals and tidy the house. The heartbreaking plans had to be made. Bedros and Ara, inseparable always, would be sent to Saint Mary's Orphanage in Malatia. Khatchadour would do his best to keep up the gun shop in a very cautious manner. The two youngest children would stay at home.

As the horse-drawn wagon pulled up the next morning, Bedros waited anxiously, clutching a small burlap sack in his tiny hands. To him it was all a grand adventure, but Ara couldn't stop crying. He had been sick since his mother gave him the horrible news. But the brave seven-year-old man stood firm, holding his head high, next to his baby brother. He put out his hand and quickly rushed Bedros toward the wagon. The two brothers climbed up into the back of the cart. They both turned and waved a tearful good-bye to their mother and grandmother, who stood supporting each other arm in arm, nearly faint with grief. The cart rolled away. The two young boys stared back toward their home. Straining to catch a last glimpse of the two ladies, they failed to notice another boy squatting in a rejected slump in the corner of the wagon. He was Garabed Hamparian.

Chapter 2

THE ORPHANAGE, 1900

A fiesta of summer clouds danced through the skies of Malatia, painting the pale-blue backdrop with splashes of crimson pinks and gentle purples. The stage was set with a vast groundwork of tawny tans and dusty beiges, and the sand seemed to glitter under the mid-afternoon sun's sparkle. A huge gull swooped down into the vivid scene, seeking his way to the massive Tigris and Euphrates River. Unlike most of Malatia, here there were abundant trees, ageless gems shooting up to the sky in thick, green pageantry. A giant cypress loomed defiantly over the rest. Its delicate leaves jostled in the soft wind.

Underneath the fine horticultural specimen stood a portly man dressed in drab, brown clothing. His head was bald but for a halo-like ring of hair encircling his head. The chubby, little man looked about with a frustrated frown on his face. He tapped his foot impatiently and firmly placed his arms on his hips. His name was Friar Cecil, and he looked no more heavenly than the tiny, black cricket that scampered quickly under his foot "When I find you, little brat, you will surely never disobey me again!"

The monk was shouting loudly to no one. Perhaps his prey would hear him and out of fear spring from his hiding place. Perhaps the poor friar would at last come to control this uncontrollable child.

Just as the annoyed Friar was about to continue his search, the sound of water trickling through the leaves above him startled him. Curiously he looked up as a stream of warm liquid poured down his shoulder and the folds of his robe, tracing his thigh and then his calf, and finally reaching down to his scuffed sandals. Baffled, he peered through the thick leaves above him to find the source of this sour-smelling fluid. Then he saw him. Perched on the uppermost branch of the tree was Bedros Vartanian, the culprit the friar had so diligently been seeking. The giggling eight-year-old child had deliberately urinated on the exasperated monk.

The little man was beside himself and the more he puffed and grimaced, the more Bedros laughed. It seemed for a moment that the Friar was going to climb up the tree, to grab the naughty child. But Bedros would have no fear of that. Friar Cecil had difficulty walking his burdensome body let alone attempting to climb the highest tree in the field. In frustration the monk clenched his fists and began jumping up and down like a foiled Rumpelstiltskin.

"This is the last straw! Only you could be so low, so filthy!"

"But Father," responded a voice from above, still choking from laughter, "I had to go so badly, and I thought you might stand down there forever."

"Enough of your insolence! You shall be punished severely this time. This time no one will save you. No one!"

With that the friar stormed back to his waiting donkey and disappeared.

Once assured that Friar "CiCi," as the children dubbed him, was gone, Bedros slid down from his precarious position. He still laughed, thinking of how well he had aimed just over the shoulder; on top of the head would really have been unpardonable. The young boy had no remorse. During his five years at Saint Mary's, it had seemed that Friar Cecil had a vendetta only for him. Bedros believed the crotchety monk was jealous of his popularity with the children and friars as well. Whatever his reason, it was obvious that the monk found pleasure in disapproving everything Bedros did. His position of disciplinarian at the orphanage gave him even more opportunity to continually badger the young boy.

This particular time Bedros's crime had been a simple misdemeanor, one with great justification. Bedros chuckled because CiCi had thought it was his first time at this particular offense. But Bedros had been doing it for almost the full five years he had been at Saint Mary's. It was the crime of the fruit basket—Bedros's fruit basket.

Since the friars, by law of their order, had to subsist solely from their own labors, Saint Mary's had an immense expanse of acreage set aside for farming. In particular, there was a magnificent orchard, which produced succulent peaches, pears, and apricots. It was a shame the delectable fruits couldn't be sold for profit. All the delicious produce could be used solely for consumption by the monks and the students. Unfortunately, during the five years Bedros had been there, these fruits had been rarely offered to the children. Yet the youngsters would continually see the monks walking about Saint Mary's, munching on the treasures they had grown.

After some six months of this, Bedros Vartanian vowed to put an end to the injustice. He began sneaking into the orchards every day, picking those beautiful edibles, and bringing them back for himself and his friends. He kept a special basket hidden under the floorboards of his large dormitory. It had been a tedious job carefully lifting the existing boards up without breaking them, then replacing them without showing any signs of tampering. But Bedros, aside from his scholastic achievements, had proved to be a remarkably talented boy with his hands. He was extremely inventive, and often the friars used his ideas for bunk beds, trunks, and other articles made of wood. He was constantly tinkering with bits and pieces of wood and metal, and in his tiny trunk piles of drawings depicting various inventions could be found.

Though the fruit basket was reserved for the boys in Bedros's own living quarters, there were a chosen few to whom he had given the secret location. Of course he had told Ara, who, though he lived in the ward with the older boys, was continually checking in on his little brother. As it had been back at home, it was Ara who was summoned when CiCi frantically looked for Bedros.

Ara was faring well at Saint Mary's. He had made many friends, and the friars highly respected him. Ara could always be counted on to add a note of sanity to the insane antics of the younger boys, led by his notorious brother.

Reluctantly, Bedros had told Garabed Hamparian about the fruit basket. Garabed wasn't well liked by the other boys at Saint Mary's. True to his heritage, he was sullen and extremely moody. He trusted virtually no one and spent most of his time in deep study or meditation. Ara and Bedros had formed an odd bond with the strange young boy, mostly because they had traveled together to the orphanage and had gone through the difficult adjustment to their new lifestyle. Of course the manner in which Garabed's father had died had also softened them to the pensive young man.

Bedros Vartanian, at eight years of age, showed not only the scholarly and charismatic traits of a leader but the physical attributes as well. What once had been rounded baby shoulders were becoming sinewy and solid. His legs were muscular and already growing shades of black hair. His hands were as large as some of the older boys', as were his feet.

Bedros's hair had thickened and straightened since his infancy. It was so black that it glistened with touches of gleaming blue highlights. The round baby nose was now more pronounced, giving him the appearance of a handsome, young bull. Above all else were his eyes. The eyes of Bedros—lucid pools into which any onlooker could be drawn down and hopelessly engulfed. They were less hazel now and showed more hues of brown and black. It seemed that no matter how the rest of him appeared, no matter if he were tired or angry or sad, his eyes remained unchanged. Always they laughed, and they danced. They reflected some inner spirit that would never cry, never be defeated, and never die.

In addition to his other talents, Bedros had shown a profound interest in music—so much so that the headmaster at Saint Mary's, Friar Vincent, had given him a clarinet to use whenever he chose. Bedros struggled with the instrument at first, giving forth only squeaks and moans. But soon he mastered the horn well enough to create his own songs. Each night his dormitory resounded in Bedros Vartanian's joyous musical interludes. Most of the monks had happily accepted these delightful sessions, all of course except CiCi.

Drinking in the cool air, Bedros reluctantly made his way back to Saint Mary's. The orphanage was several hundred feet from the field, and the walk was a pleasant one. He passed through dazzling red poppies interspersed with blossoms of purple and white. The orphanage stood by itself on the outskirts of Malatia. Saint Mary's, established by an order of monks educated in Rome, was to be totally self-sufficient and without any political or ethnic preferences. These friars dedicated their lives to farming and mechanical labors to maintain their dwelling and feed themselves and their wards. They spent mornings in closure, then onto daily Mass with the children. Their remaining hours were spent teaching. The friars came from many countries. There were Greeks, Italians, and a few Armenians.

St. Mary's provided a safe haven while the Armenians began to put their lives back together again. Many of the children were able to return to their homes. It seemed deceivingly that the terror was over. A cautious optimism overcame the citizens of the Ottoman Empire. The new young Turks had dethroned Abdul Hamid, denouncing him as a butcher and madman. They vowed a new, liberal leadership to all peoples under the Turkish yoke. What the unsuspecting Armenians didn't know was that the young Turks were actually displeased with Abdul Hamid because they felt his intention to rid Ottoman Turkey of the Armenians was neither well planned nor sufficiently brutal.

When Bedros reached the orphanage and made his way to his dormitory, the cold room was empty. It was an obvious sign that dinner was about to be served.

With the exception of a cross or religious painting, the dining hall was as unadorned and as gloomy as the classrooms and wards at the orphanage. The walls were a grayish color, which seemed even darker due to a dearth of windows. Bedros didn't mind the accommodations as they were far superior to his modest home. Except for the food and the fact that he could see his family only one day out of each week, Bedros found Saint Mary's an exciting educational and social experience. Here the young man could fulfill his penchant for knowledge, adventure, and riotous good times. If he would have changed anything in his schedule there, it would have been the daily Mass. He abhorred sitting still for more than five minutes. Furthermore, he was developing a deep personal relationship with his God. He felt he needed no more than that.

Bedros took his usual place at the long, wooden table. The bench wobbled underneath him, and he made a mental note to fix it in his spare time. His roommates were delighted upon his entry, as though a monarch had graced them with his presence. There were pats and jokes and a barrage of questions.

"I'll tell you after dinner," Bedros warned the noisy boys in a whisper, motioning to them with his head that Friar Cecil was making his waddling way to their table.

The friar's complexion took on a slow, reddish tinge as he spied his nemesis. The boys put their heads down quickly and pretended to enjoy the mushy bulghur pilaf, the scanty piece of fowl, and an offering of cucumber. The two Italian monks who served as cooks had outdone themselves that night.

As he approached the table, Friar Cecil tried to control himself so as not to draw undue attention from the other boys in the dining hall. They all sat in accordance to their ages and wards. He bypassed the others and lowered his head like a stalking lion as he came up to Bedros nose to nose.

"You have duped me for the last time, Bedros."

The monk was deliberately using a low, almost pleasant tone. He didn't wish to elaborate on the degrading experience of the day. Bedros only stared, daring not to answer, afraid of what his pride might make him say.

"You will stay in the kitchen with Friar Joseph and Friar Renaldo tonight and help them clean up. You will not leave until the job is completely done."

"Tomorrow in our arithmetic class, I will be giving extra-credit tests for the boys who are falling behind. Since you, Bedros, are so bright and far advanced in your math"—he made a face as though this fact made him sick—"you will instead spend the entire hour and a half writing for me, 'I promise I will never sneak away and pick fruits from the orchard again.'"

He drew a breath, about to go on, but saw the looks on the faces of the other boys. Bedros's expression didn't change. Fearing a loss in his already dwindling popularity, CiCi decided he had better cease his vengeance. He cleared his throat.

"Is that clear, Bedros?"

"That is clear, Friar Cecil," Bedros respectfully answered.

Satisfied, the fat man scampered off.

Back in the dormitory, the children huddled around Bedros in fascinated glee as he retold the story of the tree and the furiously wet Friar CiCi. His friends were delighted that someone had the nerve to give the miserable, old man his due. Then they dispersed, and went about their usual business of studying and letter writing. Bedros, who required very little study, sat propped up in his bed and played his clarinet in a low, soothing melody.

In this meager room gathered the future of a race. These were the teachers, builders, scientists, and artists of a new century. They were handsome, strong-willed, highly competitive young men. Inherent in them was a lust for achievement, a drive that would settle for nothing other than total success, a thirst for song, dance, and zestful living. It was these admirable traits that would eventually drive the Turks into a further frenzy.

Bedros at last settled back, hands clasped under his head in prayer. Of late he had been dwelling on the presence of God. He talked with Him. He confided in Him. Unlike some of the other boys, who had come to dispute the existence of a God so unfeeling and disinterested in the plight of the Armenians, Bedros felt a strong inspiration that God favored him. But as the night went on, he became tired and melancholy. Tears streamed down his tanned cheeks, dripping on and finally saturating his coarse pillow. He tried hard to swallow the lump swelling up in his throat. For relief he allowed a few soft sobs to escape, drawing the attention of his bedmate and good friend, Hirair.

"What is wrong?" asked the startled Hirair, who had never seen his powerful friend in a moment of weakness. "You are crying. I can tell."

"It will pass in a moment," Bedros reassured his friend. "I just began thinking about my father—how much he loved me, how much I miss him and..." He couldn't continue.

"I know," said Hirair, well understanding his friend's anguish. "I too cry often, silently, for my father."

It was the first time Hirair Plebian had ever mentioned his family to Bedros. The two boys had become good friends, and Bedros especially liked Hirair because the boy was honest. His words were straight and sincere. Bedros prided himself in evaluating people at first sight. He could read them through their eyes. And he liked the eyes of Hirair.

"You never talked of him before, Hirair. Why not?"

"It is so painful, Bedo, and I am embarrassed I will cry."

Bedros sat up, his full attention focused on his bedside friend. He remembered how the telling of his father's death story, though painful, had relieved him. Talking was important. They had all made their way to Saint Mary's because of some tragedy. No one was different; no one had been spared. He prodded his quiet friend.

"Tell me, Hirair. Believe me, you will feel better after. I will tell no one if that is what you choose. Remember, crying does not mean you are weak."

Hirair dried his tears with the back of his hand and picked up his nightshirt to gently blow his nose. Bedros chuckled at his friend's boyish ways. Then he made himself still and ready for the story that was to come. As in everything else he did, Bedros Vartanian listened with intensity. What someone he liked had to say was of great value. As brothers, the experience of one became the knowledge of the other. The weakness of one could inspire strength in the other. The very essence of life, after all, was people talking and listening to each other.

"I do not remember how many years ago it was. We lived close to the big church. My father was the parish priest. Did you know that, Bedo?"

Embarrassed, Bedros affirmatively nodded. In fact, he didn't even remember the inside of any church. His mother and grandmother would go, but the boys and Sahag, never.

"Well," continued the boy shakily, "my father—his name was Dikran—was a good man. He would tell the people in church every Sunday to be proud Armenians. 'Hold up your heads and look to God boldly,' he would say. It was his favorite expression."

He frowned a moment as if something had just occurred to him.

"I think I remember some old man warning him once not to let the Turks hear him. But my father just laughed and said there were no Turks in the Armenian Church, so how would they hear him?"

"That makes sense," interrupted Bedros, now wiggling in anxiousness.

"No, Bedo, it didn't. The Turks knew. My mother always said they had spies all over. She said they would like to make us all convert to Islam."

Bedros thought he might have gladly done just that if it would have saved his beloved father.

"So tell me, Hirair. How did they harm him?"

"Harm?" smirked the young boy, showing a wisdom and intensity Bedros had never seen in Hirair before.

"Bedo, they stormed into the church one morning, shouted crazy words to him and all of us, then dragged him out front. They forced him to kneel with his head down. Then they grabbed my mother and little sister and me. They made my mother and sister stand by Father's side. I was so frightened—I felt my stomach would come out of me. Then they made me kneel down next to him."

Bedros had sat up rigidly now, and a slow terror overcame him as he watched the color pour from his friend's smooth, young cheeks. The pain he had suffered on the morning of his own father's death was encroaching. He was sorry he had asked for this story.

"Hirair," Bedros quickly interjected, "you do not have to go on. Honestly. You have told me enough."

But Hirair was now oddly excited. Tears streamed down his face, and he shook all over. He lifted up his knees tightly against his chest to try to stop his body from quaking. He shook his head wildly and cried up to heaven as though he were telling the remainder of his tale to a somber board of the ecclesiastical listeners.

"Oh, God! What they did! What they did! As my mother, sister and I watched, they took a large sword and cut off his head. His head, Bedo! My father's head! It fell to the ground. It fell just under me. Blood was all over me. Then my eyes closed. I think—I cannot remember. I guess I fainted. I was sure I would be next since I was kneeling so close to him."

"Hirair, I am so sorry for you. So sorry."

"Bedros," Hirair sobbed in anguish, "I had to finish my story. I had to say how it happened. I couldn't speak of it since that day."

Hirair fell back in exhausted relief as Bedros came to his bedside and sat down. He stared silently at this quiet boy who had suffered so horribly. Bedros ached for Hirair; he ached for all the young Armenian children who had endured this and more. It made him sick. He got up and walked over to the jug of water the boys kept on the open window-sill. Returning with the water and a small cup, Bedros wiped his friend's face and offered him a drink.

"What of your mother and sister?" Bedros asked his now-revived companion.

"My mother lost her mind at that very moment, or so I have been told. They made her say she would accept Islam as her faith. Then they took her to some kind of hospital in Bolis. I didn't even see my sister after I woke up, but some people said the Turks had taken her for a slave. She is probably lost someplace far away."

"Sonia, my sister, was very pretty. She was older than me. She took good care of me. I wish I knew where she was. I wish she would be free and come and take me home."

Then the boys fell into each other's arms, hugging in comradely anguish.

A few moments passed, and the entire ward was hushed in stillness. One by one, the other boys had begun to eavesdrop on the private conversation. They were mostly Armenians except for one Greek boy, two Russians, and one Turkish boy who had wisely left the room. Why he was there, orphaned like the others, had never been mentioned. Rumor had it that the Turks were often as cruel to their own as they were to the Armenians.

Bedros suddenly sat up and observed the bleak pessimism that had taken over the place. The mood was serious, too serious for Bedros Vartanian. He sprang to his feet like a court jester and bounded to the center of the room.

"Is this what we are all here for? Are we to sit around like old men and sulk? We are young, we are alive. What more can we want?"

The jester was now strutting, drawing grins and giggles from his captive audience. "Let the fun begin!"

Bedros grabbed his clarinet and began to play a high-spirited dance song. The boys jumped from their beds and began to prance around in glee. They held their arms high in the air, swaying and stomping to the contagious rhythms of Bedros's music.

It was a typical Armenian-style dance—the kind the older men usually performed when they were adequately drunk. The Greek boy and the two Russians found little difficulty in the step, because their dancing styles were quite similar. It was a soul-warming scene, these young, handsome boys enjoying themselves so completely without shame or shyness. There was defiance in their gestures that declared, "See us. You have killed our fathers, shamed our mothers, but we live on. Indeed, we even dance and laugh so that you may see we will not be put down. We shall inherit our part of the earth."

It was this kind of fun that was part of the Armenian heritage. These boys would carry it with them into the future. They would thrive on it, jubilant in their survival—those of them who would survive.

Bedros put down his clarinet and began to sing. His voice was deeply mellow, crisp, and strong. He stomped his feet to the vivacious beat and soon they all joined in song. The words were happy ones. The song was one of celebration. It was a celebration of life.

Dari lo lo, Dari lo lo, lo lo
Dundigin in, ga letstustin lo lo
Oh, dari lo lo, dari lo lo, lo lo
Oh, dun a dig in in ga letstustin lo lo

Suddenly, the jubilation was shattered by the harsh voice of Friar Cecil.

"What goes on here at this hour?" asked the angry monk, not waiting for an answer. "Ha, I might have known it. I see Bedros Vartanian is behind all of this!"

Bedros refused to conceal his glee or his clarinet. Before he could answer, the other boys began to assail the friar with varied explanations for their little party. The monk grimaced at the noise, holding his hands up to his ears. At last he blasted out a bellowing shout and drew order.

"Enough! I am too tired for all your silly excuses. All of you get to bed! Remember, the extra-credit arithmetic test will be tomorrow."

He tottered out of the room, pausing a moment to look back at Bedros with righteous indignation.

"And you, of course, will remember your little assignment, Mr. Vartanian. Will you not?"

"How could I forget?" smiled Bedros, and the room fell dark and silent. Bedros lay on his back for a while, and then suddenly remembered how poorly Hirair was doing in his arithmetic. He leaned over his bed and whispered something into Hirair's ear. At first the shy boy protested, but soon began to giggle in mischievous complaisance.

"Agreed?" asked Bedros.

"Agreed!" affirmed Hirair.

The next morning after Mass, the boys entered the classroom taught by Friar Cecil. The subject was arithmetic. It was a difficult subject for most of the boys, and the instructor was intolerable. As Bedros had hoped, the puffy, old fool gave out the extra-credit tests to all but him. Each had been meticulously written by hand.

When he came to Bedros, CiCi handed the young boy a pile of plain paper for his punishment assignment. He waddled up to his desk and took his seat. True to form, the aging monk was soon snoring. With his head hanging back and his mouth comically open, he was oblivious to what was going on around him. It was as Bedros had hoped.

For the next hour, Bedros Vartanian took the difficult mathematics examination, answering all the questions with assured ease. Next to him sat Hirair Plebian, who, with the exception of an occasional groan from holding in his laughter, proceeded to write prolifically, "I promise I will never sneak away and pick fruits from the orchard again."

Then before CiCi awoke papers were swiftly transferred from desk to desk, and the brilliant plan of the little men was fulfilled. From that day on, the two boys were inseparable. On the way to the dining hall for lunch, Hirair walked along next to Bedros. Hirair grasped Bedros's arm and stopped him from his quick pace.

"Bedo," he said, barely able to get out the words, "someday I will repay you. I hope in a more important way."

"Come on!" answered Bedros, acting annoyed. "I am starving."

As he gulped down his cold lamb and cloudy chicken soup, Bedros tried to expel the growing anger and fear he harbored for Friar Cecil. The monk had become a burden to the carefree young man. He was beginning to feel as though he couldn't handle the badgering any more. Another thought ached inside him—that CiCi would notice the handwriting differences and poor Hirair might suffer for this prank. But Bedros overestimated the intelligence of the unobservant monk.

By evening Bedros and Hirair were satisfied their trick had worked. They were ecstatic. It had been a fruitful day. All the boys in ward were talkative and optimistic. An excited transfer of conversation abounded. Bedros carefully extracted several apples from his hidden fruit basket and proudly handed them out among his grateful compatriots. The young boys squatted here and there, jabbering enthusiastically. Over in the corner another group had gathered to discuss something they had been introduced to that afternoon in Friar Vincent's geography. The subject was America.

Stavros, a burly Greek boy, was the most outspoken.

"Friar Vincent talked about America like it would save everybody. I do not believe it! I have family who went there, and there was talk of how they starved. People treated them like dirt."

But Stavros was in the minority and was quickly heckled into submission. The children at Saint Mary's loved and respected Friar Vincent. In addition to being a capable headmaster, he was also a fine, inspiring teacher. Whatever he had to say was absorbed and accepted as absolute fact. And he had much to say about America, having gone there for part of his studies before returning to Rome. A few years later he came to Saint Mary's.

Friar Vincent had told of the poor who went to America and became rich. But what impressed the young boys most was when he told them everybody was created equal in this faraway land. He said a man could speak whatever language he chose, attend any church and no one would ever stand in his way. Above all else, the boys were astounded by the fact that there was a law in America, a law that said no man could steal from, torture, or murder another man, no matter what that man's ancestry might be. That such a utopia existed in their mangled world was fascinating to the boys.

A fellow Armenian named Aram, usually noncommittal, boldly spoke his mind.

"I believe Friar Vincent; I must tell you, Stavros. Before my mother and father had to send me here, they would get letters from my uncle who went to America. He got a good job, working in a big factory in a place called Philadelphia. He begged us in all his letters to come and start our lives there."

"So why did you not then?" retorted Stavros.

"Because," answered the boy, holding his head down for a moment and regaining his composure, "the Turks came and took over our house. They took our money. They ate our food. They said they needed our house for the army, and if my parents would be kind to them, no harm would ever happen to our family."

"The pigs!" someone dared to shout out, and a nervous caution overcame them all.

"We were sent out of the house, all of us, because my parents could no longer care for us. My two sisters went to an Islam home, and I and my younger brother were sent here."

Aram paused, looking about him at the sadness his story had wrought. The memories in the tear-filled eyes of his friends made him sorry he had told his story. Still he continued on.

"But I am going to leave here as soon as I can. I am going to America. I will get a job, make a lot of money, and I will bring my whole family to America myself. It is my dream."

"That's just what it is," interjected another cynic. "No Turk will let us Armenians walk out of this country just like that. We are *dimmis*, lower-class citizens. If they do not make us their slaves, then they will kill us all."

Bedros listened intently as his friends debated their points. He was delighted to see the fire that the thoughts of this brave, new land brought out in them. For himself, he hadn't thought much about the day's discussion until this very moment. His mind had been boggled with thoughts of CiCi and the examination.

America! He gently mulled the beautiful name around in his mind. America—a land of free men, a land of opportunity for all men, a land where there was no fear. He thought of his father, so brave, so good; but with it all, he couldn't withstand the Turkish dogs. He thought of Hirair and his father, whose God couldn't help him either. He thought of Garabed Hamparian's father, chopped up like food for the goats. So then even Bedros Vartanian in all his strength, in all his brilliance, in all his bravery—perhaps even he couldn't survive the brutality of the Turks?

Even if he were to survive, what kind of life would it be? He would always be a *dimmi*. He would have no rights, nor would his family. How could he achieve all the great things his young mind conjured up? Bedros thought on pensively. It wasn't weakness or cowardice that made the Armenians prey for the Turks, it was stupidity. They were stupid because they stayed there in this insane, backward land, a land that wasn't even theirs. They just waited to be slaughtered like cattle. Why? When a giant, rich land held out her hands to them and beckoned, "Come, I await you. I will give you life."

It was on this night, after sifting through these adult thoughts that Bedros Vartanian vowed to himself that he would go to that land called America and partake of her hospitality. In fact, he decided, he would make her his home. He believed he could strive and thrive there. He fell asleep with hopeful dreams.

•   •   •

A modest chapel adjoined Saint Mary's Orphanage by a long corridor. Each morning the boys were required to walk this corridor in total silence, contemplating their sins and the prayers they would be saying during the long Latin Mass. Such was the ritual every morning at six o'clock. After Mass there would be breakfast followed by classes, lunch, dinner, and then reflection—which had come to mean fun time to the boys—and at last bed.

Two hundred young men were huddled into the small building. They sat, as elsewhere in the orphanage, according to age. Bedros and the boys from eight-to-ten ward filled the middle rows, in between the four- to seven-year-olds and eleven- to fifteen-year-olds. It had been carefully planned that Ara would sit directly behind Bedros and periodically poke the squirming boy or once in a while slip him a piece of candy.

Saint Mary's chapel was a dust-speckled mass of sunshine on this warm September morning. The haze from the morning mist infiltrated the building and mingled in melodious swirls with the puffs of smoke that wriggled to the ceiling from the burning incense on the altar. It was a most-solemn scene—the monks gathered around the altar, their bald heads gleaming like so many melons under the peeking sunlight. The candles flicked furiously but were no match for the gilded light streaming through the windows. Adding to this mystical scene were the mournful chants of the Gregorian Mass, sung in ancient, laborious Latin.

As the friars loudly blared out, *"Dominus Vobiscum,"* their audience, a group of young boys—all dressed in the same drab gray with a hint of a tiny, white collar—answered not so authoritatively, *"Et cum spiritu tuo."*

Bedros sat oddly still for one usually so fidgety and disinterested in the tedious Mass. He stared up at the large, wooden crucifix, which hung from two ropes high above the heads of the chanting monks. There was a look on his face that had a faint trace of piety; his lips opened and closed in quick gestures like a bird chirping. He was oblivious to all around him, even Ara, who waited for the first wiggle from his brother, astounded that it hadn't as yet come. The evening before, Bedros Vartanian had thought a lot about his life and his past. Now he decided it was time to confer with his God.

"Father, I have been thinking a lot lately. I need your help. I have been thinking about America. I have heard many stories about it. I need to get out of Malatia. I want to get away from this whole part of the world. I want to go to America and be a great man. Help me Father. Please!"

Suddenly Bedros's head fell back in a spasm so rigid that Ara quickly grabbed him. Bedros' face was white, his eyes glassy and distant.

"What is the matter with you?" whispered Ara, shaking his little brother.

"Brother," replied Bedros with a serene smile on his face, "He answered me. He said he would help me."

"Who? Who are you talking about?" insisted Ara.

Bedros didn't answer. He rose from his seat and walked out of the chapel. Walking out during services was considered a grave sin, but he didn't care.

Ara reached forward and tried to snatch his brother, but the slippery, little fish was already free. The boys of eight-to-ten ward began to murmur, craning their heads to see what Bedros was up to this time. As it would happen, in the middle of a loudly bellowed "Alleluia, alleluia," Friar Cecil casually turned around just as Bedros Vartanian was making his escape.

Bedros went out the door and flew down the stone path to the fresh, wet-smelling orchard. His muscular legs leaped like a gazelle. His head was turned upward to heaven, as though some invisible string were attached to his chin, pulling him along like a human puppet. The young boy was ecstatic and full of hope. The same God who had failed his father had spoken to him! It was as the priests had tried to explain; God had to let his own son die in order that the world might live. So that was why Sahag Vartanian had to die, so that Bedros might live. And live he would, for he wasn't about to mishandle this precious gift.

At last stopping, breathless, Bedros reached up for an apple, which drooped just over his head. He yanked it loose, grabbed it tightly, and jammed it into his mouth with gusto. The splashy crunch was so loud that it frightened away the birds peacefully nestled above in the bony apple tree. He munched and laughed and cried. It was as though this day were his first. For some time he stood there, among the apples and pears, dreaming of his father, his God, and his beautiful America.

His prayerful daydreaming came to an abrupt halt with the faint sound of someone approaching. Bedros was immediately alert, like a doe about to be shot by a steadfast hunter. He quickly ran to a clump of bushes nearby. As he crouched down he listened intently. The harsh bellow of Friar Cici shattered the serene hush of the orchard.

"Bedros, where are you, boy? I know you are in here!"

He sounded more furious than Bedros could ever remember, and for the first time, the young boy feared that this man might actually do him harm. He was so overjoyed with his experience at Mass he considered surrendering himself, assured that his spiritual experience would move the religious man. But Friar Cecil's second outburst quickly dispelled the thought from his mind.

"Listen to me, you brat! I saw you leave Mass. You know that is inexcusable. This time you will not fool me." The man was puffing and snorting like a rabid dog. "I will stay here and not move until you come out."

Bedros remained silent, planning his strategy.

"You do hear me, do you not, Bedros? Stay there if you will, but night will come and I, Friar Cecil, will remain here until you come out."

There was no doubt Bedros could outrun the arthritic, old man. But just how far could he run? How long could he hold out? No matter how fast or far he ran he feared CiCi had him sooner or later. He paused a moment, bowing his head, and asked God to get him out of this one.

Then a thought came to him. Bedros grinned widely. He cautiously got up on his feet, trying not to rustle the heavy, reddish-green brambles that surrounded him. He ran with great speed out of his hiding place into the orchard, past a small pond, and out into the vast, open farmland of Saint Mary's.

Friar Cecil couldn't believe the audacity of this boy—to show himself and then run off into the openness of the crops and low fields. He bounded after him, his fists clenched and waving wildly in the air. This time he would get him. This time he would get this boy who considered himself a man, this boy who thought himself different from all the other children. This time he would quell his spirit. How dare he believe himself gifted, special, beyond need of normal restrictions and regimentations? Perhaps Friar Cecil saw in Bedros all the strong attributes he himself lacked, but that was of no matter. The hunter had at last encountered his prey. He would finally stifle him, break his will, and extinguish his hopes.

As Bedros raced out toward the open farmland, he could see the shabby row of outhouses lined up like wooden soldiers, looking like caretakers guarding the crops. The outdoor bathrooms had been placed far out there for a specific reason, and it was that reason that drew Bedros there, to the culmination of the hunt. Since the friars couldn't afford fertilizers, they used the waste collected daily from these outdoor latrines. About twenty-five feet behind the outhouses rested a large mountain of human manure. Already the smell had reached Bedros's nose, and he faltered. Looking back, he could see the round monk wobbling after him with a maniacal look on his face. CiCi came closer and closer, and Bedros braced himself. He had to do what he had to do. Survival at all costs. Steadfastly he ran past the tomatoes, stomping on the leafy squash and tangling in and over the lithe cucumbers. He slipped and scrambled up and onto the ghastly-smelling pile of decaying feces.

When the panting Friar Cecil finally reached the field, he hesitated. No doubt Bedros was in one of the latrines. It was just a matter of which one. As he made his way closer to begin his inspection of the outhouses, he detected a sound from behind them. Although the monk was overcome with nausea from the foul smell, his determination won out. He turned and walked behind the first bathroom and was appalled to see young Bedros perched high atop the sickening hill.

The old man was beside himself. The odor made his stomach turn upside down. Flies buzzed all around him and the defiant boy above him. CiCi was dizzy with nausea, yet Bedros stood undaunted, his hands proudly placed on his hips, a grin on his face.

"Now I know you are insane!" shouted CiCi up to his archenemy.

Bedros looked down with a naughty smile, which was somewhat distorted by a growing grimace. He thought he would pass out and roll down the big, brown hill right into CiCi's waiting lap. Bravely, he fought off the sickness, and defiantly he held his nose.

"I am crazy, Father, but you would be crazier to come up and get me."

Bedros laughed while swatting savagely at the buzzing insects. Friar Cecil, even in all his vengeance, so close to his pursuance, quickly reneged. He was too old for this kind of madness. He was temporarily beaten. The egregious boy had thwarted the monk.

As he stomped down an angry foot and took his usual hand-on-hips stance, he declared loudly up to Bedros, "I will not be so mad, but your brother Ara will be summoned to fetch you. And upon returning, which I have no doubts you eventually must, you will answer to me alone."

Off strutted the exasperated friar, leaving Bedros Vartanian perched in uncanny regality on his brown mountain.

As sick as he was, Bedros wouldn't dare slide down the fertilizer hill until he at last saw Ara approaching. He yelped with glee at the sight of his brother and slid down the slimy pile, oblivious of his clothes, his skin, and the chunks of brown matter clinging to him all over.

"Ara, you made it!" shouted Bedros, running up to his brother as if he were about to hug him. He considerately stopped himself short, realizing his undesirable looks.

Ara stood for a second, his mouth dropped open, unable to speak. The scowl he had worn into the field instantly fled from his face, and the twelve-year-old burst into uproarious laughter. Tears gushed from his eyes, and he bent over to one side, holding his stomach in the pain of his laughter.

"Now I believe you have done it all, little Bedo. Look at you! You are a smelly mess."

Bedros looked down at himself, surprised by the extent of his disgusting condition. He put his hand up to his mouth as though he would become sick but instead fell down on the ground, laughing.

Once again brother Ara led brother Bedros down the path to his reckoning. But it was in fact the younger of the two who would eventually lead them both out of hell, away from the manure pile that was Malatia and on to the Promised Land.

"I guess CiCi is going to give it to me good this time, eh, Ara?"

"No, as a matter of fact," Ara replied, "it is Friar Vincent who wishes to see you this time."

Friar Vincent's office was modest and unpretentious. The floor was hard, hand-sanded wood. There was a heavy wooden desk and stately ladder-backed chair, in which the robust man sat. In a bookcase to the left of the desk were more volumes than Bedros had ever seen. The books were of all different colors and titles. For a moment the sight of them distracted Bedros from his purpose there. Friar Vincent cleared his throat loudly to regain the young boy's attention. He motioned to him to take a seat in one of two chairs facing the front of his desk.

As the young boy stood warily in front of the headmaster, he noted how handsome Friar Vincent was. His graying hair was vividly speckled with hues of reddish brown. He had deep, pensive eyes, which were kind like his father's. And there was something else about Friar Vincent. He looked like a priest should. He had the countenance of peace, the eyes of love, and the brow of understanding. Perhaps he was something of an earthly counterpart to the God Bedros had just come to know.

Slowly Bedros took his seat, looking up at the lonely, black crucifix, which hung on the wall just above the good monk's head. Friar Vincent looked back with a most compassionate smile. Though his eyes wanted to show displeasure, it seemed they couldn't. It had taken much time, water, and scrubbing but Ara had prepared his brother well. Friar Vincent marveled at this good-looking, shining, clean young man. He perceived the wisdom in Bedros's eyes, the self-assurance in his manner. As the two acquainted themselves with each other, a mutual respect was immediately evident. Bedros knew it would be a fine meeting, not a confessional scolding.

"Bedros," began the headmaster, peering out from under bushy eyebrows, "you have greatly upset Friar Cecil."

"I know, Father," responded the respectful Bedros.

"Friar Cecil tells me you are rude, dirty, and impossible to teach. He says you steal our produce and sneak out of Mass. Is this so?"

Bedros tried to control his rising anger, though he knew his reddening face was a giveaway. "Father Vincent, I do not like Friar Cecil, and he does not like me. No matter what I do, he will find fault."

"I see," mused the monk, surprised by the boy's candid reply. "Go on, Bedros. Tell me how you feel about all this."

Well, thought Bedros, suddenly trusting that this wonderful man would understand whatever he had to say. "Father, I do think I am special, I suppose. That is, I feel strong. I feel like I can do anything I decide to do. Friar Cecil thinks I am bold and immodest. Those are the words he always uses. But I do not feel like I am better than everyone else... just...just luckier, I guess."

"Hmmm," responded Friar Vincent, "and what do you think we should do about this intolerable situation? You know it cannot go on. It will soon interfere with your schooling, and I do not want to see that happen."

Bedros didn't know what to say. He truly felt that nothing could help his relationship with CiCi, and he told Friar Vincent so. He insisted that he couldn't change his personality for anyone and explained his reasons for the fruit thefts and for running out of Mass.

Friar Vincent listened and was deeply moved by this articulate young man.

"Bedo," interrupted the friar kindly, "I have a suggestion."

"Yes, Father?" asked the curious young man.

"Firstly, I will see to it that the cooks include a large portion of fresh fruits and vegetables in all meals."

Bedros's face lit up, and he nearly jumped out of his seat.

"In fact," continued the wise man, "I think I will have a large basket of fresh fruit kept on a special table in each ward. That way the boys will not have to resort to seeking out hidden fruit baskets under floors."

Friar Vincent spoke with a note of soft satire. He was delighted to have startled the young man with his knowledge.

"You knew about that?" Bedros asked, mortified.

"Yes, Bedo. I knew about your secret basket for a long time. And I know much more. I have learned from your work in my class and from your other teachers that you are an outstanding pupil, far advanced for your age."

Bedros said nothing but modestly squirmed a little in his chair.

"I have a certain plan for you, Bedros, something you will have to consider carefully."

Bedros felt a surge of excitement overcome him.

"Yes, Father?"

"I am going to send you to Rome at the beginning of the next school term in January."

For the first time in his life, Bedros Vartanian was speechless. He managed to squeak out the word—"Rome?"

"Yes, my son, Rome. You will go to Italy. You will attend our finest school there. It is run by the Mekhitarist Fathers. They are strict but wise and dedicated teachers."

"Father, there is nothing I would want more." Bedros softly interjected, feeling most unworthy for once in his life.

"Yes, I am sure you would thrive there, Bedros. Rome is a beautiful, exciting city. It is sophisticated, unlike here. There they have modern conveniences and advanced European teaching methods. Yes, my son, you will fare well there."

"Father, I will make you proud. I will write to you and tell you everything I am doing. I will—"

"Before you get packed," laughed the delighted friar, "I must, of course, write to your mother for permission. I am sure she would be most proud to see you so favored and given a free education in so fine a place."

Yes, of course, thought Bedros suddenly, a little uneasy. He was seized with a fear of the thought that anything, or anyone, could awaken him from this blissful dream.

Absent-mindedly he jumped out of his seat and began to run out of the office.

"Excuse me!" shouted Friar Vincent, understanding the young man's anxiousness. "There is still one more thing."

"One more thing?" asked Bedros, wishing he were already in the eternal city.

"Yes, Bedros." continued the kindly priest, leaning back in his chair and folding his determined arms. "Though I sadly realize you do not have a religious calling, for the remainder of your days here, you must respectfully attend daily Mass."

"Of course, of course." insisted Bedros, still itching to get out the door.

"Wait a moment, my son.

Friar Vincent walked over to the impatient, young boy and whispered something serious into Bedros's ear.

The next morning Mass was celebrated as usual in Saint Mary's chapel. Everything seemed quietly the same. The monks gathered in solemn unison, heads up to heaven, chanting their Latin songs. The boys sat like statues—unmoving masses of gray and white—feebly responding in their ceremonious voices. On the altar the candles flickered. The incense puffed. The crucifix loomed above. But today on the altar, amid the chalices and statues and crisply folded, white vestments, there was a new, most attentive altar boy. It was Bedros Vartanian.

Friar Cecil looked on with satisfied accomplishment in his eyes, assured that he alone was responsible for this miracle. The boys from his ward snickered, wondering how hideous CiCi's punishment must have been to bring the unconquerable Bedros Vartanian to this. And Ara wondered, as he gazed up at his little brother who meandered about the altar, carrying golden plates and tiny candles. What in heaven had God said to Bedros after all?

At breakfast all rumor was made fact as Bedros excitedly told his story to his friends, pausing only to gulp down a glass of goat's milk, some thin bread, and a delicious, green pear. After eating, he ran over to Ara and breathlessly explained what had happened the day before.

Ara Vartanian silently listened to the chattering of his excited baby brother. It didn't come as a surprise to him that someone would discover the greatness in this little one. He was so very proud, so very happy, for his beloved brother. There was no envy in him, no remorse, only a slow growing sad realization that he would lose his precious, little partner. He would no longer be his brother's overseer, laugh with him, and delight in him. Casually Ara Vartanian explained away his tears as signs of happiness for Bedros's extreme good fortune.

A week later, Bedros awoke on a rainy, dismal morning to the sight of Friar Vincent standing over his bed, staring down at him with a look of sadness on his face. The young man was frightened by what he saw in this normally complaisant man. He sat up. He couldn't speak, but his worried, inquisitive eyes spoke for him.

"Bedros, I am so very sorry," Friar Vincent began, taking the boy in his arms and embracing him in an unusual show of emotion. "Your mother has come for you and Ara."

"What?" asked Bedros, not understanding what this meant.

"She is furious with all of us here, my child. You must forgive her. She does not understand."

"Understand...understand what? Please, Friar, do not tell me...I do not want to hear."

The kindly priest clasped Bedros's shoulders tightly, rocking him gently.

"Your mother feels she cannot let you leave Malatia. She says all this talk about Rome and education is foolishness. She claims she needs you and Ara home to begin working so you can help the family by earning wages."

Bedros fell back into his bed, sobbing. "No, no. Please, make her understand!" he begged.

"I have done and said all I can, my son. Your mother believes I have filled your head with nonsense. She is taking you home today."

Bedros sat up defiantly. Stubbornly he thrust the tears off his face with the sweep of his trembling arm. He threw his few meager belongings into the same sack he had brought with him years ago and bravely walked out of the ward, not daring to awaken his friends or create a scene of anguish with long, pointless good-byes. Friar Vincent accompanied him to his office, where an impatient, infuriated Yughaper Vartanian awaited her sons.

Ara was sitting morosely in the chair by Friar Vincent's desk. Yughaper stood by the door, her arms tightly folded. The look on her face was stoic. Taking one look at her, Bedros knew there was no use in crying or begging. The woman had made up her closed mind. Ara and Bedros exchanged tear-filled, understanding glances. They had seen their mother on occasion during their time at St. Mary's, yet they never really knew her. Today they learned quickly what kind of woman she was. If wrong or right, she was doggedly determined. No one, not even the great and intelligent Friar Vincent, was going to change her mind.

Irene Vosbikian

A few polite but cold words were muttered between Yughaper and Friar Vincent, and then quickly Ara and Bedros found themselves next to their mother. She grasped each by the arm, roughly escorting them out of the office and into the waiting carriage.

It was a familiar scene but with reversed emotions. Now the two boys were leaving Saint Mary's, a home they had come to love. They would miss the influence of the beautiful man who stood at the front doorway of the orphanage, bidding them farewell.

"Remember, boys," shouted Friar Vincent to the donkey cart, which was already pulling away. "When God closes one door, he opens many windows!"

So saying, the monk lowered his head and turned his back on the disappearing carriage, which carried the mother with her two despondent but obedient children.

It was three days later, and Friar Vincent was taking his usual stroll through the gardens in the atrium at the entrance to Saint Mary's. He customarily took these silent, lonely walks right before Mass. They allowed him the only time in his day to be completely in solace—alone with his thoughts and his God. He bent down to pick a bunch of purplish-blue asters, which he thought he would bring to adorn the altar. He marveled at their delicate beauty and wistfully wondered what Bedros Vartanian would be doing with this refreshing fall day. As he started back in to prepare for Mass, he heard the sound of a cart approaching. He looked around, flabbergasted, to see that driving it was a leathery, old woman, and behind her Ara and Bedros Vartanian.

"Father," called the crackling voice of the old woman, "I have come to deliver two packages to you."

Friar Vincent could barely contain his joy as he watched the two young boys hop off their transport and run toward him. They were both carrying the same satchels they'd had when they left. Friar Vincent gave an amused smile, wondering if they had ever even unpacked.

Not waiting for words, Bedros and Ara flew into the orphanage and quickly disappeared. Friar Vincent walked up to the donkey cart, where

64

the elderly lady sat. She had an odd look on her face, which seemed a cross between extreme joy and profound sorrow.

"Good morning to you, madam," Friar Vincent bestowed upon the woman.

"And you, Father. I am Yester, the boys' grandmother."

"I am happy to meet you, Digin Yester. I am Friar Vincent, headmaster of Saint Mary's."

"And not a very good one!" scolded Yester, pointing an accusing, rickety finger at the startled priest.

"I beg your pardon!" retorted the astonished and slightly annoyed monk.

"Just as I have said," continued Yester. "You send home two boys to us? Well, they are of no use. They know nothing of the working world. They are lazy and disrespectful to their mother. They do not even know how to clean themselves properly."

Friar Vincent suddenly realized this old lady was toying with him. They were many things, but these two fine young men were none of the distasteful things this woman was suggesting. He had always considered both boys two of the finest children at Saint Mary's.

Playing along, he asked Yester, "What would you have me do?

"The clever old woman answered, "Perhaps you had better just keep them here a little longer. Heaven knows they could use more polishing."

"But what about their mother?" The headmaster frowned.

"That is all taken care of, sir!" Yester responded, flashing a toothless grin.

Friar Vincent gave Yester an understanding smile and took her shaking hand. "I understand perfectly, Digin Yester. They will be in good hands."

Yester had done all she could to pretend anger, but her eyes gave her away as they freely spurted tears down her wrinkled cheeks. As she yanked impatiently at the donkey's yoke, she looked down timidly at the compassionate friar.

"Take care of them, Father. They are my life."

"I know that, Digin. They are mine as well."

As the donkey slowly began to move his burden along, Yester turned around with one last remark to Friar Vincent.

"Remember one last thing!" she shouted in the original voice with which she had greeted him. "No Rome!"

"Agreed, my friend, agreed!" Friar Vincent shouted out to the lady, who was already on her way home.

Friar Vincent walked slowly back into the orphanage. He was most impressed with the courageous and wise woman he had just met. She had coyly convinced her daughter of her hastiness, and though it must have broken her heart, she had let go of her precious grandchildren now for a second time. He vowed he wouldn't take her trust lightly.

As he entered Saint Mary's chapel, he saw Ara nestled comfortably in his place among the other boys. Then he looked up at the blazing altar in joyous astonishment to see Bedros Vartanian kneeling in respect under the statues of the Virgin Mary and Saint Joseph, who seemed to nod in contentment that he was back.

Ara and Bedros were to spend five more years at Saint Mary's. They were fruitful years, filled with extensive studies and devout religious training. Both boys had been requested to help with various expansion efforts at the orphanage, through which they learned multifaceted techniques of building.

During those years, many of their friends had left. Hirair received a letter from his mother, which said she was completely recovered and had remarried in Bolis. He was overjoyed but saddened to be leaving his dearest friend. Friar Vincent, his worth sorely needed, was temporarily recalled to Rome. CiCi died of a heart attack. And so, as God so magnificently manipulates, Ara and Bedros were more than ready to leave on the morning Yughaper came to retrieve them.

One of their first functions upon returning home was to attend the funeral of their grandmother, Yester. The cause of her death was unknown. The villagers believed she was nearly ninety. No one knew, least of all Yester herself. She had been chirpily harvesting chamomile, a prized herb she frequently used to concoct her medications, only a few hours before she fell into her final sleep.

Chapter 3

MALATIA, 1909

Like the Vartanian brothers, Malatia had matured during the fourteen years since Sahag Vartanian died. Homes were being built more frequently, and their construction far surpassed the muddy, feeble huts of adobe, which had been prevalent before. Roads were better paved, lumber was now available in abundance, and the town took on a relatively modern appearance. Still the town was by no means advanced. Malatia, by virtue of her central, isolated location, still progressed at a much slower rate than other villages, such as Adana and Trebizond. These were closer to major rivers, and therefore the sophisticated influence of the Western world flowed more frequently into them.

Even Yughaper Vartanian, now a perfect replica of her mother, had acquired a fascinating new invention called a *furoon*—a coal-burning stove. Nevertheless, even with a few minor improvements in her lifestyle, the years had taken a tremendous toll on her. At fifty, she looked closer to seventy. She still smoked her coveted Turkish cigarettes. She still worked the garden and tended her prized herbs. She had at least gained a renewed respect for her medicinal powers.

The torrid summer of 1908 turned into the harsh, blustering winter of 1909, and most of Malatia remained locked up indoors. By the spring of that year, an evident ray of hope overcame all of Malatia and her surrounding vilayets. Armenian women dared to speak their mother tongue freely, except in the markets where the Turks were still the predominant nationality. There was notable interaction between the

Turkish neighbors and the others; some of it even bordered on friendship. It seemed like the dawning of a new age for all.

Politically there was cautious optimism since that same year brought with it the organization of the Ittihad-Terraki Party, still commonly known as the Young Turks. Sultan Abdul Hamid stepped down, and a constitutional government was formed. These young Turkish leaders had established themselves throughout the world as liberals, seeking peace and equality for all ethnic groups living under their reign. They had even begun consulting with prominent Armenian activists in their new regime, one of whom was a noted man, whom many had earlier considered a dangerous rebel. His name was Garo Vartanian.

Garo had sent word to his family that he had left Aleppo, where life had grown serenely dull. He had gone to Adana, a progressive town where Turks and Armenians were congenially manipulating the future of Armenia. Garo excitedly joined in with the political goings-on there, assured that he would now peacefully achieve the same ends he had earlier sought through more precarious means. He had traveled to Adana by boat up a small tributary of the Euphrates River. The trip had taken him nearly one month through bitter cold to make the simple, northwesterly journey. He wrote often, saying he was well and extremely optimistic.

Khatchadour was now a young man of twenty-six. He was handsomely dark and tall. He had taken a wife, who was not of Yughaper's liking, because she wasn't originally from Malatia but rather from Arabkir. There had always been an amusing rivalry between the Armenians in these two neighboring towns, each claiming to have the finest cuisine, the most beautiful dance styles, and the loveliest women. But when Khatchadour and Anna had their first child—a son, of course—Yughaper was at least more civil to her daughter-in-law. Nevertheless, the two decided to move out of the house and build a small home for themselves near the gunsmith foundry where Khatchadour worked.

Hovsep was now fifteen, and his younger brother, Sahag, was only one year behind him. The two had grown up so closely together that they not only acted like twins but also even took on the same expressions and mannerisms. Each had a reddish color to his very curly hair as well as hazel eyes and lighter complexions than those of the other brothers.

Their days consisted of Armenian school in the mornings and then work in the foundry with Khatchadour in the afternoons. Their evenings were contrived of cavorting and philandering with older boys. Unlike Ara and Bedros, who had lived with sadness in the eyes of their fellow orphans, the memory of Sahag Vartanian wasn't a part of their fun-filled minds. To them life had always been, and would always, be great fun.

At twenty-one Ara had grown taller and much stronger in appearance than the seventeen-year-old Bedros, but still possessed his simple, quiet ways. In the very manner he walked and talked, he portrayed peace and solemnity. So Bedros gave the appearance of being physically larger than Ara, mostly because of his emotional, impetuous, and rambunctious nature. It was as it had always been—the two young men were extremely different personalities, yet each imparted inseparable influences on the other. After four years of daily schooling and boring hours in the foundry, they both soon agreed that it was time they set out to make a living on their own.

Ara and Bedros spent most of that spring helping Khatchadour build his simple home out of lumber, adobe, and a few hard-to-get roof tiles. They had become gifted craftsmen due in part to their labors at Saint Mary's. When Khatchadour's home was completed, the two Vartanian brothers decided they would become builders.

After his mother's fine dinners, Bedros spent most of his evenings at Vahak's, which had by now regained its carefree café image. The clientele was well mixed. Turks and Greeks could often be seen drinking together. Bedros now and then involved himself in a skilled game of *tavloo* with one of the local Armenians, unless Ara might be there, but he most often wasn't. Though women didn't come into such places, it wasn't uncommon for the more forward young Armenian girls to wait outside for a coveted glimpse of the handsome Bedros Vartanian. He had become a tremendous-looking young man, whose pitch-black eyes peered luminously out from under well-formed, thick, black eyebrows. His body was sculpted to perfection, with rippling muscles that peeked out from his short-sleeved shirt, making many a young lady swoon.

It was the morning after one of these tiring evenings that Bedros Vartanian awoke to the sound of a knock at his front door. He lazily lay in bed, hoping someone else would open the door, but apparently no one had else heard the knock. Angrily, he got up and splashed some cold water on his bristly face. The young bull stomped over to the door and swung it open. A seven-year-old girl stood bashfully before him.

At the sight of this abruptly awakened, unshaven mountain of a man, the little girl turned on her heels to run away, but Bedros quickly caught the back of her long burlap dress.

"Hold still, little girl!" he growled. "You do not wake me up after a night like I had last night just to go running away." He pleasantly changed his tone and softened the hard frown on his prickly face to a casual smile. "I am sorry if I frightened you. What is it that you want?"

"I am Syrvart Hamparian," announced the trembling, soft-spoken little girl. "My cousin Garabed sent me to fetch you."

For a moment Bedros was speechless that this strange, little messenger should bring up a name he had left somewhere far behind him—Garabed Hamparian. All he could visualize was the always unpleasant, disinterested disposition of the boy who had spent his time loitering around in dismal daydreams. He momentarily recalled a time back at Saint Mary's when he had startled the strange boy.

Bedros had gone into the older ward, which, like most of his practices, was forbidden. He had been looking for Ara; the reason why now escaped him. There, sitting in a far off corner of the dormitory, huddled over a small box, was Garabed. The engrossed boy was so busy fiddling with his little possession that he didn't hear Bedros approaching. When he finally looked up, Garabed quickly closed the box and thrust it behind him, as if Bedros had brought some criminal intent with him.

Bedros teased him about his silly secret and the ridiculous, little box, about which he said he couldn't care less. Garabed became indignant. He called Bedros over and pompously opened his wooden treasure, displaying more *piastres*, Turkish coins, than Bedros had ever seen in his life. Proudly satisfied, Garabed explained that his father had left him this fortune. Hovnan had told his son of its hiding place if anything were to happen to him. Garabed had concealed the treasure, even from the monks.

After this revelation, Bedros had sworn secrecy to his friend.

What Garabed Hamparian could have to do with this little girl or why he had come back to Malatia at all instilled curiosity in Bedros. He asked the young girl to wait while he freshened up. He then obediently got into her carriage, which she had remarkably driven there herself. Being a well-bred gentleman, Bedros Vartanian took over the reins for the short journey to Hovnan Hamparian's home. The place had been deadly deserted since his mutilation fourteen years earlier.

As he drove the bouncing donkey cart along, Bedros now and then looked sideways at the silent little girl, who sat cautiously away from his reach. She amused him, and he was surprised that he had never seen her before. His life had always been filled with boys, boys of all sizes and personalities. It was a gruff social circle. This delicate, little flower was a pleasantly fragile change of pace. She had said her name was Syrvart, which meant "flower." It was an appropriate name, he mused.

Bedros remembered meeting Syrvart's mother once or twice. Her name was Mariam. He had run a few errands for her, as he recalled. Yughaper had explained that he had to help the woman out, because in some distant mingling of ancient bloods, Mariam Hamparian was a cousin to Yughaper. Bedros then realized that if Garabed was this young lady's cousin, then that meant he, Bedros, was in some way related to Garabed. He preferred to dispel the thoughts of this complicated family tree for the moment. Besides—he laughed to himself—everyone knew all Armenians were related to each other in one way or another. Such familial dinner table discussions had always made him laugh with amused confusion. Then, in the middle of his muddled thoughts, chirped the voice of the lovely young girl. She had been so silent for so long that Bedros was astounded that she dared speak to him at all.

"Your mother tried to save my father's life last week," she said softly, "but he died."

Bedros was embarrassed. In all his wanderings lately, he had rarely spoken to Yughaper about her comings and goings. He politely bestowed his condolences to the now less-nervous Syrvart.

"I am sorry. I didn't know."

"She said he had something called pneumonia. She gave him many different medicines. But he died anyway."

She was matter-of-fact in her sorrow, showing a remarkable austerity for one so young. Bedros was impressed.

"I had met your mother a few times," Bedros said, finally breaking a long silence. "I didn't know your father."

"His name was Manoog," explained the child. "He was a wonderful man. I was his only daughter, and he treated me like a special doll." She drew a long breath, and then turned her head, embarrassed by her tears.

"So," Bedros dared to question further, "what has Garabed to do with you?"

"My mother had a baby, my little brother, Hagop, about two months ago." She continued their conversation reluctantly, still staring out distantly, her head turned away from Bedros. "She has been very weak, and then when my father died...Well, we had no one."

"I see. So Garabed came to help you?" asked Bedros, not imagining that Garabed had a compassionate bone in his body.

"He is our only living relative. Through the years my family has been scattered and killed off. Garabed left the orphanage as soon as he heard about my father. He made us leave our old house. He said it was too small with too many memories. He has taken us into his childhood home."

Though still not allowing himself to believe Garabed's motives were totally honorable, Bedros was at least pleased that someone had come to take care of this unfortunate girl and her mother and brother. Bedros knew all too well that Garabed Hamparian had the money to support his newly acquired family. Still puzzling him was what Garabed could possibly want of him, unless it was to boast of his new worth in life—instant family and responsibility. Whatever it was, he would soon find out. The home of Hovnan and Arpine Hamparian loomed before them. A shudder ran through his body as he remembered the horrors the old place had seen. As a child, he had played there in search of the ghost rumored to be lurking about the place. He wasn't playing now.

Garabed was waiting at the door. He walked triumphantly out of the gated courtyard and on past the great well, in which the spirit of Hovnan was said to linger. Garabed had already begun to clear the thick weeds, which had taken over the once-meticulous garden. Repairs had been made on the roof and windows. Ulysses had returned home to gather his booty, reclaim his birthright, and father a fatherless family. Or so it seemed.

Bedros halted the cart. Syrvart slid down and was out of his sight without another word. She vanished into the house. The sounds of a baby crying came from within.

Bedros got down and made his way toward Garabed. The two men gave each other a quick hug and made the motions of being happy to see one another. It had been four years. Bedros took note of Garabed's frailty. He had always had a sickly sort of look. Garabed was twenty-four years old, but seemed much older. Garabed's face was extremely thin. He had never been one who enjoyed food, drink, or anything else of life. His hair was already thinning and lacking in specific color. He was well dressed in new, Western-style clothing—a white shirt, suspenders, and gray flannel knickers. His hands were clean and unmarked—the sign of a gentleman.

"You are looking well," lied Bedros.

"And, as always, you are looking handsome and healthy," responded Garabed with some disdain.

"I work outdoors a good deal," answered Bedros, as though excusing his rugged handsomeness to this hapless man.

"Yes, I have heard. You have a reputation for being an accomplished builder around Malatia. That is why I had Syrvart call you."

Bedros thought Garabed was trying hard to sound polished and westernized, though it did little to help his meek presentation, he decided.

"What did you have in mind?" asked Bedros.

"Well, you see, now I have three people living here, and the place is not made for all of this." He motioned with his arm back toward the house, which contained his newly acquired wards.

"Mariam is only thirty-eight years old and without a husband. It wouldn't be proper for us to live, even as cousins, in such proximity. So I was hoping you and Ara could come up with a plan to redo the house, giving me a separate living area from the others, especially the women.

With pleasure, Bedros silently thought, agreeing that this whole arrangement appeared rather seedy. "Of course, we can manage something," he said finally.

"You will have to do more than manage!" retorted Garabed. "As you know, I can pay you well for your labors."

"I know," responded Bedros with a sly smile. "Well then, we will be back tomorrow to begin work."

"That will be fine," Garabed coldly exclaimed and turned to walk back into his domain.

Bedros considered Garabed for a while before leaving. Though he loved to build homes, he felt menial and patronized working for this man. Still he felt sympathy for little Syrvart and her family. As he pensively walked home, he found a certain note of delight in the fact that he could, at least, occasionally oversee the relationships of this newly formed household. He vowed that he would keep Garabed Hamparian under close scrutiny whenever he could. There was something wrong, something peculiar, about the whole situation. He had no idea what it was, but it bothered him. The thought consumed him until he at last came upon his home and the aroma of something delicious. As anticipated, the food was beyond compare.

The next morning Bedros took extra care with his appearance, making sure his face was properly shaven, his unruly hair somewhat subdued. He put on a blue work shirt and gray pants. He fooled around with a pair of suspenders Khatchadour had left behind but found them to be not only foolish looking but totally unnecessary. His broad, upsweeping shoulders, thick waist, and firm buttocks did the job of holding up his pants quite well.

Ara and Bedros sat down to a hearty breakfast of coddled eggs, creamed wheat cereal, thin Armenian bread, and tomatoes. It was like a cafeteria in Yughaper's kitchen of late, with the boys all coming to the table at different times, then running off in different directions. She didn't mind. In fact, it delighted her to be so incessantly busy in her culinary domain.

Ara eyed his shiny, clean brother curiously. "You are dressed rather fancy for a day of hammering and sawing, are you not?"

A little embarrassed and truthfully not knowing why he had taken such pains with himself that morning, Bedros simply laughed the remark off.

"Well, Ara, we do not want the cultured Garabed Hamparian to call us sloppy laborers just because we have hard work to do. Remember, we are gentlemen first and always, no matter what road the day may take us on."

From that day on Bedros Vartanian continued to take immaculate care of himself, being ever mindful of how he looked and sounded to those around him.

Finishing their breakfasts, the two brothers gave Yughaper a hasty good-bye. They went out to a fine shed they had just built and gathered up their tools. Garabed had told them he would have all the lumber and stones they would need available to them. The two brothers mounted their carriage and drove off to the Hamparian home.

On the way the two brothers, were engrossed in gay conversation. There was serious talk from Ara about how the money they were slowly gathering would one day build a fine construction business in Van or Bolis. Bedros laughed at his brother's naïveté, assuring him that if any money would be spent, it would be spent in America. They formed a perfect business twosome—Ara, the craftsman, whose hands worked endlessly and flawlessly; and Bedros, whose mind and heart worked in similar fashion.

After a moment's silence, the two marveled at the wasteland over which they traveled. The barrens of central Turkey had been spared the burden of beauty. Only an occasional far-off mountain or cluster of trees could be considered scenery of any account. Bedros bent over and whispered something obviously naughty to his brother. Ara just turned away with a look of disgust, scolding his baby brother as he had been doing since Bedros was born. To add a serious note, Bedros volunteered that they should build a separate bedroom and bath area for Garabed, joined to the rest of the house by a sizable door. Ara agreed, not knowing that his brother's architectural plans were merely an attempt to keep Garabed as far away as possible from the vulnerable new widow and the seven-year-old little girl.

As they finally approached the Hamparian house, Bedros was startled to see Syrvart running out of the front door, her dress pulled up against her sweet face. Not noticing them, she rushed past the donkey cart. She was sobbing. As Ara pulled the donkey to a halt, they both turned around to be of assistance, but the little girl had already disappeared somewhere behind the house. Ara and Bedros looked at each other, questioning what might be the matter with the young lady.

"Girls!" exclaimed Ara, shaking his head as they hopped down to begin their work. "They are a mystery to me."

Piles of wood, boxes of nails, and a large mound of roof tiles had been placed just next to the area where the brothers were to begin their work. Garabed came out when he heard the sounds of lumber being dragged and rearranged. Ara and Bedros stopped and greeted the master of the household.

"*Pari luis*," called Garabed pleasantly, bidding good morning as he walked toward the two builders.

"*Luis pari*," responded Ara while Bedros merely gave a nod of his head.

"You see I am all ready for you. So, you have your plans?"

"Yes," answered Ara, who rapidly went through the explanation of a separate apartment for Garabed, which would be accessible to the main house by a door.

Hmmm, the proud landlord thought carefully. "It sounds fine. After all, why should the others not have the most room? I am only one man. They are a growing family."

Ara agreed, satisfied that Garabed had accepted their renovation format. But Bedros eyed him suspiciously, turned to pick up his hammer, and then looked back as Garabed was walking toward his brand-new donkey carriage.

"What was the matter with little Syrvart?" asked Bedros to the astonishment of his big brother.

Garabed turned around with a look of cool anger on his face. For a moment he glared at Bedros, wondering what business that was of his. But thinking better of a rash remark, he responded kindly.

"Children, you know. They are so temperamental. This little one especially, I find. I guess I will have to keep a firm hand on her." With that he gallantly marched away.

Bedros began hammering violently on a nail, as though he wanted to demolish it. He worked on with disgusted anger as Garabed rode off toward town. Bedros was mumbling to himself.

"What in God's name is wrong with you, Bedo? I have never seen you show such dislike for anyone." Ara was annoyed at his brother's immaturity.

"I cannot explain it. I just do not like him. I never have."

"Why? You must have a reason," insisted Ara.

"No, no reason. That is, not yet."

"Well then, you are being unfair. Surely, I think he is strange, too. But look how he came here to help this family. He didn't have to do that, did he?"

Bedros hammered a moment and thought deeply. "No, he didn't. But then, answer me this, where else was he going to go?"

Ara looked away in disapproval and continued working. The two brothers worked on until dusk. They could hear Mariam fussing about inside over her infant. Garabed hadn't yet returned. Just as they were leaving, they saw Syrvart skipping up the path to the house. She held an armful of blazing, red poppies with puffy, black centers. She was singing a little girl's song and ignored them both as she ran into the house.

"Trouble?" blasted Ara sarcastically to the baffled Bedros. "Brother, you are too suspicious for your own good."

Exhausted, they returned home, anxious for a fine dinner and even finer sleep.

Ara and Bedros worked on the Hamparian home well into the summer. There were few other disturbances there. Once or twice Bedros noticed Syrvart running from the house. Now and then she would sit alone in the garden, dig out weeds, and pick some of the abundant crop of plump, red tomatoes and skinny, crisp cucumbers. Bedros watched the little girl constantly, trying to figure out what it was that he detected in her otherwise-beautiful face. Then on one of his last days at the building site, he finally confronted her. She had fled the home and sat sobbing in a web of dancing eggplant leaves.

"What is the matter, Syrvart?" Bedros asked, shocking the little girl into embarrassment over her tears. "Please answer me. You must know by now that I would never hurt you." He paused, brushing the thin, long, brown hair back away from her troubled face. "Come now. Tell me why you seem so afraid of something."

Syrvart Hamparian looked up cautiously at the large, masculine prince who bent over her. She had known no men in her short life except her beloved father and now Garabed. This Bedros was too overpowering, too big, and too handsome; she couldn't allow herself to trust him, yet somehow she did. He seemed to care, and she felt she had to tell him something. Finally she spoke.

"I guess," she said, shaking her head in confusion, "I guess Garabed just does not know how to be father, like my real father."

"What do you mean?" pumped Bedros.

"Well, it is just that he is very stern. He is so cross with my mother. He hates it when Hagop cries and my mother tries very hard to keep him silent." She looked down at a purplish eggplant peeking through its protective leaves. She fiddled with the vegetable, trying to avoid saying something else.

"And?" insisted Bedros. "What about how he treats you?"

Syrvart frowned, wondering why this young man could possibly care about any part of her life. But yet he did have a kind, sympathetic face, and she felt a sudden courage to go on with their discussion.

"You see, it is not so much how he treats me, but more how he..." She turned her head, stood up, and began nervously pacing around the garden, shuffling her feet through the entangling vegetables.

"Yes, go on!" prompted Bedros.

"I cannot say exactly," she said shyly. "He seems to hate it if I comb my hair or try to care for myself in any way. He says it is vain foolishness. He treats Mommy the same way. In fact, yesterday—"

The singing voice of her mother, calling from indoors, sharply cut off her words. "Syrvart, time to come in. That is enough dawdling. There is work to be done."

Before Bedros could stop her, the seven-year-old had flown into the house, leaving behind her a confused, angry, impetuous young man, who vowed he would one day get to the bottom of this mystery. To his dismay, Bedros's opportunity wasn't immediately forthcoming.

Less than two days before the extension work on the Hamparian house was completed, Garabed arrived at the Vartanian home. He presented the brothers with their wages in full for a job very well done. Then he explained that due to family matters and what he considered impending trouble in the area, he was taking Mariam, Syrvart, and

Hagop and moving to Constantinople. He asked that they put his renovated home up for sale. Then he disappeared.

• • •

After Garabed and his adopted family left for Constantinople, which was also called Bolis, Bedros's yearning for the enticing world outside Malatia intensified. It seemed that his every labor had become insignificant, wasted. He talked continually of Bolis and America. He watched with suppressed fury as Turkish gendarmes marched from one end of his small town to the other, not causing trouble but obviously defying anyone to do so. At dinner he would nervously swing his foot, sometimes kicking Hovsep or Sahag and causing an explosion of bickering and accusations that exasperated Yughaper. When he wasn't working or sleeping, he would sit around the house, humming a song of no origin except in his mind. He was behaving like an insulted child whose friends had all been invited to a very special birthday party, excluding him. Garabed was at the party; Bedros wasn't. And at seventeen closing in on eighteen, he felt that life was passing him by.

Ara tried hard to renew his brother's interest in their building enterprises. The work was always there, but now Bedros did it begrudgingly, leaving Ara with most of the finishing touches and wage collecting. Often Ara could be seen helping his young brother home in the overcast hours of the morning—the discontented Bedros overcome with whiskey, staggering, shouting words of a Promised Land and fortunes and new worlds. Yughaper was beside herself over him. The younger brothers couldn't understand what had overcome their big brother. Khatchadour was involved with his wife and child. And so as always it was Ara who brought Bedros home, listened to his ramblings, calmed his discontent, and prayed that the fire and stamina that had once been in Bedros would soon return.

It was July 1909, and Bedros was numbly fumbling with a piece of dried beef for his breakfast when a messenger came to the door with a letter for Yughaper. It was from Garo, postmarked Aleppo.

At first Bedros and his brothers chomped on with their breakfasts, not caring about the letter but their concern grew as they watched their mother's reaction. Yughaper held her hand tightly to her forehead. She then flopped down weakly into a chair. The family, one by one, gathered around their troubled mother with mounting curiosity. As Yughaper read each new word, the pain deepened in her eyes. Sobbing, she crumpled up the paper and threw it to the ground. Only Bedros dared to retrieve the note. He read it aloud to horrified ears.

Aleppo
May 19, 1909

Dearest Mother and brothers,

As you can see, I have left Adana and am safely back in Aleppo. I left Adana, not by my choosing but for survival. I saw things there, dearest family that my heart and mind refused to believe, but my eyes couldn't deny. I report them to you, not to make you sick or to reap enjoyment in its gruesomeness, but to justly frighten you all. Frighten you enough that you will now watch everything around you. Be wary of any stranger, any change in the mood of Malatia. If you perceive the slightest hint of a change in the air, I beg you; leave, all of you, quickly! Go anywhere! Bolis, Beirut, even Aleppo, but get out at all costs.

For several months with the arrival of early spring, Adana seemed a haven for me and our forces. We had weekly meetings with the mutessarif and his Turkish officers from the kaimakam, down to the local gendarmes. Everyone seemed in accord. Armenians were given their equal say along with the Greeks and Russians. It seemed that peace had at last come. They named me local leader of the Armenian community there.

Then it began. First slowly, then so swiftly that no one had a moment to protect themselves or their families. In early April the mutessarif began arresting several dissidents, or so he called them. He claimed there were Armenians who wanted to demise his authority and incite a revolution.

I began to feel the same terror that overtook me several days before my stepfather was killed. Wisely, I went into hiding. A friend of mine—a Syrian girl—let me live with her. Our flat was two stories above a local café. One night we heard a tremendous amount of noise and looked out our window to see a group of gendarmes boisterously singing and stomping about in the middle of the street. At first we were amused by their drunken antics, but we learned later that this disturbance was a ploy to distract the villagers from a carefully planned massacre that was occurring at the very same time. As I was about to return to my room, I heard Tavit call up from the street below. He was hiding behind a watering trough. The jubilant Turks didn't hear him call me. I looked down, and Tavit motioned to me to come down to the street, which I did. He whispered that something terrible was about to happen in the Armenian sector. We crawled on our bellies behind the café and into his waiting carriage. As we approached the Armenian section, we couldn't speak for the screams and shouts that filled the air. Flames and smoke shot up into the black sky. We saw naked women running past us, screaming in insane frenzy, oblivious to us or our attempts to help them. Little children wandered about, crying for their mothers. Horses and donkeys ran wild, snorting and whinnying. Homes were in flames; carriages were turned over. It was a holocaust!

We quickly jumped down from the wagon and ran for the church, where we hoped to find sanctuary. It was there upon that sight, Mother, that I lost my soul, my spirit, my will to fight any longer. Saddest of all, Tavit and I stood there, terror struck, frozen, unable to rescue our slaughtered brethren. It was a scene of madness- a living hell!

Before our eyes, we saw the gendarmes with their drawn bayonets decapitating men one by one. We saw the heads rolling down the street, tripping the terrified horses under whose hoofs they rolled. Then we saw the worst of all, Mother. God, help me. I must say the words. The soldiers took their swords and disemboweled some of the villagers as they tried to escape. Many of them were trampling their own screaming children. With my own eyes, I saw the body of an unborn child impaled on the sword of a galloping soldier. Under his horse lay the body of the infant's mother, her stomach opened up, her insides spewed across her tattered dress. I vomited. Tavit went into a convulsion of horror. I suppose it was after that when we both lost consciousness.

When we came to. the section was completely deserted. Only a few smolders of smoke remained as signs of life. We learned later that in that one night 30,000 Armenians had been murdered. How we were not noticed is unimportant now. To be sure, we left the next evening. First we walked at night discreetly. Then we began taking rides whenever we could from travelers we were sure of. Tavit went on to Van. I shall remain here, in Aleppo.

I am sorry, but I can write no more. Just the words make me sick to my stomach. Be assured, Mother, that I am here. I am safe. I have learned now that we cannot fight back. We are to remain the ruled, and we must obey. Our lives are worth the degradation—of that I can assure you.

Heed my word, beloved family. The nightmare is just beginning. If there is a God, let him be with you.

I shall always remain,

Garo

A reminder, Mother, destroy this letter immediately. I couldn't bear to have you punished twice for my foolish sins.

Yughaper had retired to the kitchen table and was frantically puffing on the remainder of a cigarette. Hovsep and Sahag had run out halfway through the letter and didn't return until that evening. Ara and Bedros sat staring hopelessly at one another, neither having the words to speak. Bedros crumpled the blood letter and took it over to the *furoon*, lighting it into fast-burning flames. He came back to Ara and suggested a brief walk. They needed the fresh air. Their stomachs were nauseous and twisted.

"What shall we do, Brother?" asked Bedros, hoping Ara could soften the terror inside of him.

"We can do nothing, Bedo. We do not have enough money to leave, and there are too many of us. We could never all make such a long trip safely. We must stay here and hope for the best."

Bedros turned around sharply and grabbed his brother's shoulders. "That is madness!" he screamed. "Are we all chickens, waiting in our coops to be slaughtered? No! We cannot! We will not!" Bedros Vartanian was crying for the first time since his friend Hirair had told him his sad story so many years before.

"Be calm, Bedo. Do not overreact as you always do. We are safe here. The Turks respect Mother for her doctoring. We are a part of her."

As Bedros was about to answer, he saw two soldiers walking down the dusty road, probably heading for the kaimakam's office in town. Suddenly Bedros stopped, frozen in his tracks. His eyes were aghast, and his mouth flew open. He seemed to be in a catatonic trance.

Ara was frightened. "What in heaven's—"

"Ara!" Bedros shouted, tears still streaming down his cheeks. "I know now what I must do! To fight them, I must join them!"

He took Ara in his arms and gave him a crushing hug. "Ara, you are my favorite. I shall never leave you, not for long. But there is something I must do. Remember, I love you, and I shall never abandon you."

Without speaking, Ara agreed. There were no more words as the brothers walked home arm in arm, their hearts in each other's hands—their souls intertwined.

Hovsep, Sahag, Yughaper, and Bedros fell asleep very early that night. Garo's letter had exhausted them. Fear bade them to bed. Ara had gone out after dinner to tell Khatchadour of Garo's story. He returned home well after dark to find the family in a sleep.

He undressed quietly and walked over to his tiny bed, which had been pushed uncomfortably up against his younger brother's. He looked down on the face of Bedros. It was a beautiful face—so much more handsome than the rest. Though Bedros's eyes were closed, they seemed to be rolling restlessly in his head. His brows formed a deep frown even sleep couldn't erase. Ara said a silent prayer as he sat on his bed, contemplating his sleeping brother.

"Bedo, you are my life," he whispered. "We have gone through everything together. Now I fear that you will leave me. I know I cannot go on without you, but I will try to show the strength that you have always thought me to have. It is you, Bedo, who are really the strength of this family. I know in my heart, baby brother, our separation will not be for long. God will see to it."

He bent over and kissed the scowl away from his brother's forehead. "I love you, Bedo. Do what you must. We shall be together again. Of that I am positive." Ara washed his tearstained face and settled back into a restless sleep.

The next morning the family woke in a frenzy. Bedros was neither in his bed nor anywhere around the house. His few belongings and a tiny traveling bag were gone. On his bed lay a hastily scribbled note.

Beloved family,
    I must leave you for a short while. I do this for you, no matter what you may think or hear. Trust me, believe in me. Remember, wherever I go, God is with me. I love you all.

With my heart,
Bedros

For a very long month the Vartanian home became morbid in the absence of Bedros. He had always been the jester, the kidder, the one who transformed intolerable dullness and poverty into hilarious folly. Ara, handicapped by sensibility and his tendency to be stoic, was particularly at a loss without his closest brother. He felt a sense of being overburdened by what Bedros had left behind. Yet Ara Vartanian went on, as did the rest of his family, consoled that at least they hadn't received news of any harm to Bedros.

Ara went full speed into his construction business, saving money carefully so that he would one day carry his brothers and mother from this violent, unfriendly land. Yughaper protested this continually. As the captain of her household, she refused to abandon it. If need be, she convinced herself, she would stay there and die with the rest of Malatia's Armenians.

By now Yughaper had achieved a very coveted position in her town. Many considered her to be indispensable, including the Turkish population. Though she was now aging and tired, her fingers creaking with arthritis, she continued to deliver the town's babies and cure its colds. For these reasons alone, the woman felt immune to the terror many insisted was forthcoming. There were also many townspeople who laughed off the gossip as doomsday gibberish and morose rumor.

One stifling June morning, another letter carrier came to the Vartanian home. He rode up on an aging horse, dismounted deftly, and pounded on the door. A precious letter was clutched in his hand. Ara opened the door and snatched the letter. It was from Bedros. Once again, Yughaper and her remaining sons gathered intently around the narrator—Ara.

Bolis,

June 1909

Dearest Mother and brothers,

I am at last settled in my new life. The morning I left you, I did so secretly because I hate crying and sad good-byes.

I walked quickly into town and went to the mutessarif's office. Do not worry. He remembered Grandmother and the day she came to him for the pension money. He was sympathetic toward all of us and that made me feel much more at ease in leaving.

Well, I enlisted in the army! Yes, Bedros Vartanian is now a member of the imperial Turkish army. Many of our young Armenians are doing the same, do not be shocked. It is a good way of getting inside and finding out just what is going on in the minds of the Turks.

We left that very morning, twenty-three of us, most of them my age. Over half of us are Armenians. We traveled by two wagon loads, each pulled with a double team of healthy horses. We carried all our provisions with us. We did our own cooking and made only an occasional stop at designated Armenian homes used for the comforts of the soldiers.

When I tell you it took nearly three weeks to reach Constantinople, you may believe it, my family. We came upon a huge, expanse of dry land. For miles and miles, there was nothing but hot sand, air with no smell, sky with no color. Now and then, thank God, we would come to an oasis to refresh ourselves and our horses. I will never forget that endless journey.

We did a lot of drinking. I kept a little bottle in my bag; some others brought some whiskey too. We sang all kinds of songs, mostly Armenian. Once, during a very long stretch on the desert, we got out to relieve ourselves and then started dancing and singing right there on that hard, hot sand. Before long, we had our Turkish commanders laughing so hard that they even joined in with us for a while. I tell you, they seem like fine people. All of us on the trip—the few Greeks and Russians and our leaders—we were like one family. It is hard to believe that these same Turkish leaders come from a breed of murderers, the kind we have seen. I would like to believe that those days are gone, that we shall all live again in peace.

When we reached Bolis, my eyes nearly fell out of my head. I cannot tell you of its size, its excitement! The people! There are thousands of them, all kinds, and all languages. I am fascinated here and know that I am in the right place to begin my great plan. I shall get myself and all of you to America soon, very soon. Perhaps you will come here first. You will not believe this place!

My deepest love and prayers are with all of you. Please write to me. I am at the Imperial Army Training Center in Pera, Constantinople.

With all my heart,
I love you.
Bedo

Chapter 4
CONSTANTINOPLE, 1909

She was a grand and pompous lady, standing high above the rest at the northwesterly tip of Turkey. By the very nature of her prominent position, she pointed a beckoning finger to the Western world, bidding it to come and partake of her splendor. As is befitting of a queen, two great protectors properly flanked her on either side. To her right, stretching for miles directly into Russia, lay the foreboding Black Sea. At her left side, less massive but equally protective, lingered the Sea of Marmora, which wrapped itself seductively around her southern and western boundaries. It was this latter body of water that boasted rightful claim to her glory, for it was through the churning white caps of Marmora that travelers from the Western world reached the shores of lavish, sultry, elegant, notorious Constantinople.

As is true of most rich and famous women, Constantinople was not only delightfully spoiled by her admirers; she was profoundly complex and unsettled as well. Her soul had been captured by too many lovers, and she found herself engulfed by all of them. Though she ignored the Americans as uneducated roughnecks from an unchartered wilderness, she was most arduous of her European neighbors. It was perhaps just as well, for the Americans, ecstatic in their growing pains, had little time for the mysterious and archaic cultures of the Far East.

Through the centuries diversified, highly cultured peoples infiltrated Constantinople. The French captivated her with their fine, romantic language and coveted educational experiences. She owed the Greeks her financial livelihood, since they controlled over 8 percent of her business ventures. The Armenians—some three hundred thousand of them—bestowed upon her their finest philosophers and scientists so that her mind wouldn't wither. And the British dotted her domain with missionaries, who educated and cared for her children. Added to these were the Germans, who further nurtured her children and tended to her sick.

She was a most fickle lady, giving her body to all and her heart to none. In the comfort of her realm, she was oblivious to the suffering and backwardness of her communities, which were scattered in isolation throughout her southern and eastern ends. To her, they simply didn't exist; ignoring them was easier than facing up to their miserable presence. In fact, Constantinople gave herself to but one lasting suitor, and that was the Turks. After all, were they not her true natives, her chosen sons, her blood relatives? It was only fitting that they should command her and rule her very spirit. True, they didn't fill her overflowing purse, but nevertheless, they pulled its fragile strings with great authority. It was they who kept her chaste. Now and then they would tolerate her flagrant flirtations with the foreigners, but to be sure, they would exterminate those who would dare to violate her.

Constantinople was made up of many segments, which cut her into several little cities, each totally different from the other. She had her unsightly slums, where beggars squatted by filthy, decrepit homes with flies buzzing about their outstretched hands. But these were surprisingly scarce.

More to her fame were the two magnificent sections of Pera and Beshiktash. Pera was a gorgeous community of predominantly single homes, mostly built of brick with red-and-black tile roofs. These elegant dwellings had gracious interiors and lovely courtyards with formal gardens. It was in such homes that the wealthy Greeks and Armenians lived, along with some lower-ranking Turkish officers. Pera housed the officers' training school for the Turkish army, a modern hospital, several Armenian and Greek churches, and several schools, missionaries, and mosques. Pera was the commercial center of Constantinople. There were also some less ostentatious brick row houses in Pera. They were adequately comfortable, tending to the few lower middle classes of Constantinople.

But as lovely and advanced as Pera was, Beshiktash left her behind to dwell in mediocrity; for Beshiktash was the rich and futuristic core of Constantinople. It was here that the sultan's winter palace, Yildiz Kiosk, loomed in marble and glistening glass, surrounded by superbly maintained gardens and fountains. It was here that the elite of the Turkish bureaucracy lived and played. To this day Beshiktash boasts of Istanbul's most extravagant bath houses, finest restaurants, artistic cathedrals and mosques, and lavishly posh residences. It was also here that a few favored foreigners could afford to live—the political leaders, many of whom were Armenian; the restaurant owners, most of whom were Greek; and the artists and performers, who came from all nationalities.

One could travel about easily in Constantinople using a system of horse-drawn trolleys, called tramways. The trolleys ran throughout the city on an intricate series of tracks. Even as early as 1900, Constantinople had managed to lure fine art, elegant shops, renowned universities, and sophisticated communications techniques to her bosom. It was difficult to fathom how a meek, backward farming town such as Malatia could exist at the same time and in the same country as this mecca of culture and excitement.

Finally to her credit, the political climate of Constantinople was tranquil and balmy. This fact was due not to any maturity or sympathy on her part but rather to a far more rational reason. The Turks lived in a fishbowl in this great city. Constantly watching them were curious cats from every part of the world. If they cared to stir up trouble, they held back because of the continual onlookers, who would broadcast their naughty activities to the entire Western civilization. Here the Turks didn't enjoy the undeterred renegade romps that they did in the poor vilayets far from the city walls. In these remote areas they answered to no one for their crimes. What few decent Turks were around were themselves too busy surviving to keep their sardonic brothers in check.

It was no wonder Bedros Vartanian's eyes fell from his head when his wagon pulled into lustful, luxurious Pera. The young men jumped to their feet and stood speechlessly within the cart, holding onto the wooden sides of the jostling vehicle for balance. Their heads rolled from one scene to another, and their young eyes shone in disbelief. It was as though they had traveled into not a different city but rather a different time, a different dimension.

Bedros was particularly overcome. He gasped, roared, and stomped his feet with each new sight. Here—a snoring old man crouched by a barricade of various-sized baskets. There—a proud, tanned man, who wore a bright-red, velvet fez, drove a gold-and-bronze carriage. To his side—there were brilliantly attired marching soldiers. Behind the wagon, screaming, giggling girls followed them. They were of all varieties and accosted the soldiers with indecent suggestions. The air was permeated with the mingling of nasal chanting, galloping horse hoofs, crying babies, huckstering merchants, and the aromas of charred chickens, spices, cheeses, fruits, and vegetables. It was a tantalizing potpourri of life. Pera was—like Bedros—alive, aggressive, and indefatigable. He had found his place, or at least the place that would pave his way into posterity.

The wagonload rolled on into the city past the Turkish baths, past the huge brick homes, past the brothels, past the children playing in the school yards, and on to the officers' training school. The school was a bland, long, low building of endless brick and windows. The center was bustling with soldiers of all ranks and uniform. Horses swayed, snorting uneasily in their stalls. Wagons were lined up by the hundreds. When his wagon at last pulled into the livery area and the soldiers disembarked, Bedros felt his stomach first leap, then drop inside him. His new life had begun.

• • •

From the moment he entered the mammoth building, which housed several thousand young men and schooled them for the rigid life of the military, Bedros was aware of one thing—there would be a life of regimentation within these walls. That was something he had always abhorred. But this time it would be far more serious, more insistent that it had ever been at Saint Mary's. It occurred to him that this facility was similar to the orphanage in its vastness. It was a cold maze of corridors, but it lacked the occasional warmth of the strolling monks and the canticles and the pillow fights in the night. He wondered how he would fare here. Would his outspoken manner and penchant for good times be an asset, or would he be squelched? His thoughts rambled, and an uncharacteristic feeling of inadequacy overcame him. He walked along with his fellow *nefers*—privates—down a long hall behind a tall, thin soldier, who was their orientation guide.

Subservience wasn't in him; he was incapable of it. But here, he knew he would have to endure it, at least for a while. On and on he walked behind the haughty soldier, who dared to think he knew more than the young men behind him. Bedros chuckled to himself as the condescending guide pointed out first the mess hall, then the showers and bathrooms, which were at least indoors with cold running water. What a significant job this bore has, he thought. He decided to put up with this folly and pay attention. It was a new environment, and he would be wise to familiarize himself with it, even though he knew it would take him less than one day to know the place inside and out by heart.

Finally the men were led to a dowdy room with two dozen bunk beds and a few scattered wooden chests of drawers. This was to be his dormitory. There would be forty-eight young men in this room, all privates. Here, unlike the orphanage, they would be mostly Turkish. The Armenians and Greeks would be in the minority. They were to unpack and place their clothes in the appointed dressers. They were assigned bunks and to his dismay, Bedros discovered that a slovenly-looking Turk named Nooredeen occupied the bed above him.

The hairy, young Turk hung down a sleepy head and bade Bedros welcome. Bedros tried to size him up quickly, but Nooredeen quickly retreated back into his embryonic position. Bedros began to put away his few belongings. He was glad he had brought so little since ten boys shared one dresser. He went back to sit on his hard bunk as the guide explained in Turkish that each private would be assigned a companion who spoke his native tongue. This was to help them more easily acquaint themselves with the training center. Bedros thought the whole idea was immature and idiotic. The guide left the dormitory with a final statement that the *yuze-bashi*, their captain, would be in momentarily to introduce himself and assign their companions.

Shortly the man appeared. He seemed formidable and kind though rigid in stature. He had a thick, curled-down, black moustache, which gave him a frown; and as an interesting accompaniment, his eyebrows curved down in similar fashion.

"Good afternoon, men. Welcome to the Pera Training Center."

He perused the group of young men stiffly standing at attention. "You have made a noble decision in becoming soldiers. Your country needs all of you. Life here will be regulated and hard, but you will find your commanders understanding as long as you comply with our orders. Most of your time will be spent in classrooms. After six months you will be assigned to the training centers outside of Pera. There are three—Erenkeuy, Nakrkeuy, and Maltepe."

Bedros felt an uncharacteristic wave of apprehension, which he cast aside by a long, cool stare out a nearby window. He allowed himself to refocus on the meticulously dressed captain, who was now fumbling with a three-foot-long scroll. The man cleared his throat.

"Gentlemen! Your companions will be in charge of explaining daily routines and directing you about the center, until you become acclimated. Right now everyone except the few men you see sleeping here are on their daily jobs. These others are on evening duty. So I will read the names, and this evening as the men return, you will each seek out your companion and introduce yourself. This list, by the way, has been carefully prepared according to nationality and place of birth wherever possible."

As Bedros listened to the long list of names, his mind began fleeing in boredom. The names were strange, many of them Turkish and foreign to him.

"And now we have, ah, Bedros Vartanian, whose companion will be, ah, Hirair Plebian."

Bedros snapped out of his daydreaming in disbelief. He felt his heart surge. He put his hand to his chest as though trying to stop it from escaping his body. His eyes bulged in excitement. He gawked at the captain.

"Is there a problem already?" said the yuze-bashi sarcastically.

"Ah," fumbled Bedros dumbly. "No, sir, but if you would not mind, sir, could you repeat the name of my companion again?"

The captain scowled at Bedros under bushy eyebrows. He turned on his heels abruptly.

"We say things once here, Nefer Vartanian! Remember that from now on!" And then he was gone.

Bedros flopped back on his bed, not daring to be overjoyed yet hoping there had been no mistake. Could it be another person with the same name? It seemed unlikely. If it indeed was Hirair—oh the joys, oh the times they would have! The young men bustled about, busying themselves in unpacking and conversation.

Night began to lay its black veil down on humanity, and one by one the veteran soldiers returned to the dormitory, greeting their new companions. Bedros sat like a statue, his eyes glued to the door, waiting for whoever Hirair Plebian was. When the young man in question entered the room, the ensuing yelp by both young men at the sight of each other left no doubt that there had been no mistake. Hirair rushed to Bedros, who was already leaping upon him. The two shouted each other's names, cried, embraced, and threw one another flat on the floor. They were two bullish bodies pounding upon one another in blissful reunion.

Hirair and Bedros plopped down on a bed together and began to ramble in excited chatter. They breathlessly tried to cram almost ten years into the few precious minutes before mess call. Hirair explained how he and his stepfather were not getting along well. His mother, he felt, had never really been the same, even though the hospital had released her. He had spent several months searching for his lost sister, Sonia, but he had failed. He then decided, like Bedros, that perhaps the army offered some obscure promise for the future.

Bedros, through tears and bursts of laughter, ambled through his tales of building homes and Garabed Hamparian and Garo's frightening experience in Adana. He told Hirair of his plans to raise enough money to take his whole family to America. Then a harsh, whistling horn sounded, and all conversation ceased. Hirair threw a strong arm around his friend and led him to the mess hall, where they ate ravenously—not tasting, not knowing, not caring what they consumed. It was just as well. The hall was filled with such a clamor that it was nearly impossible to carry on a conversation. After dinner, Hirair suggested a walk around the Pera Center. They were permitted to have one free hour after dinner, during which time most of the young men strolled about the bustling city streets, looking for trouble and finding it.

This evening they didn't wish to go into the city, because the joy of finding each other could find no match in the streets of Pera. Hirair spoke first as a gentle rain began to fall on the two inseparable heads.

"It really is not bad here, Bedo. The food is fair, better than Saint Mary's, or at least there is more of it. I spend my afternoons after classes in the west side of the center, where we build the ammunition boxes and some furniture."

"Great!" shouted Bedros. "I am a builder by trade. I will request that they assign me to that job. Then we can be together day and night."

Hirair let out a roaring laugh, slapping his friend on the back in jest and shaking his head.

"You have not changed at all, my friend. We do not request things here. This is the army. But I am friendly with the *hassarbed*. The Turks call him *binbashi*. His name is Ismael, and he has charge of one thousand nefers. Tomorrow I will talk to him about putting us together."

"What do you think he will say?" asked Bedros, slightly embarrassed by his naïveté.

"I think when I tell him of your building experience, he will agree. Some of the boys in the shop are poor workers. They belong on the road work teams instead of doing skilled labor."

Bedros dropped his head a moment and the two walked around the barracks in silence, listening to the misty whispers of the rain tinkering all about them. A strong smell of manure came whizzing by as they approached the livery area, and Bedros chuckled under his breath.

"I know!" said Hirair brightly. "You are thinking about CiCi and the fertilizer pile!"

"How did you guess, old friend?" laughed Bedros, not expecting an answer. "They were great days. We had such fun." A somber look overcame him as though his youth had just died. Hirair quickly shook him by the shoulders.

"Hey, not you, Bedo. Never you! I do not ever want to see sadness in your eyes again." He gently smacked his friend's cheek. "It does not become your handsome face, eh?"

The two strolled on, encircling the training center, following the boundary of a large wrought-iron fence. As they reached the side entrance, which led directly to their sleeping quarters, Hirair stopped shortly as if something had occurred to him, which he had meant to discuss before.

"You know, there is something I need to tell you about Garabed."

"What about Garabed?" asked Bedros, wrinkling his nose slightly as though he still smelled the livery stables.

"He is here."

"Here? Where here?"

"He is right here in our sector, in Pera. The family lives in a brick row house not far from the port area."

"How do you know? Did you see him?"

"Yes, I have seen him now and then in town. The first time I saw him was at the Tokatlian, a big Armenian restaurant in the downtown area."

"What was he doing there? I would have thought he'd have run out of piastres by now."

Hirair laughed, looking askance at his friend's angry eyes. "On the contrary, he was dressed like a nobleman. He had Mariam and her little girl with him. Ah, what was her name?"

"Syrvart," answered Bedros, quickly feeling the blood rush to his head.

"Well, at any rate, he was acting like somebody very special, and the waiters were treating him quite well. When he saw me, he showed off even more."

"Naturally. Did you go up to him?"

"Yes, I introduced myself, and he acted as though he had forgotten me, but I knew he had not. The lady, Mariam, politely offered her home to me. She said she always had a fresh Armenian meal on the stove for a hungry soldier."

"Did you mention me?" asked Bedros with growing concern.

"No, old friend. Garabed didn't give me a chance. He clearly wished me to leave them to their dinner, which I gladly did." Hirair wondered about the strange look on his friend's face. "Tomorrow night, if you like, we'll take on Pera, and I'll show you where they live."

Bedros sublimated, forcing a wide grin. He threw his huge arm around Hirair's shoulders. The latter stumbled slightly under his weight.

"That sounds like a fine idea. If you think Pera is ready for Bedros Vartanian," he jested, and took off jogging down the corridor to the barracks.

"Now that is more like it!" laughed Hirair, running after his friend, who was rounding a corner and disappearing.

Upon entering the dormitory, the two boys quickly undressed and prepared for bed. Bedros, noticing that the sleepy Turk Nooredeen wasn't in his bunk, asked Hirair about him.

"Nooredeen? Oh, he seems harmless enough. He has guard duty all evening long, so you will not have much contact with him."

"That's good!" sighed Bedros.

"Listen, friend, you will have to get used to having Turks hanging around. We are in their territory now more than ever.So far, there have been no problems."

"Let us get some sleep," suggested Bedros, not wishing to go on further with this conversation.

Hirair was in the bunk directly across the room from Bedros. His bed was by the windows, and a glow from the new moon lay on his face as he tried to sleep. He was thanking God for sending him Bedros and just as he was about to fall asleep, Bedros's voice awakened him.

"Hirair!" came a loud whisper across the row.

"What is it?"

"I am sorry, but, I was just thinking..."

"Yes?"

"How did that little Syrvart look?"

"Look? What do you mean, look? She is a little girl, not much more than seven or eight. She is pretty, in a way."

"No, I mean, did she look frightened or sad?"

There was silence for a while as Hirair tried to remember.

"She looked, well...shy, I guess is the word. She would not even let her eyes meet mine. But, no, I would not say she looked frightened. All right?"

"All right." And the two old friends fell into a mutually comfortable sleep.

At dawn, a soldier entered the quarters and loudly called for all the day workers to awaken. There were disbelieving groans and shuffles as one by one the young men made their beds, prepared themselves in their uniforms, used the baths, and shuffled down to the mess hall. Bedros felt as though he had just fallen asleep, and he hated the loud soldier who dared to disturb him. Most everyone in the dormitories disliked that early-morning rooster of a man.

Bedros and Hirair sat together, enjoying fresh coffee, eggs, and oatmeal. As Hirair had said, the food wasn't especially tasty but plentiful. It had to be so, for the men spent the rest of the morning doing calisthenics and various tiring military routines. Hirair and Bedros grunted together through the grueling ups and downs, jumping jacks, and running in place. Then they went on to the classrooms, where they were taught a medley of fighting techniques, rifle practice, and livery work. For those few months, the fighting would be done on paper; the experience would come out of books. Bedros didn't want to think about the distant training areas with the strange names; he would take them as they came.

During lunch Hirair suggested that Bedros join him in meeting the Binbashi Ismael in hopes of altering his work assignment. It would be worth a try, and Hirair knew that if anyone could turn a head or change a mind, even a staunch Turkish officer, it was Bedros Vartanian.

When they reached the administration offices, Bedros was overwhelmed. They were all too stuffy and official looking. There were hand-carved chairs, red Oriental carpets, and rifled guards everywhere. Hirair boldly walked up to a pair of gendarmes, who stood at the door of the binbashi's private office. Bedros was amazed at the cool self-assurance of his friend. He had become a strong, brave man, as Bedros always believed he would. After a few words from Hirair, the soldiers turned and gave Bedros a suspicious stare. One entered the general's quarters, then momentarily returned and motioned the two boys to enter.

The room was decorated in plush, crimson carpet and flowing folds of similarly colored draperies. There was a wall filled with books, many of which were military manuals. There was a bronze statue of a warrior on a valiant steed, a looming tapestry depicting a gruesome battle, and a grand, mahogany desk, behind which sat the powerful binbashi. The man rose from his chair, using his hairy hands to lift himself up. He leaned forward, curiously perusing the two young men, who stood nervously before him. The first courtesy the ruler showed was to address the boys in Armenian. He spoke it fluently and presumed it would relax them somewhat. Immediately Bedros read his eyes, searched his receding forehead, dove into his soul. This was a powerful but kind man.

"Hirair." The binbashi's voice was gravelly and quite deep. He sounded as though he had a cold or needed to clear his throat. Bedros soon learned that he always sounded this way. "You wished to see me?"

"Sir," answered Hirair proudly as he lifted himself to full attention. "This is my companion and very dear friend, Bedros Vartanian."

Bedros stiffened, saluted, dared not to speak. He gulped down the heavy lump in his throat. "How do you do, sir?"

"I do fine," smiled Captain Ismael as he carefully absorbed every line and breadth of Bedros's countenance. "You seem to do fine also, nefer. You are new here in Pera's center?"

"Yes, Hassarabed, I am."

"And how do you like it here thus far?"

Bedros looked admiringly about the large, warm room. "I like it well enough, sir."

"Good, we try to keep our soldiers happy here. But as you have no doubt discovered we work them hard, very hard." He looked aside at Hirair, who smiled in respectful agreement.

"Yes, sir," answered Bedros, and then felt he had to go on. "But hard work is not unusual to me. I built houses in Malatia before I came here, and I am well accustomed to labor."

The binbashi rose and walked around Bedros with his hands clasped behind his back. "Yes. I can see that, young man."

It seemed that Hirair had frozen in his position and that there were but the two of them in the room—the general and the new private.

"Yes, sir! Sir, if you please, that is why Hirair and I came to see you. I would like to work with him in the woodshop. I am a fine craftsman. You will see."

"I imagine you are Bedros...Vartanian, was it?"

"Yes, sir. Vartanian."

"You say you are from Malatia?"

"Yes, sir. My mother and brothers live there on a government pension."

"And why is that?" continued Ismael, becoming more and more taken in by the virile, intelligent young man before him.

Bedros looked to Hirair for help, but his friend was momentarily silent. Hirair didn't want to mar this fine rapport with his stories of murder and hatred, but in an effort to help his friend he decided to speak.

"If you please, sir; Bedros's father was killed by the Turks in 1895."

General Ismael looked back at Bedros with genuine sorrow on his face. He lowered his head and lumbered back to his desk. He sat, rested his forehead in his hands, and rubbed at his temples.

"So you are another of the leftovers, the burdens we must now face due to our own stupidity." He was talking to himself, and the two young men listened without daring to respond. Ismael lifted his head and smiled at the boys. He got up and put his arms around both of their shoulders, drawing all three of them into an uncomfortable huddle. He then escorted them to the door.

"Hirair, you will take Bedros to the shop tomorrow and teach him our techniques in making the ammunition boxes."

Hirair and Bedros looked at each other and burst into wide grins. They blurted out simultaneous thank-yous to the kindly commander. As they began to leave, he added a final note.

"I will stop in tomorrow before dinner to check on your progress. If I see your closeness to each other interferes with your work—"

The young men interrupted him with a barrage of assurances that such wouldn't be the case. Then Hirair left, and Bedros began to walk out behind him, looking back for one moment at this unique man.

"Sir, you are a most kind person," Bedros politely offered.

"Thank you, Bedros; you may leave now."

"And sir, one more thing."

"Yes?" replied the general, now impatient with the lingering young man.

"You will see that I will do a better job than anyone in the wood-shop. Perhaps I will even improve upon the methods here."

Astonished, the binbashi glowered at Bedros. "Is that so, nefer?"

"Yes, sir," answered Bedros, not faltering. "I believe you will see that is so."

And with that, Bedros Vartanian rushed after his friend.

The next morning after the usual exercises and lunch, the dayshift soldiers were divided up to begin their various work schedules. The Turkish soldiers were usually assigned together, and it was most always work of a military nature. Only the Turks were permitted the prestige of working with ammunition and weapons. As for the others, most were assigned government tasks of road repair and general maintenance. The very skilled built new barracks and sometimes homes for the elite in the upper echelon of the military bureaucracy. Then there were those, Bedros and Hirair among them, who had the coveted distinction of being able to make things with their skilled hands—things like bunk beds, ammunition boxes, and clothing chests.

Bedros became quickly acclimated. His fingers worked steadily and flawlessly, building an endless stack of ammunition boxes. Though these crates were used mostly for rifle shells, they were also utilized for other small paraphernalia such as nails and bolts. After Bedros and his crew completed the boxes, the Turkish soldiers would fill them with ammunition.

Within his first two hours of work, Bedros Vartanian decided that the technique used in finishing the bottoms of the boxes was archaic and too time-consuming. After some thought and a bit of scribbling on a pad, he found a more precise way to seal the boxes. His technique made them neater looking and stronger as well. He proceeded to prepare one as a sample. No sooner was the box completed than the general, as he had promised, entered the workshop to see how the novice had fared.

With folded hands, the skeptical binbashi listened and watched as Bedros explained his new process of inlaying the wood in such a pattern as to need fewer nails, to increase strength, and to add a certain aesthetic improvement as well. The general was captivated. He walked silently over to the sample box and began to run his fingers along its perimeter, turning the box over again and again. Without saying a word or a change in his expression, he inspected the original boxes in the same manner. Then he went back to the new box and examined it one more time. He turned and examined its maker as well. Bedros stood still. What could the man be thinking? Hirair hovered shyly in a corner. Disinterested, the other soldiers had left for dinner.

"Bedros, fine work!" Ismael spoke in a disturbed fashion, surprised no one else had thought of this method before. "You have indeed found a better way to make our ammunition boxes."

"Thank you, sir," responded Bedros, assured his words were no longer necessary.

Absent-mindedly the commander asked that the room be cleared except for Bedros. He walked about, pacing, for several minutes. The commander's behavior baffled Bedros. The binbashi looked at the boxes, then at Bedros, then back at the boxes again. As he meandered around, it seemed that his mind was formulating some intense plan. At last, to Bedros's relief, General Ismael spoke to him.

"How old are you, soldier?"

"I am eighteen, sir," responded Bedros, wondering what purpose this question might have.

"Eighteen!" mused the leader to himself. "Do you have a girlfriend?"

"A girlfriend? No, sir." Bedros answered in astonishment.

"Do you think you could make regular furniture—that is, residential furniture?"

"Yes, sir. Of course."

"Good! I am in the process of remodeling my home in Beshiktash. I am in need of some quality benches, a few tables and chairs. Do you think you could help me, nefer?"

Bedros was shocked. Surely his meager invention didn't qualify him for such favor? But he wasn't one to look any opportunity in the face.

101

"Sir, I would be most honored to help you."

Ismael eyed him carefully, admiration written on his face. But there was a look of something more, Bedros thought. It was almost a look of fatherly concern, a look close to, perhaps, love.

"Good, very good. From now on you will have your dinner with me in my home. You will work on your task after dinner and return to the barracks in time for bed check."

"Sir, that is not necessary. I—"

"Enough, Vartanian! I am your commander, or have you, in your self-esteem, forgotten that?"

"No, sir."

"Bedros, I live with only one daughter. Her name is Sheida. And I have a most capable housekeeper who will prepare our dinners. I am sure she can include some Armenian cuisine in our weekly menus." He paused, seizing Bedros with his alluring stare. "Please, private, you will do my home an honor."

"It will be as you wish, sir." Bedros, exhausted and overcome, excused himself and returned to his dormitory, where he told an incredulous Hirair the story of what had just transpired.

Bedros Vartanian fell back on his bed, thinking about Binbashi Ismael and what had possessed him to choose him for so fine a job. Also in the back of his mind was one gnawing question. Why did it matter if he had a girlfriend or not?

While dining on roasted lamb, curried pilaf, and fresh eggplant fried in olive oil, Bedros and Hirair decided they would celebrate the occasion with a night on the town. This night was to be their one evening off for the week. As such they were not required to be in attendance for bed check, only for morning roll call. Pera would have to brace herself for their arrival.

They manicured themselves, donning fresh, gray, woolen knickers; crisp, beige shirts; and metal-buttoned military jackets. They were both quite handsome and striking: Hirair with his sandy-colored hair and boyish face—and Bedros with his dark, wavy hair; and his brown-black eyes glistening with intense excitement and mischievousness. The deep, dark Middle Eastern night would meet its match in the person of Bedros Vartanian. For he outshone her, bade her no reverence.

The two friends left the military complex and decided to walk from the compound and into Pera proper, which was a little over a mile and a half of pleasant strolling. It was a clear night—no rain fell—but there was a misty fog lingering, carrying with it the smells of the city: liquor, stale tobacco, incense, perfumes—the aromatic potpourri of humanity.

At first the outskirts of Pera appeared dull and lifeless, displaying only a meager shop here or a tiny, unappealing market there. The two soldiers passed a large hospital and a fish market. Bedros was becoming disappointed in the scenery, but sharply, without warning, Pera turned into the vamp she truly was, like a plain-looking lady who doesn't immediately reveal the sensuality she hides within. Sounds began to fill the air—harsh, lively sounds of tantalizing music: of old ladies chatting on corners, of babies wailing, and of ladies of the night singing out in seductive whines to their prospective mates.

Bedros began to perspire in response to the fascinating sights and sounds he encountered. Like a child at the circus for the first time, he would halt, turn, point, and even jump up and down with chagrin. Now and then he would shriek with disbelief, and then quickly cover his mouth to mask his naïveté. Hirair put aside his astonishment. He remembered how it had been when he and Constantinople first met.

"What is that?" shouted Bedros, pointing to a gaudy-looking building with red-and-purple candles glowing from behind flimsy lace curtains. Then, noticing the young, veiled girls loitering in front of the place, he answered his own question.

"Guess?" Hirair laughed with a naughty grin, shaking his head in disbelief at his friend's inexperience.

"You mean, it really is a—"

"Yes, it really is, Bedo," interrupted Hirair, trying to spare his friend the words. "When I first came to Pera, I thought most of these women wore veils to cover their faces and bodies as a sign that they were lesser than the men or at least for modesty. But I quickly found out that is true of only the most devout Muhammadans. Instead I discovered most of the young girls wear the veils to make themselves more tempting." He laughed a hearty laugh. "You know, it's the old idea that what you cannot see is more interesting than what you can."

"I see," snickered Bedros, his eyes wide with astonishment.

"You can see—that is for sure! These particular ladies do not wear anything underneath all those pale fabrics. It does not take a discerning eye to find that out."

Hirair looked eagerly at his gawking friend. Then he frowned. "Ah, do you want to go in, Bedo?"

Bedros seriously considered Hirair's proposal as he eyed a gorgeous, raven-haired girl who was softly humming and waving a beckoning hand at him. His innocence seemed to sweep through the channels of his heart and out of his body. For a few reckless seconds, he was ready.

"Hirair," Bedros answered, "I think I would like to...to take a bath."

"A bath!" shouted Hirair, choking in surprise.

"Yes, what else? I have been waiting to see what these Turkish baths are all about. Have you ever been?"

"No," admitted Hirair.

"So, let us go!" announced Bedros, walking decisively yet occasionally glancing back at the beautiful creature leaning suggestively against the door of the ill-reputed house.

They chose one of the most luxurious public bathhouses in Pera. It was the one patronized by the most prominent people in town. As they passed through the city, Bedros captured mental photographs of specific stores and cafés. He indelibly marked the location of the brothel in his mind, and when all spots of importance were carefully sequestered therein, he relaxed, enjoying the remainder of their brisk walk. The light fog was slowly lifting, allowing bright, and sparkling Pera to proudly display herself.

Shortly they approached the Galata port area, where the smell of fish and oil-stained, murky waters reached their noses. Hirair stopped a moment and pointed toward the water, which was some distance away.

"There, see the tops of those ships over there?"

"Not too clearly," answered Bedros, squinting.

"Well, it is a little far from here, but just off to the right of the port about a mile is the housing complex where Garabed lives."

Bedros suddenly showed great interest, and he carefully plotted the location of the homes, then turned and calculated the direction they had just taken.

"Ah, let me see." Bedros paused, scratching his head lightly. "The barracks are where?"

"Back that way. See the fish market? Then we passed the lovely ladies." Hirair winked while pointing the way.

Bedros looked about, as though he were retracing his steps for some future trip he might have to make through these streets—a trip he might have to take quickly and accurately.

"Yes, I remember. I have it now. On with you, Hirair!"

The two continued on, approaching an elegant building of carved marble with ornate golden trim scrolled about it. It looked more like a palace than a public bathhouse. Hirair grabbed Bedros's arm excitedly.

"Here we are, old friend. I hope you are ready for this. Fancy, is it not?"

When Hirair turned to see his friend's expression, he found that Bedros's head was turned. He was pensively staring back toward the Galata Port area.

"Bedo! Wake up! We are here. You said you couldn't wait to see it!"

"Hirair," responded the young man without turning. "What is the house number?"

"What house number?" Hirair was confused and exasperated at his friend's untimely preoccupation from the subject at hand.

"Garabed's house. What is the number? You must remember; you said you were there."

Hirair shook his head in disbelief, and then rubbed his temples, trying to remember the time he had gone there.

"Uh, I think, seven. Yes, I am sure it is seven."

"Seven! What do you know? That is my lucky number!"

"Really?" asked Hirair, engrossed in this new discussion. "Since when?"

"Since now," Bedros laughed, slapping his friend squarely on the back. "So, come. Let us take our bath. I do not know what you are waiting for, Hirair."

The two wrapped youthful arms around each other and boldly entered the marble atrium of the looming bathhouse. Hirair looked over at his friend and gave him a confused but affectionate smile. He would never understand him, but he would ever love him. Bedros looked over at his friend's apprehensive stare.

"Hirair, you must not be afraid. Never fear when Bedros is here!"

"You are crazy, Bedo. You know that?"

"Hirair," smiled the young bull. "I have only just begun to be crazy."

The two novices entered and paid their money to a fat, fuzzy-looking man wearing a red fez and a green, velvet jacket with gold fringe on the shoulders and bodice. Bedros thought he looked like a clown. The puffy, ornate man immediately spied that Hirair and Bedros were new to the bathhouse based on their wary glances. He made up his mind not to make the experience any easier for them than he had to.

"Men to the left!" He pointed in a military fashion.

Jokingly Bedros began walking to the right, and Hirair froze as the chubby man flew after him in a dither.

"Did you not hear me, soldier? I said men to the left!" He huffed and grabbed Bedros's arm to bring him back in the proper direction. Bedros jerked away angrily. The look on the young soldier's face made the little man tremble and quickly pull away his hand. The flabby cashier wisely softened as Bedros intimately pushed his great nose against his quivering forehead.

"I guess you didn't understand?" giggled the cashier nervously.

"I understood!" growled Bedros in a deep, strong voice. Then he grabbed Hirair's arm and started toward the left entrance, ignoring the ramblings of the silly, old man.

Grumbling, Bedros swung open the heavy wooden doors by their great brass pulls. "There is nothing I hate more than people who become carried away with their authority. Serious! Everyone is too serious!"

When they entered the steam-filled room, Hirair and Bedros stood speechless, overwhelmed by this new world of flesh and lavishness.

The glistening, titled room was fifty feet square. In the center of it was a slab of gold-swirled marble, which was about three feet high. Under the marble a small fire burned, creating intense heat on the stone slab. The bodies of men lay strewn over this altar of marble. They were of all sizes, all shapes. Many of them were bulging with fat. The men were nude, lying on their backs, turning red from the heat beneath them. They were wet with perspiration.

Then, as each man was sufficiently heated, he would step down into the tepid pool, which encircled the heated marble altar of bodies. For several minutes each would soak and dunk in the clean, clear water. A snap of the fingers brought a skinny, young boy with a large absorbent towel, widely opened in his outstretched arms. After being properly dried, the bathers retired to a side bed of marble, which wasn't heated. There each received a massage with fragrant oils and perfumes.

Hirair and Bedros, without embarrassment, quickly disrobed and lay on the hot bed of marble; then they enjoyed the cool, soothing bath and final massage. For over an hour, the two were in sublime ecstasy.

"This is the only way, Hirair," Bedros said, his voice shaking from the pats and rolls of the masseuse. "We must be rich and enjoy a luxurious life like this! For us, the best. Only the best!"

Hirair just closed his eyes, refusing to answer his philosophical friend. He was so peaceful, so relaxed. No one could make him think of the future or the dreariness he feared was in store for all of them. He wished only to bask in the moment at hand and reflect on nothing more. The thought of wealth was beyond him. They had spent nearly a week's wages on this one night, and his foolish friend dared to dream of riches. He chuckled to himself as the masseuse pounded away on his thick, young body.

Before long, they each had enough of the pampering and became restless to go. They quickly dressed and walked once around the blue pool of water, where a gentle vapor rose from it. It swirled around the rippled bodies lying helter-skelter on the marble throne. As they passed through the doors into the atrium, Bedros noticed that the cashier wasn't at his post.

"Look, Hirair, he is gone! Come, let us go to the right and see what the ladies are up to."

Hirair was aghast. "*Asdvadz*! Bedo, no! I cannot."

"Come!" Bedros had a gleam in his black eyes, his finger astutely pointing toward the women's entrance. "Just one look!"

"No!" insisted Hirair, his hand on the pull of the front entrance doors.

"All right, then. I will go myself, my cowardly friend." And Bedros started down the hallway.

Hirair wanted to run out in panic, but suddenly he turned around and ran after his daring friend. He stood behind Bedros as though trying to hide behind his muscular body. Slowly Bedros opened the doors and took two quiet steps into the bath hall. Hirair was still glued to his rear. In impish satisfaction, the two young soldiers absorbed the sensual sight of oiled ladies, firm and flabby, bobbing breasts floating on the blue water, rounded rears being pounded into pink flatness, sumptuous sinews stretching and turning in beautiful rhythmic calisthenics.

It took one elderly woman's discovery of their presence to set off a chain reaction of shrieks and screams, which shook the very walls of the plush room.

The intruders made a fast exit, and on their way to the front door, they whizzed past the confounded cashier, who hadn't yet realized what had happened. When he finally did, he flew after them, his dimpled fists rotating like two tiny eggbeaters. But Hirair and Bedros had already disappeared into the mass of humanity bustling about the crowded city streets.

Breathlessly, the young soldiers ran, finally resting when they were sure they were safe from the cashier's feeble chase. They paused, exhausted, their heads down, their faces still red from the bath and the ensuing excitement. They found a nearby trough and happily sat back in respite. At last revived, they looked up simultaneously at one another and burst into uncontrolled laughter. It was miraculous they didn't flip backward into the warm, rancid water, which stood in an entwinement of algae in the large, wooden watering trough.

Bedros spoke first, still slightly out of breath.

"I think I am ready to meet the veiled ladies, my friend."

Hirair quickly lost his pink glow. "I—I do not think I am ready for that yet, Bedo."

"Well." Bedros smiled, understanding his friend's reluctance. He himself knew nothing of women as yet. "Let us walk back that way. If you change your mind, you can join me."

They rose and started on their way toward another new experience in life. It would be the first of many—the most exciting, the most sensuous of all.

The veiled ladies were still at their posts. Some boldly walked out into the street. A few stayed quietly back, as though hoping not to be noticed.

Bedros saw that the lovely, blue-black-haired girl was still standing there, leaning her shoulders against a statue of a naked woman holding up a laden bunch of grapes. The young girl seemed in a trance. Bedros dared to draw closer and saw that she was a beautiful, young thing, who was not nearly as hard looking as her cohorts.

Hirair stopped short of actually walking into the midst of the night-time ladies. He tugged on Bedros's sleeve and then reluctantly shook his head.

"Sorry, my friend. This is not for me- at least not tonight."

"It is all right, Hirair. You go on. I do not even know how far I will get, but I must investigate these delicate creatures, particularly that one in the pale-green veils."

Hirair looked over at the sweet, young girl, to whom Bedros was pointing. Noticing that the two soldiers were eyeing her, the girl stepped back shyly, turning her head toward the statue of the grape lady. Bedros was surprised. Earlier she had seemed to be accosting him, presumably wanting him to spend the evening with her.

"She is lovely," remarked Hirair sadly. "But, believe me, I do not even know how much—let alone how to—old friend."

The two laughed heartily as Hirair sped away, leaving Bedros surrounded by the howls and indecent gestures of the prostitutes. He cast his eyes on only one. Annoyed by his indifference, the other women quickly found other passersby to prey on as Bedros cautiously walked up to the black-haired girl.

"*Parev.*" He cleared his throat, but she didn't turn. "Well, perhaps I should speak Turkish. Which are you?" No answer. "Are you Greek?" No answer. "Ah, then I have it. You are Chinese." he joked.

It worked. The young beauty turned around slowly. There was a wary bend to her well-shaped, black brows, but she giggled like a tiny child. Bedros could see now that her eyes were as black as her hair, and her skin was nearly white. If she were Armenian, she had an unusual coloring, he thought.

"So, you are not Chinese," he boldly continued. "Armenian then?"

She shook her head to say yes, and then closed her huge eyes to reveal a soft fan of thick, black lashes nestled against her high, pink cheekbones. Under the veil, which covered her face from her nose to below her chin, Bedros could see that a fine craftsman had chiseled her features; they were very small. Her rosebud mouth blazed from beneath the green chiffon in a burst of brazen red. Under three or four folds of the same pale-green chiffon, he could see hints of two small, round thighs. Bedros felt his heart thump, and he knew his face was reddening.

"I am new to all this, my little lady friend."

"It is all right," she spoke in a whisper, her voice that of a little girl—soft, mellow, with just a hint of seductiveness. "It is not new to me."

Bedros felt his heart sink. So young, so precious, so beautiful—yet to her, this sort of thing was second nature. She took his hand gently and led him into the dark hallway of the house. She bent her head down as though she wished not to be noticed. Once safely in the hall, she looked up at him, standing on her toes to speak into his round, red ear.

"Whatever you wish to give me will be all right, soldier."

She was making the whole thing so easy for him. Bedros was chagrined that instead of him leading her, this young girl was leading him for his first time.

As they walked together down the dimly lit corridor, lined with rows of numbered doors, Bedros could hear the sounds of performing women and loud, cursing men. There were moans, grisly laughter, and shouts. Some of the doorways gave off only deadly silence. He thought these sounds were not as he would have expected love to be. The voices of the men were not tender. The women were bold and loud. He felt a chill run from his toes up into his legs, causing his knees to quake. How could he invade the body of this beautiful girl? How could other men have done so for so long?

At last, after an eternity, they reached her room. She opened the door, leading him in and then turned to lock it securely. There was one window, covered with the same pale, green chiffon the girl wore. There was a low bed with an animal skin thrown across it. On a small basket-like table, one hurricane lamp glowed, casting light on her eyes and causing them to sparkle in an eerie black, blue, and green fireworks display.

She sat on the bed and lifted her veil, proving to him that he hadn't overestimated her beauty. Bedros just stood, staring stupidly, as she began to remove the first of the layers of veils. He quickly sat next to her and grabbed her hands.

"Wait, can we not talk a moment?"

"If you wish, soldier."

Bedros frowned, wondering at the manner in which she spoke. He knew the accent; it was unmistakable, it was his own. "Can it be girl that you are from Malatia?"

Her eyes widened, and filled with tears. She immediately put her head down and controlled herself. She couldn't show weakness to any man. If she did, she would pay the price of his brutality. She merely nodded to show him he was correct. She wished the discussion would go no further.

"I thought so," Bedros went on, trying to be as gentle and sincere as possible. She seemed to be responding to him slowly, but he was afraid of alienating her by saying the wrong thing. "Well, at least, you can tell me your name."

"My name is not important, soldier. As far back as I can remember, the Turks would call me SaSa. That is good enough for you."

She had become melancholy and cold toward him.

"SaSa. I am also from Malatia. My name is Vartanian. Bedros Vartanian. Did you know of my family there?"

"No. I was taken from my family many years ago. I was young. The Turkish generals used me as a slave at first. And then..."

She got up quickly, embarrassed for being so open with this man.

"I know. You do not have to say it. I know how they have always taken the pretty Armenian girls as their concubines."

The young girl turned toward him, and, seeing the compassion in his liquid eyes, she softened and sat next to him. She lifted a piece of her remaining veil and wiped away a trickle, which was seeping from her nostril and making its way toward her lips.

"I ran away about two years ago. I tried to find my mother, but it was impossible. So, I turned to this. It was the only thing I ever knew."

At last she could hold in her grief no more, and she wept bitterly. Bedros took her head into his arms, caressing her soft, shining hair.

"Cry, little one; you have the right. But please, tell me if you can—what is your Christian name? You must remember it. Perhaps I know of your family or at least can find out."

In a few moments the girl had controlled herself and looked up at the handsome soldier, who kept her warm in his great arms. She didn't answer, only gazed into his eyes with such intense desire that Bedros felt his whole body tremble. She didn't speak another word but only took his large, strong face into her hands and kissed him in a way he didn't know existed.

In seconds the two were entwined. Bedros was fearful of crushing her delicate body, but she cajoled him with innocent delight, and the deep, dark, young boy turned quickly into a sensuous man. It was as he had always imagined it would be —gentle, sincere, warm.

The two young bodies lay together, covered in the coarse animal skin, and then SaSa fell into a child's sleep. Bedros quickly dressed and tried to quietly leave. He paused for a moment, pondering this beautiful creature. He felt great desire mixed with aching sadness. As he turned to go, he thought he might return, might try to help her change her lifestyle. He stopped short at the sound of her voice.

"Bedros," she said groggily, "if you should want to return, you may call me by my Christian name. It is Sonia. Sonia Plebian."

• • •

How or when he got back to the barracks he didn't know. Sonia's incredible revelation had shocked him. Bedros's mind was in turmoil with questions and no answers. He felt sick and ashamed and no matter how many times he told himself he had no way of knowing who the girl was, this truth didn't help ease the gnawing pain inside him. Would he tell Hirair? And if he did, what good would it do? Could this girl be saved? How could he tell his dearest friend of what he had just done with his sister? He couldn't sleep that night. He was unsure if he would sleep well ever again.

The next morning Bedros ate breakfast silently next to Hirair. He decided he wouldn't tell his friend about the encounter with his sister. Fortunately Hirair didn't suspect Bedros's dark mood. He was gentleman enough not to ask him anything about the previous night. They made small talk. Privately, Bedros decided he would ask Binbashi Ismael for help.

The entire day Hirair was cautiously quiet with Bedros. The two friends seemed afraid to confront one another about the evening before. Several times Bedros was ready to reveal to his friend the sad story of the fate of Sonia, but the words stuck in his throat. They sat through the usual boring classes, making drawings of war zones and military formations, and listening to exaggerated stories of great Turkish warriors. They ate lunch without gusto and went on together to the woodshop, where they would be working in close proximity. Bedros grew more and more uncomfortable. It was Binbashi Ismael who at last broke the thick silence in the room.

"Nefer Vartanian, I wanted to be sure you didn't forget our date this evening."

His booming voice startled the young men out of their hammering, and Hirair looked at Bedros in shock that this busy commander should take the time to seek out a mere private. They all stood rigidly at attention until Ismael motioned them back to work. Bedros remained standing, wondering how much the others must have hated him for this show of preference. Even Hirair seemed to sullenly turn his back on him.

"No, sir. Of course I didn't forget."

"I thought not. Here is my address in Beshiktash. The driver will know where to let you off."

He tossed the tiny piece of paper into Bedros's hand and was quickly gone.

Bedros walked over to Hirair and joked about how, after his first piece of furniture, he would surely be fired. He lightheartedly laughed about his inferiority. But the damage had been done, and he well knew it. Hirair thought Bedros's silence that day was a sign of haughtiness, and Bedros couldn't tell him the truth at any cost.

As the bumpy tramway trotted him along to his destination in Beshiktash, Bedros found himself thinking only of Hirair and how he loved him and how he could ever tell him of the evening with Sonia. There was an answer somewhere, and he would find it. The binbashi would help him, he felt sure. If not, he promised himself he would tell Hirair the truth in the morning. It might cost him their friendship, but at least then Hirair would be free to seek out his sister and try to help her. That is, if she was in the realm of help.

The beautiful, dark soldier rode with his head down, not seeing this lovely and dignified sector of Constantinople. His sad eyes didn't enjoy the stately buildings and ancient architecture that abounded—the fine churches and mosques standing astutely side by side in marble and stone. The homes were far more elegant than those in Pera. As the horse-drawn tram came deeper into Beshiktash, Bedros didn't see the magnificent Cathedral of Sophia, which was acclaimed as one of the finest specimens of Turkish architecture. It had been built during the Byzantine Empire, yet it was perfectly unmarred. It was a breathtaking sight which Bedros didn't see. His eyes were tired, his mind befuddled. The high-pitched voice of the tramway driver forced him out of his sullenness. The driver pointed up toward a stunning home surrounded by a brick wall.

"That is it, soldier. Up there is the binbashi's residence."

Like a timid child Bedros Vartanian made his way up the path, bounding up brick steps and strolling through a wrought-iron gateway which led him to the entrance of the plush home. He was overwhelmed and felt rather insignificant as he reached for the brass horse's head knocker on the large oak door.

A cheerful, heavy woman answered the door and bade him to come in. She motioned to him to wait in the foyer while she scurried off to fetch her master.

Half man, half boy, he stood in wonderment of the majestic interior about him. His army boots, dirty and worn, stood on a pink marble floor. The walls were resplendent with tapestries and oil paintings with golden frames. Next to him, there was a vase of fresh red poppies and ferns perched on a gilded carved table. The smell of success and comfort and security was in the air. Around and around he turned, his head held up in awe when the binbashi entered the room.

"Good evening, Bedros. Did you have any trouble getting here?"

He was in civilian clothes, gray Western-style slacks and a gorgeous crimson velvet dinner jacket. His salt and pepper hair was slicked back and his eyes were gentle, without authority.

"Good evening, sir. No, no trouble at all. Your home is just exquisite. I do not know what to say."

"Say nothing," laughed the general. "Come let me show you around."

Bedros was then led from room to sumptuous room, and his eyes reached a point at which no wonder could amaze them. The place was paradise on earth. It was a lifestyle he would never have believed existed. To be sure, his family back in Malatia would scorn him if he dared tell them only half of what he saw. It was the way he wanted to live, vowed he would live one day.

"Ah, Sheida, you are down at last!" The binbashi startled Bedros from his dreaming. He looked up from his preoccupation with the vast and glorious parlor to see a tall, thin young woman enter through a curtained archway. She was elegant in a long blue satin dress, which looked like nothing he had ever seen before. She wore dangling gold earrings and a matching necklace around her long white swan neck. She acknowledged him with cold brown eyes and a toss of her haughty head, which was crowned with a sleek brown chignon. Immediately Bedros knew this girl thought she was something very special. He couldn't readily dispute her thoughts.

"You are looking lovely as ever tonight, my child." The binbashi beamed as he walked over to his daughter bestowing her with a kiss. "This is the soldier I told you about. Nefer Bedros Vartanian, this is my daughter, Sheida."

The pompous lady gave Bedros a disinterested nod and sat quickly down in an ornately scrolled chair. The two men politely waited, then found seats on a burgundy velvet loveseat hugged between two brass statues of lions.

"Cook says dinner is nearly ready, Father. She has prepared a strange meal tonight; I do not know what it is."

Her Turkish was so pure and flawless that Bedros had difficulty understanding her. He tried not to show his confusion. He was overcome by the girl's stature, and if she wasn't totally beautiful, her stance and manner made her so.

"That is not a strange dinner." Binbashi Ismael laughed. "I asked cook to prepare an Armenian meal tonight for our guest. After all, he needs a good dinner before beginning his tasks around the house."

"To be sure." Sheida curtly responded.

After what seemed like hours to the uncomfortable young Armenian, a reddish-skinned lady entered the parlor and announced that dinner was ready. They entered the huge dining room and sat at its endless pine table. They appeared lost, filling up only three of the sixteen chairs. Conversation was sparse but the food, which consisted of many courses, wasn't.

There was a crisp but bland salad, a soup that was mostly chicken broth and a few square-shaped noodles, and then came the supposed Armenian meal. Bedros laughed to himself at the dolma with too much rice, pilaf that had been boiled in plain water and overcooked green snap beans. He remembered Yughaper and her fine, painstaking cooking which would have put this to shame. Politely he complimented the cook and finished his mediocre meal, outwardly displaying enjoyment with each bite.

After a rich black Turkish coffee, Sheida excused herself and gingerly fled from the elegant room, leaving the two men staring awkwardly at one another. The housekeeper brought in a large oval brass platter brimming with succulent apples, pears and golden grapes. After this came a smaller tray that was abundant with nuts and assorted cheeses. It was enough dessert for five times the people and Bedros felt silly picking out his meager handful.

"Did you enjoy it all, Bedros?" questioned the burly host.

"Sir, it was the finest meal I can remember!" Bedros lied.

"I am sorry for Sheida's rude exit. She becomes uncomfortable in a world of men and their talk."

"I see," answered Bedros, looking at the doorway through which the fancy lady had disappeared.

"She has been a rather catered-to young woman since her mother died three years ago."

"I am sorry, sir," said Bedros sadly.

"It was pneumonia. Her mother's death was very painful for both of us. Now Sheida has consumed my whole life. I live for her pleasure alone. But I fear I cannot give her the happiness she deserves."

Bedros considered the man across the long table with great amazement. He had profound feelings and deep consideration. He was a family man, a moral, loving man. He wasn't as anyone from Malatia might believe a Turk to be.

"Sir, she is a lovely girl and I am sure she will find happiness one day. Sir if I may, before she returns I would like to discuss something with you. It is man's talk, something I am deeply troubled over."

Binbashi Ismael was touched by Bedros's confidence.

"Please, speak now. That is what I am here for." He leaned back in his chair intently waiting for Bedros's story.

Bedros began to tell the difficult tale to this man whom he had barely just met, and hardly knew. He felt his face reddening and his voice sticking in his throat as the story of his evening with Sonia began to unravel. He watched Ismael's face for some sign of a reaction. Surely the man must have thought him insane. Even to Bedros the tale was an unbelievable twist of fate. At last he finished, and the fancy room fell silent.

Finally, the commander spoke. "Interesting, Bedros, but why do you tell me this and not Hirair?"

"Sir, you must understand. Hirair is my dearest friend from many years back," he paused, looking up at the ceiling, "I suppose I am only thinking of myself and the shame I feel."

"Understandable." The binbashi nodded, and then leaned forward in his chair peering directly into Bedros's large, sad eyes. "And what would you like me to do about this...Sonia, was it?"

"Yes, sir. I want Hirair to find her, of course, but not as she is. Her mother is unstable and married to a man who I believe would only abuse the girl more. I had hoped you could get her out of there and perhaps give her some small job in the military. Once she felt she could make her own way, we could happily lead Hirair to her."

Binbashi Ismael didn't immediately answer, but Bedros felt a sudden surety in what he was saying and went on. The general pulled a long cigar from his jacket and lit it.

"If you please, sir, I believe it is the only way. If I may say, I believe the Turkish government owes her something."

Bedros couldn't believe he had said it aloud, but the words were out before he could stop them. He sat back, awaiting the explosion he was sure was forthcoming. Binbashi Ismael scowled at him, got up hastily, and paced angrily about the room.

When the general at last turned around, Bedros was shocked to see a glaze of liquid over his eyes. It was the same look but perhaps more agonized than Binbashi Ismael had showed him on the day the binbashi learned of Bedros's father's fate. Bedros froze, unable to speak or look at his commander.

"Bedros," he spoke shakily at first, and then gradually cleared his throat to its normal tone. "You are a most unusual young man. If I thought it before, I am assured of it now."

"Sir, I—"

"Let me speak. You are right in all you say, and you are fortunate that you have said it to me and not to several of my peers. I have heard of the massacres in the south during your father's time, but I tried through my years to discount them in any way I could. I know now that they were all true, and it sickens me. It sickens me that fine military men, like the ones I train every day in honesty and valor, could have been transformed into murdering imbeciles. I cannot undo what took place, Bedo; I can only try to help the victims of those terrible times." the binbashi took a long, hard breath, pacing around the room once again, staring out a window with a grim look on his face—"and we can all only pray, to whatever God we choose, that such atrocities will never happen again."

Bedros's head hung down. He was overwhelmed with the compassion of this fascinating man. He felt warmth toward him that he couldn't remember having for any of his elders. He had loved Friar Vincent but not like this. No, this feeling was closer to—he dared to remember—that which he felt for his father.

"Bedo, I will take care of the girl for you. When I am sure she is settled and has given up her former life, I will arrange to have Hirair find her. "

"Sir," Bedros jumped up from his chair. "I do not know what to say."

"There is no need, my boy." He attempted a facade of sternness, but it didn't work.

Bedros came closer to him and looked directly into his eyes. Four mighty, gleaming circles confronted each other, each pair trying to delve deeply into the inner reaches of the other.

"There is one condition I would like to add, if I may."

"Yes?" The general frowned under thick brows.

"Sonia must promise that she will never reveal her past life or fate as a child to her brother. You must make her promise."

Binbashi Ismael smiled at him so affectionately that for a moment Bedros thought he might embrace him.

"And so it shall be, Bedros, if you in turn promise me something."

"Of course, sir, anything."

"You shall promise never to seek out this girl again in any way. If by chance you should encounter her, you will act as though you have no memory of her." The commander stared deeply into the black pools of Bedros Vartanian's grateful, glowing eyes. "That is a fair exchange, would you say?"

"Yes, sir. Very fair. Thank you, sir."

"And now, young man, enough of this weighty conversation. You have work to do. Come with me."

And so it was that boy and man walked together through the glorious estate. The binbashi took Bedros out to a pleasant courtyard in the rear of the home. It was lush with flowers and shrubbery so plentiful that the plants pushed up against one another to form a massive afghan of bright green interspersed with splashes of gold, yellow, purple and crimson. Here on the patio Bedros was to build outdoor furniture.

After brief instructions, the binbashi disappeared, leaving Bedros in this miniature paradise with slabs of wood and sufficient tools to do his work. He had only the flickering light of several hurricane lamps to ease his labored eyes, but he didn't care. With each pound of the hammer, he implanted a nail of fortitude into his soul. Bedros knew he was on his way. He didn't know exactly where, only that he would get there. That was enough for him.

After several hours of uninterrupted work, Bedros heard someone approach him from behind. He dropped his hammer and turned around suddenly. There, glimmering in blue-and-white satin among the lamplights and moonbeams, was Sheida. He felt embarrassed. He was disheveled from his sweaty work.

"Hello," he meekly said.

"My father has sent me to tell you to stop your work for tonight."

Her voice was so mellow, she almost sounded as though she were singing. Still she had that pompous air. He felt patronized, sloppy and undignified in her presence.

"My father has requested you to spend the night with us. He has also arranged for you to spend the day with us tomorrow; I believe he wishes to show you around the area."

Bedros brushed back his hair, which was wildly flopping in every direction. He politely turned his back to gather up his tools. "I am grateful, but he has done enough for me already."

"And he will continue to do so if you are not so foolish as to refuse his hospitality, soldier."

He turned and stared at her stupidly as she granted him a curt smile. "Follow me, please."

Bedros put aside his tools, looking down at his dirty uniform in disgust.

"There will be clothing for you in the guest room."

He didn't like following anyone, especially girls—especially *this* girl who thought herself something rather sacred. He wished he looked smashing in a fine shirt and velvet knickers. She couldn't see him for what he really was in his present state, and it bothered him. She rambled on past the living quarters through a narrow pantry area and then down a corridor to the boudoir wing. He caught glimpses of the other bedrooms filled, like the rest of the home, with expensive furniture and fine fabric which covered beds, walls, windows—everything.

They came to the end of the corridor. Sheida pointed out a bathroom, and then opened another door. They entered the guest room, a small but elaborate room with a highly polished wood floor, which only barely showed under a thick, ornately patterned Oriental carpet. The curtains were deep red velvet. The bed was covered with a large throw cover of hand-knitted squares, all golden and bronze hued. He was still staring at the splendor when Sheida bade him a pleasant evening and was gone.

Tossed loosely but neatly on a high-back chair by the bed was a brown flannel nightshirt. Folded on the seat of the chair were street clothes - a pale-beige shirt, brown khaki pants and sandals. They appeared to be the perfect size. As the young soldier took in the lovely room, it occurred to him that this was the first real bedroom, except for Sonia's, he had ever slept in. In fact, this was the first real bed that wasn't a bunch of boards nailed together and placed on a cold floor. He laughed at it all as he prepared for bed. In the guest room was a small sink with running water and a fresh bar of lavender-smelling soap. Bedros realized, the soap, the room—everything in the house, was feminine and frilly like Sheida.

Once settled in his bed, Bedros tried to rest his mind and alleviate the burning in his eyes. His thoughts fled through the amazing events of the day and all that had transpired. Could all of this have anything to do with luscious, aloof, turned-up nose Sheida? The question came and went and at last sleep overcame him.

The next morning the same elderly housekeeper awakened Bedros and announced that breakfast would be served in fifteen minutes. He spent every bit of the time preparing himself the way he used to during his triumphant Malatia days. As he perused himself in the fuzzy, full-length mirror by the sink, he decided he had spent his time well. Today Bedros Vartanian was ready for anything, including the little lady of the household.

When he entered the dining room, Ismael and his daughter were already seated next to each other, engrossed in conversation and laughter. His entry abruptly ended their little tête-à-tête. Ismael motioned for Bedros to sit next to him. They were served a large breakfast of eggs, Syrian bread, soft, white cheese, *zatoons* (moist black olives) and freshly sliced cold lamb. The coffee was strong and hot. Sheida ate delicately, while Bedros voraciously devoured his meal. Ismael watched the two youngsters as if in a trance and he hardly touched his breakfast. He did, however, enjoy several cups of the housekeeper's rich coffee.

"Today, Bedros, Sheida and I would like to take for a tour."

Bedros thought to himself that Sheida had nothing to do with these plans. Bedros remarked, "I have seen a good deal of the Pera sector, sir."

Ismael and Sheida shared a private chuckle, which annoyed Bedros.

"We do not mean to laugh at you, Bedo. It is just that Pera, as exciting as it is, has nothing on the places you will see today."

Bedros looked over at Sheida, who smiled a condescending smile.

"Well then, sir. I would be delighted.

The binbashi cleared his throat. "Shall we go?"

They rose and walked out to the atrium to await the carriage. A young, Polynesian-looking servant came scurrying along, leading a sleek, black horse, which was harnessed to a classic-looking cabriolet. It was the most ornate carriage Bedros had ever seen, with its rippling, red fringe hanging from its silky hood and all along its rim. The servant helped Sheida up into the swaying wagon. She was lovely looking again today, wearing a long, tan-colored skirt, a ruffled, yellow blouse, and a matching plumed hat, which was cocked over the side of her perfectly coiffed head. She looked to Bedros like the pictures he had seen of French aristocratic ladies. He felt a surge of excitement at the sight of her, but he controlled himself for she was a Turkish captain's daughter.

Ismael hopped up next, motioning to Bedros to take the rear seat behind him and his daughter. With a brisk tug, the horse began to totter along and Bedros looked back at the beautiful brick house as it disappeared behind a lush hill, laden with palms and thick, colorful vegetation. It was going to be a perfect day. He just knew it.

"We are heading toward the Sea of Marmora first. It is a short journey through some very aesthetic countryside. You will enjoy the scenery, but more so, the spot we are going to see."

"What is that?" asked Bedros excitedly.

"We will go to Sophia, a small but beautiful city. She is home to many famous mosques, cathedrals, tombs and so on. She is a tourist's delight!"

"There we will see Dolma Baghche," offered Sheida.

Bedros laughed at the word "dolma", which literally meant "stuffed" in his native tongue. Then, catching the cool glances of Ismael and his daughter, he apologized.

"In this case, Bedros," Ismael informed him, "*Dolma Baghche* means 'enveloped with gardens.' *Stuffed*—if you choose to use that word."

"I see," said Bedros. "And what is this place?"

Sheida quickly answered him. "It is the summer residence of our sultan. It is acclaimed as one of the finest architectural and horticultural wonders of our times."

Bedros thought how nasal her tone became when she used her fancy words. He couldn't decide whether he liked or loathed her.

Ismael, aware of his daughter's haughty nature, broke the chilled silence. "Today, Bedros, I hope to show you the great accomplishments of my people so perhaps you will see a side of the Turks of which I am most proud. We are a fine cultured people, Bedros, not the barbarians you understandably think we are."

"I do not think that way, sir. I hope I am intelligent enough not to throw a whole nationality into one large basket."

Sheida looked back at him in surprise that this giant bull of a man was so well spoken and indeed so sensitive to her people.

"Well spoken, soldier," she complimented, but Bedros didn't reply.

Ismael drove the cabriolet around the famous sixteenth-century mosque called Bayazit. He explained to Bedros that it was considered one of the finest specimens of Byzantine architecture known to mankind. Bedros gazed up at the structure in wonder. It had a domed roof which jutted out into the clouds. The magnificently carved dome was completely made of gold. The windows were shimmering lead glass and the stones with which it had been constructed were four feet in length and nearly three feet high. Its entire facade was covered with blue and gold inlaid tiles. It was incredibly beautiful and creatively built. Bedros was impressed and he told them so.

They then took a quick turn to view another mosque several miles away. The Turks called it Sarayli. It was smaller than Bayazit but just as lavishly constructed—a masterpiece of human accomplishment.

The refreshing morning lapsed into a balmy afternoon and the threesome stopped in a café just a few blocks from the Sarayli Mosque. The little restaurant was alive with veiled women, puffy old men and mischievous children scampering about. Dark, wooden fans hung from the ceiling, circulating the smell of coffee and tobacco. They each ordered a cool punch for which the place was noted. It tasted like a very sweet combination of exotic fruit juices and some form of whiskey. The waiter then brought a large tray filled with assorted Greek and Armenian appetizers. There was *yalanci* dolma, cheese *boeregg*, and choeregg, along with a pale yellow, stringy cheese.

As was her custom, Sheida barely touched anything on the tray. The two men ate arduously and partook of the excitement around them.

"Next, we will head for the sea, Bedros. It will be cool and tranquil there and you will see the Dolma Baghche."

"I am most impressed with everything, sir. I cannot wait to see this place." Bedros looked at Sheida for some assistance in the small talk but he found her to be staring mistily at him. When she realized he was aware of her daydreaming, she collected herself quickly, nervously tapping at her mouth with her napkin and looking elsewhere with her eyes.

"How far are we from there now?" Bedros asked the binbashi, giving up on their female companion.

"We will ride another half an hour or so. Then on the way back to Pera, we will ride again through Beshiktash to show you where the sultan lives in the winter. It is where all the nobility and wealth of Constantinople abide."

"You do not have to take me back to Pera. I am happy to take the tramway."

"That is all right, Bedros. I have things I can do there, and Sheida will be company for me on the way back. Let us go."

The afternoon grew hotter, with only the fragrant, nautical breezes carrying with them the cool sensations of water to relieve the burning sun. As the archaic splendor of Sophia faded away, the cabriolet made its way into the typical desert wasteland Bedros had known as a child.

"You see, it is like leaving the world once you are outside of Constantinople. Civilization is left behind and medieval primitivism abounds." The binbashi was a brilliantly eloquent man, whose every word seemed like it was carefully contemplated before spoken.

Bedros sighed and rested back in his seat. "It looks just like Malatia now."

"This is nothing, Bedros!" interjected the usually reserved Sheida. "Father has taken me to the training areas of Erenköy, Maltepe. They are truly desolate places. They are not fit for any man, as far as I am concerned!"

Bedros felt the same nausea overcome him as when the yuze-bashi mentioned they would be stationed in one of those horrid-sounding places after general training. Bedros had preferred not to think about those days to come, but the caustic sound of Sheida's voice reminded him. He laughed, though, and tried to make light of his feelings.

"Yes, I remember hearing something about those fine-sounding places when I first arrived in Pera."

They all had an enjoyable chuckle at the soldier's sarcasm. Somehow Bedros couldn't help thinking that Sheida and her father were having a great deal of fun at his expense. Binbashi Ismael then broke the laughter abruptly, saying some words Bedros would carry with him for the rest of his life.

"Bedo, this conversation has been implanted for our jovial benefit. Sheida and I wanted to mention those grueling training centers to remind you..."

The general stopped short and looked over at his daughter with a sheepish wink. Bedros felt his seat growing extremely uncomfortable underneath him.

"What was I saying? Oh, yes, we wanted to remind you of where you are <u>not</u> going to go."

For several minutes there was nothing—no glances, no words, no laughter, just the incessant trotting of the horses' hoofs and the sandy rotations of the carriage wheels. At last Bedros leaned forward, nearly flopping over into the front seat.

"Sir? Where I am <u>not</u> going to go?" Bedros was dumbfounded. He tried to erase the stupefied grin on his face but saw that Sheida and her father were displaying equal delight in the moment.

"No. Bedo," the binbashi answered, his voice mellow with pride and his eyes moist with the joy he had evoked from this favored young man, "Sheida asked that I use my meager power to allow you to remain in Pera. After all, how can we ever find a carpenter as fine as you to complete the endless work on our house? It wouldn't be fitting for a man of my rank to settle for a lesser craftsman. So, permission has been granted for you to remain in Pera and continue your work for us."

Bedros fell back and yelped in glee. His feet flew up in the air, kicking the back of Sheida's seat, and he quickly apologized. She didn't answer—just kept her stare focused on the barren countryside, but Bedros could make out from the side of her turned head the creases of a broad smile.

The binbashi then added, as though more were needed, "I have also arranged for Hirair to remain with you. Morale, after all, is of the utmost importance when a man is doing a task. Don't you agree, Bedo?"

"I agree, sir, with all my heart," responded Bedros happily.

The afternoon flew by and a lighthearted evening took its place. The three had become an odd sort of family. It was incredible that mere words could change the feelings of one man for another—one young boy for one young girl. Bedros Vartanian began to feel love for Binbashi Ismael, and he at least had become warily fond of his daughter.

Soon they found themselves standing on a rocky platform, which jutted into the Marmora Sea. The rocky ledge was directly across from the most breathtakingly beautiful spectacle Bedros had ever seen. It was a plot of heaven that had fallen to earth - the baroque Dolma Baghche! The sea breezes tangled and played twisting games with his hair. The mist seized his black eyes and infiltrated the bristles in his nose. He was tantalized. He cautiously looked over at Sheida to see whether she could be as exhilarated as he was by the breathtaking view and invigorating air, but he found her looking at him in the same daydream stare he had noticed on the ride here. There was one difference. This time she didn't care that he saw her staring at him, didn't try to mask her feelings in an air of loftiness. Sheida looked at Bedros Vartanian with nothing short of desire on her beautiful face, and Bedros was now the one who didn't know what to do with his eyes. He turned his head to follow a gull and felt Sheida's hand reach out for his. He had no choice but to gently grasp it. Ismael took Sheida's other hand and the three walked back to the carriage. Sheida sat next to Bedros in the rear of the carriage for the ride back to Beshiktash. They were a charming sight - the enamored young girl, the succumbing soldier, and the peacock of a father.

• • •

On returning to Pera, the threesome enjoyed a lovely, late dinner at the Tokatlian Restaurant. They were fussed over like royalty, and Bedros wished Garabed Hamparian could have been there to see him. It occurred to Bedros, as he munched on exquisite Middle Eastern delicacies, that his nest was quickly becoming feathered.

When Bedros sank into the hard bunk back at the barracks, he looked up at the loudly snoring Nooredeen, who would probably be awakening soon for his evening duties. Try as he might his churning insides wouldn't permit him to rest and Bedros finally rose, sneaking over to the sleeping Hirair. He gently tapped him; then, not getting a response, he shook the boy. He could no longer hold back his bursting desire to share his good fortune with his dear friend.

Hirair awoke, startled by Bedros's alarming behavior. "What in God's name, Bedo?" Hirair was too groggy to show the displeasure he had felt earlier with his friend's secretive manner.

In the still blackness of the bedroom, replete with tired bodies, Bedros chattered on and on to his wide-eyed friend. The conversation culminated with a dual exclamation of glee and an embrace. Fearing that the other boys might have awakened, Bedros stealthily made his way back to his bed. He wasn't surprised Nooredeen had ceased his snoring and was bending down from the above bunk like a dangling possum.

"So, you have gained the favor of the binbashi, have you?" he grunted.

The perceptively accurate ears of his Turkish bunkmate annoyed Bedros.

"That is right, Nooredeen," Bedros answered, not wishing to continue the conversation further.

"Some people get all the luck," grumbled the young Turk as he jumped down from his perch and began dressing. Bedros quietly watched him from his bed, pretending to sleep.

"I am happy for you, Bedros," exclaimed Nooredeen as he hurried out of the room. Though nothing could take away his delight this night, though nothing could make him worry, Bedros still fell asleep wondering if Nooredeen was really happy for him.

In the following months, Bedros continued his fine work for Binbashi Ismael along with his duties at the Pera Center. Though he and Hirair spent a good deal of time together during the day, his evenings were consumed with Ismael and Sheida. Soon there was no question in his mind that the general had picked him for his precious Sheida to marry. Whenever he could the commander left the two alone, affording them every possible opportunity to fall in love. Though Sheida was obviously convinced Bedros was to be her husband, the soldier was still cautiously slow in his advances. The feeling he believed to be love wasn't exactly developing as he had hoped it might.

One afternoon as Bedros was busily constructing a new batch of ammunition boxes, Hirair came bounding in with fiery excitement in his eyes. He grabbed Bedros's arm and pulled him over to a corner away from the ever-watchful eyes and ears of the envious soldiers who had become aware of the favoritism being shown to these two inseparable friends.

"Bedo, you cannot believe what just happened!"

"What?" asked Bedros, pretending a question but knowing the binbashi had kept his promise about Sonia. Nothing else could have wielded such elation on his friend's glowing face.

"At long last I have found my sister, Sonia!" Hirair wept with joy and threw his arms around Bedros's neck.

"This is wonderful, Hirair! How did it happen?" asked the actor.

"The binbashi sent me to the kaimakam's headquarters inside Pera this morning to fetch some papers for him. To my surprise I saw a girl sitting behind a desk in the lobby there who looked very familiar to me. We started talking and eventually I realized who she was."

"That must have been some reunion!" exclaimed Bedros, thrilled for his friend.

"You can believe it was! We made so much noise the kaimakam himself put us out into the street so that we could continue our celebration outside."

"I am happy for you, my friend," said Bedros, finally feeling the guilt flee from his soul, a soul that had borne it so painfully for too long. "How does she seem to you?"

"Fine," continued Hirair, now slightly less jovial and a bit thoughtful. "She did seem a little reserved, as though she wished to tell me many more things, but she was cheerful and of course, just beautiful. She said that she was taken as a house servant after our father died. She insists she was treated with great respect, and not once was she touched by any of the Turkish men. It was her last employer who recommended her for this office work in the kaimakam's headquarters."

"Wonderful! Now you can set your mind to rest about her."

"Yes, at last. I am delighted that she is close so that I can see her often. Perhaps you will find the chance to meet her with me one day, Bedo. I know you would love her immediately."

Bedros smiled a difficult smile and turned to pick up some fallen nails. "I would like that, Hirair, but you know I am very taken up these days."

"Yes, I forgot," teased Hirair. "Your lovely Turkish lady and her kindly father."

Bedros laughed slyly, slapping Hirair on the back. "Come on, soldier. Let us get back to work. There are boxes to be made."

Bedros was delighted, as this had been the final proof that the binbashi was indeed a man of his word. He would make a perfect father-in-law. He would not only protect and advance Bedros, but the soldier knew he could be the savior for his entire family. If he didn't end up in America, for sure he would inherit the earth here in Turkey under the protective wing of the powerful binbashi.

After dinner that evening, Bedros was solemnly thinking about his family. He had never received a return letter from them since his arrival in Constantinople. Though Sheida was alluring and the meal was one of the finest the cook had ever prepared, Bedros was preoccupied and sullen. Sheida knew immediately he wasn't himself.

"What is the matter with you tonight, Bedo? I feel as though you are with me only in body. Where is your mind?"

Bedros looked fondly at her. She was a picture to behold—her brown hair always perfect, her clothes meticulous. He had yet to see her wear the same dress twice. She was, to any man, the ideal woman. Yet why was she not so to him? He had convinced himself that he would learn to love her and that her position and this grand comfort he enjoyed could make his effort all worthwhile. He had also noticed that Sheida no longer wore her status like a shawl. She had become a fine, sensitive young woman, whose sole purpose was his enjoyment and satisfaction. No man could ask for more.

"I am thinking of my family back in Malatia. I have found such comfort and luxury here in your beautiful home Sheida that I feel some sorrow and guilt that they all remain in the backward poverty of Malatia."

"Bedo," she said softly, kneeling by his side as he sank into one of the overstuffed chairs in the elaborate parlor. "When the time comes... I am sure you know my father will be happy to arrange for them to come here and live with us. It will be our pleasure."

And so it would be. He could ask for no more. If he couldn't sacrifice love for his own comfort, then he would have to for his family. He would be crazy to refuse this kindest of all gestures.

While the two would-be lovers amused each other, Ismael entered the room. There was a pout of burden on his face. His face brightened at the sight of Sheida and Bedros in their engrossed conversation.

"I see you two have found each other once again," he laughed as the youngsters nodded politely.

"Yes, sir," responded Bedros, rising. "But I think it is time I boarded the tramway and got myself back to Pera. There is much to do tomorrow. The box order this time is quite large."

"Yes, I know, Bedo," Ismael agreed. He looked thoroughly exhausted. "But before you leave, I must tell you that I will be leaving the city for a few weeks."

Sheida jumped and embraced her father. Bedros came to his side in concern as well.

"Several weeks? Why, Father? You have never been gone that long before."

"I know, my child," her father said, gently caressing her hair. "There is political trouble. Some overzealous rabble-rousers are starting up again. I feel I must go out to the training centers and say my piece. In good conscience I cannot let madness overcome our ranks again."

His face was drawn, his eyes red and puffy. The two who loved him so deeply felt his pain. There was something terribly wrong, and they knew they couldn't dissuade him. He had to go.

Bedros said the very thing Ismael was about to ask him. "Sir, you can be sure I will look after Sheida and the household for you, if that is your wish."

"That is my wish, Bedo. If anything happens here while I am gone, anything that you feel is unfair or bordering on the volatile, you must send for me immediately." He paused, looking at the concern on his daughter's lovely face. "At any rate, it will only be a few weeks. Too short a time for anything serious to occur."

Within a few days of the binbashi's departure, Bedros sensed a change in the barracks. The other officers had become short-tempered with him, picking on insignificant details. He was sure the Turkish soldiers were snickering and collaborating behind his and Hirair's back. He put it all aside, viewing it as aimless folly. He knew it was a chance for those jealous soldiers to gossip and whine while the binbashi wasn't there to defend his chosen protégé. All this, he was sure, could cause him no harm.

The childish behaviors of his fellow soldiers were further put aside when at long last a letter arrived from Ara. Bedros tore it open hungrily and basked in every precious word.

Dear Brother,

It has been too long, I know, but be assured our prayers and thoughts are with you daily. Mother is well, though she still smokes constantly. She is busy with her doctoring and has become even more popular around the town. Between the offerings of her patients and the pension, we are able to eat and dress quite well. I am still building houses as much as I can and saving diligently for the day when we can all leave here, though Mother still insists she will never go.

Khatchadour and Anna have another son, and they have named him Sahag, after our father. They are doing well in their own little home and she seems a good wife to him.

Sahag and Hovsep are inseparable, like twins! They run all over the place, creating havoc. I think they are more mischievous than we ever were. I am sure they will soon join the army as you did. There is really not enough work for them in the foundry with Khatchadour, and to be sure, the building business is poor. Our Malatiatsi neighbors have little money to spend on new homes or even expansion of their existing ones. Our brothers think your life must be so exciting and have already warned Mother of their intent.

I am sure, by now, you have met hundreds of beautiful girls! Here, it is the same ones we grew up with. I do not know what it is, but I cannot seem to find anyone of interest. Perhaps when we get to Bolis, the selection will be more interesting. I have heard so many stories about the veiled women and the baths and all sorts of other things I dare not mention in my letter. But I know you must be having a high time.

I must tell you one more thing before closing. It is probably just the hallucinations of this bored young man whom you left behind in this dismal land, but I feel there is something in the air. I hope to God it is all talk. Some people say that the Turks are again planning to annihilate all Christians. The word is that their primary targets will be us, the Armenians, because once again we are progressing too far, too fast.

I wonder how it seems to you in Pera? If you ever get any hint of trouble, I know you will let us know so that we can get out in time. You know that I will do the same.

For now it will be my place to take care of Mother and stay with her. For sure, there is no other woman who could lure me away from home as yet!

Care well for yourself, brother, and be assured of my love always. My heart tells me we will be together soon, the way it used to be.

My fondest love,
Ara

It was the perfect tonic, a sleeping medication second to none. Bedros was momentarily one with his beloved family. More than ever, he was sure he would inevitably marry Sheida and bring his family to Bolis. If they had to bow to the Turks to at least maintain their dignity that would be all right. Satisfied, he fell asleep soundly. In the morning before roll call, he scribbled a fast letter, telling all about Garabed and Hirair, Binbashi Ismael and Sheida. He knew his family would be delighted.

After writing his letter, Bedros still had time until breakfast, so he decided to go to the woodshop and inspect the ammunition boxes. With the new scrutiny of his superiors, he couldn't afford any flaws or inventory discrepancies. The rest of the dormitory was still asleep. As he made his way across the room he stopped, looking up as though something had just occurred to him. He went back to his bunk, and after being sure everyone was asleep, he fell to his knees and began intensely praying. In his recent endeavors, he had forgotten to discuss his plans with the one person in whom he had complete faith—complete blind, trusting love.

"Father, I know you must have thought I forgot you. You must never think that of us, you and I, for you will always be in my mind, even if I forget to tell you so.

"I want to thank you for caring so well for my family while I am here. I feel so inadequate, still unable to release them from their plight. But I know, with your help, we will get them out safely and soon. I know too that you have great plans for me. I can feel it deep inside. I am not afraid, not of anything or anyone. Whatever the Turks, this land or America may have in store, we will meet it head on, and together we will conquer it. I love you, Father."

Bedros quickly rose and made his way through the vacant corridors down to the woodshop. When he opened the door, he surprised three of his Armenian coworkers, who quickly jumped up from their huddled positions over one of Bedros's ammunition boxes. He didn't know the men well. They were a cliquey threesome, rather heavy bores with whom he couldn't be bothered. Their names were Sebouh, Stepan and Vahak. He knew little else about them.

Sebouh was the first to speak, the look of fear easing from his face. "Bedros, you nearly frightened us to death. We didn't expect anyone to come barging in like this!"

Bedros retorted with a deep frown, "I didn't expect to find you here examining my ammunition boxes either."

Sebouh put his arm around Bedros and led him over to the other chagrined soldiers, who were now standing in front of the box, foolishly trying to cover up their scheme.

"Look." Sebouh pointed to the box, the cover of which had been pried off and was lying on the floor.

When Bedros drew closer and looked down into the box, he was horrified to see it was filled to overflowing with rifle shells.

"In God's name!" he said, glaring furiously at them. "You three are mad! You will be put to the torch for this. You know we do not handle any ammunition here. You better unload this fast!"

Vahak immediately grabbed his arms. The looks on the faces of the three culprits had changed from shock to anger.

Vahak continued to squeeze Bedros's arm. Bedros pulled away and the two began grappling. Stepan and Sebouh intervened.

Sebouh addressed Bedros in a patronizing tone of voice. "We cannot fight one another. We are Tashnags, Bedros. This has been planned for a long time. Once each week we fill a box and smuggle it out of the barracks. No one knows."

"Except him," snapped Vahak, ready to lunge at Bedros again, but his companions held him at bay. "Do you really believe our secret is safe? Everyone knows he is the binbashi's golden boy!"

No amount of strength could restrain him further. Bedros flung his arms free, and his fist sent Vahak flying across the room. He smashed into the box, and bullets scattered all over the floor. As if the first punch were not enough, the infuriated young bull started after the crushed soldier again. This time the other two held him back. Sebouh rushed over to pick up Vahak, while Stepan held his arms in struggling difficulty around Bedros's waist.

Sebouh rose up, with his moaning partner slouched over his shoulder. Sebouh held out a peaceful hand toward Bedros. "Forgive him, Bedros. We all know this is not true. If we can trust anyone in this center, I would stake my life on you, as would all our Armenian soldiers."

"All right," puffed Bedros, "and now what?"

"Let us continue silently. It has nothing to do with you. The boxes will not be missed as long as you overlook the discrepancies."

Bedros looked uncomfortably at the three apprehensive faces. They were Armenians. They were his people. He wanted to believe how he felt about them or their mission didn't matter.

"All right," he said. "Let us clean up this mess so you can get on with your work. Hurry now; it is almost dawn, and there will be much activity here shortly."

For himself, Bedros thought it best to get out of there and leave the dregs to his countrymen. He left the room quickly, passing down the corridor toward his dormitory. He didn't stop to look behind; didn't think of anything except getting away fast; didn't notice that Nooredeen had been crouching secretly behind the door adjacent to the room from which he had just fled.

At breakfast, as he and Hirair were about to eat, the yuze-bashi stormed into the room, accosted Bedros and took his arm rudely, pulling him from the dining hall. Hirair was horrified but knew better than to interfere at that particular moment.

"What is the matter, captain?" questioned Bedros, who was sick with the feeling that he knew all too well what must be the matter.

"Never mind nefer. You come with me! I have some friends of yours locked up and I would like to know if you should join them."

"Friends..." But he didn't get the chance to finish, for they had already reached the captain's office. The yuze-bashi flung open the door, pushed Bedros in front of him and then pulled him furiously down into a chair by his desk.

"I am in charge here while the binbashi is away. You will not receive any special treatment from me, Vartanian!"

"I did not ask for any, sir," said Bedros, still wondering what this power-wielding madman had in store for him.

Six armed gendarmes entered the office escorting the three Armenian soldiers Vahak, Stepan, and Sebouh. Bedros felt the urge to vomit at the sight of these overzealous idiots, whose foolish, insignificant shenanigans might very well cost him his future—or his life.

"These are your friends, Nefer Vartanian?" questioned the yuze-bashi sarcastically.

Bedros eyed the three soldiers. It took him a few moments to consider an answer or perhaps a definition for the unwarranted word *friend*.

"I can only say they are fellow Armenians, sir." He said the words coldly without emotion. His only thought at the moment was that he was telling the truth. It was a truth his inquisitors already disbelieved.

"What do you have to say to that, nefers?" asked the yuze-bashi with a demonic gleam in his searching eyes.

Sebouh, the self-appointed leader, decided to speak after a short, silent conversation of glances among the three.

"Bedros is our friend by nationality, sir. Nothing more."

"Is that so?" growled the captain, growing furious at the careful protectiveness of the accused. "Then why is it that a fellow private discovered him in your presence this morning during your little party?"

Bedros felt his face turn white, and the room spun around him. He had been seen with these fools. There was no hope.

"Sir," responded Sebouh, "Bedros walked in on us; that is true. But he had nothing to do with the ammunition box affair. As I have tried to tell you, neither did we. We found the box there and were trying to cover up our surprise when Nooredeen came upon us. That is why we behaved so suspiciously."

Nooredeen, thought Bedros. Of course! The slimy spy who always pretended sleep and kindness and disinterest. He had been waiting for a chance to discredit him all along.

"Bedros, what do you have to say to this?"

"Sir, I do not know of any wrong doing. I entered the room and found them trying to pick up the bullets. They had accidentally knocked over the box and spilled the shells onto the floor. They were as frightened as I of the consequences of being found."

The words just came out. He was too horrified to try to think of a more elaborate tale.

"Interesting stories, gentlemen. My compliments to all. You Armenians are sly creatures, but you have overlooked one point." The yuze-bashi peered at them from under his thick, graying eyebrows, wrinkling his nose as though he found them repulsive. "What were the four of you doing in the woodshop at such an unusual hour?"

The three criminals stood stone-like and silent, their eyes focused on Bedros, searching for help. Bedros rose without permission and stood valiantly by the side of the infuriated captain.

"Sir," he began coolly and was shocked at his own fortitude, "I thought it would be a good idea to begin taking inventory of the ammunition boxes in the shop. I felt, to avoid just such a happening as this, we should keep a careful tabulation. I asked Sebouh, Vahak, and Stepan to help me early this morning in the count."

Silence shrouded the room. No one dared to speak. The yuze-bashi got slowly up out of his seat. He glowered at Bedros as though he wished the young man would disappear. He hated Bedros for his intelligence, his sophistication and more importantly, for his logical answer to what he thought was an inescapable question. He paced the room precisely, peering first out a window, then at Bedros, then at the three Armenians still flanked by the unflinching gendarmes. At last he made his way back to his seat and mused on his words carefully before continuing.

"We shall not pursue this further until the binbashi returns. I would not like to take it upon myself to make a decision in this matter, especially considering the great fondness Ismael has for you, Nefer Vartanian." He made his last remark with a glare of distaste and a crooked smirk, both bestowed directly on Bedros.

Too soon the three Armenian rebels relaxed, but the yuze-bashi had not yet finished his decree. They stiffened respectfully as he went on.

"Now then, Bedros, you shall remain confined to the Pera center with no nights off or privileges to leave the barracks boundaries. I allow you your freedom only due to your auspiciousness in the eyes of Binbashi Ismael."

Bedros was furious. He wanted to strangle this man, but upon hearing the continuing verdicts, he was grateful to have gotten off so easily.

"Furthermore, you three—Stepan, Sebouh, and Vahak—shall be confined to prisoners' cells without any military activities whatsoever. Upon the binbashi's return, we shall have a trial in order to make a decision in this matter."

He began strutting in front of them with a look of superiority upon his face. "I assure you, once the binbashi sees the evidence of the ammunition box so perfectly filled with rifle shells, there will be no question of your guilt. This of course includes you, Vartanian."

There was no more to say. Perhaps they all felt fortunate in not being immediately executed without trial, a fate that would be commonplace in the near future. The gendarmes yanked the three defeated Tashnags to the prisoners' cells located outside near the livery complex. Bedros was permitted to leave the room and return to his daily routine. He was sick with worry but determined to dismiss the thoughts of anything other than the formation of a vivid plan for self-preservation.

After the four accused soldiers were well out of the way, the yuze-bashi summoned Nooredeen and a few local Turks, all of whom had mutual hatred for Bedros Vartanian and Armenian soldiers. In the midst of a sizzling Turkish afternoon in the captain's office, a meeting took place. It was a meeting of treacherous triumph. Once the bin-bashi returned and the box was opened, the four Armenians would be executed as traitors. Binbashi Ismael would learn a bitter lesson—that no Armenian, no matter how good or advanced, could ever be trusted let alone cared for or embraced. They would be an example for all the military, so at last the charade of any compatibility between the Turkish soldiers and their dhimmi peers would perish. They drank from a bottle of bittersweet whiskey, which the yuze-bashi kept stashed away in his lower desk drawer. In vulgar drunkenness they laughed and contemplated the glory of the day when the binbashi would return and be told the news. The box would be opened, and the slippery little fish would be caught, dangling helplessly from the hook of hatred.

There would be other clandestine meetings. There would be other places—other dark, seedy rooms—filled with people of different faces but similar hearts, hearts of sorrowful confusion, souls that thought themselves superior, spirits that believed themselves masters of the world. For them no act was too gruesome or inconceivable to attain their distorted ends. These meetings would spark the beginning of a five-year, rampage of hatred, which would eventually regurgitate in the near elimination of a nationality from the face of the earth.

Bedros didn't go to the mess hall for the rest of the day, and just as Hirair was about to seek him out, the shaken soldier entered the dormitory. They greeted each other with only their eyes and a cautious gesture of silence. Bedros walked wearily over to his bunk and lay back; his great arms became a nest for his heavy, troubled head. He gazed up at the upper berth, which was empty. He smiled to himself, assured that Nooredeen had wisely decided to seek other sleeping quarters. But Bedros knew he still wasn't safe. There were others in the ward, many others, soldiers he thought he knew. Now he realized he knew no one, only himself and Hirair. It was an unstable, unfriendly environment.

Hirair could bear it no longer and came over to his friend. He looked around uneasily, but there were no soldiers nearby. Still he whispered so softly that Bedros could barely hear him. He bent low over his companion's stiffly prone body.

"What happened to you? I thought they would carry you off, and I would never see you again. I tell you, Bedo, I was sick to my stomach the whole day."

Bedros sat up and the two spoke nervously in the hushed blackness of the room.

"They tried—with that damn Nooredeen—they tried to accuse me of consorting with those three—Stepan, Sebouh, and Vahak—in the shop. They have been smuggling ammunition out of the barracks using our own boxes. Do you believe it? They are ardent Tashnags, and now I am sworn to secrecy in their conspiracy."

"I would never have believed it of those three!"

"At least they tried to release me from suspicion in the matter, but even if I get off the officers have the filled box as proof of guilt. To be sure, they will be tried and executed."

"What can we do?" asked Hirair.

He looked like the frightened, shy little boy he'd been on the afternoon Bedros first met him at Saint Mary's. It made Bedros even sicker to realize that he himself was harboring the same weak feelings of inferiority and doom. Bedros Vartanian was a young man who would, in the altitudes of life, accept no level less than the very top. At this dismal moment, he was wallowing in the earth's deepest, darkest ravines. He could bear it no longer. He gazed up at Nooredeen's bunk with a sudden smile of understanding. He had reached another turning point in his life.

"Hirair," he thought, "we both know that there is no future for us here in Turkey, or in any other part of this Far Eastern world. If we make it beyond this hurdle, my dearest friend, will there not be other Nooredeens, other yuze-bashis, other madmen, the kind Binbashi Ismael so fears and hates? Turkey belongs to the Turks, and by God, we will gladly let them have it. No Armenian, even if he is fortunate enough to survive these times, will ever inherit this part of the earth or claim heritage to his birthright. As for me, even the mighty binbashi and his beloved Sheida cannot offer me what I must have- the safety and freedom to build my own life with no interference or treachery". So there it all was. Upon the blank pages of his future, Bedros Vartanian had just indelibly written the blueprint from which he wouldn't deviate.

"Have no fear, Hirair." He smiled. "*Hos em.* Bedros is here!"

Hirair held back his laughter and faked a punch at his friend's nose. "Now go to sleep. Tomorrow there will be sunshine."

Bedros shooed him away and lay back, still as the night around him. He spent the next hour in collaboration with his Lord. Finally Bedros was told—no, ordered—and he knew what he had to do. He got up, his heart pounding, his hands shaking, his blood turning to ice water in his veins. He made sure that all the other soldiers were in deep sleep. And then the stealthy cat crept out the door, down the tomb-like corridor to the woodshop. In there the deadly evidence lay. Not daring to breathe, he opened the door and inhaled the room's blackness. He walked in and could vaguely see that the box was in its same position, and it seemed, as he had hoped, that it was left unguarded.

He encroached farther into the room, hunched over, stumbling in the dark. He got down and slowly scrambled his way over to the box. He drew close to it and found that the lid had been securely replaced. He ran his nimble fingers along the perimeter of the top to find that each corner had been steadfastly bolted with iron brackets and large construction nails. There was no possible way he could open it and try to reseal it without the appearance being ridiculously obvious. There had to be another way—a way to open the box and remove the evidence without anyone noticing.

He crept over to the long, sentinel-like line of ammunition boxes, which stood in stately inventory just behind the sealed box. He hid behind this perfect barricade a moment, and then reached up to a windowsill for a hurricane lamp, which he lit. There for several minutes he lay like a harmless snake, which had unknowingly slithered into enemy territory.

The soldier lay still for some time, with the hurricane flame angelically illuminating his flickering eyes, which were cast deeply in his rigid, determined face. He didn't know precisely what he was going to do. He didn't even care if they caught him. After all, his coffin, like the box filled with rifle shells, had already been sealed; of that he was sure. He could do himself no harm at this point than to at least try to save his fellow Armenians and consequently himself.

For a fleeting moment, his memory took him back to Saint Mary's. How insignificant his childish folly now seemed—now when maturity allowed no games. He felt a warmth flow through his chilled body when he remembered the tenderness of Friar Vincent, who even then had known Bedros's worth. He remembered poor, old CiCi, the man he'd taken such delight in torturing. He thought of his notorious fruit basket nestled secretly under the wooden boards in the floor of his dormitory, when suddenly it came to him. Under the floor! That was where he would hide the bullets!

He would have to open the box somehow without removing the lid. But what did he fear? Was he not a master at placing wood into wood, forming perfect patterns of workmanship? If he could create something with his talented hands, couldn't he then take it apart and then recreate it with no one being the wiser?

Sliding the lamp and his body along the cool floor, he made his way to the area just between the sealed box and the line of inventory behind it. He then dared to rise up a moment to go to the tool crate and get a screwdriver, a hammer, and some tiny wood nails. He returned to his belly, with his tools grasped tightly in his hand, and crept back to the floor area behind the box. It took nearly half an hour of arduous labor to remove just three small panels of wood from the floorboards, leaving an opening only about one foot square.

Next he carefully examined the ammunition box itself. He had built it and knew its every line and seam. He admired his meticulous craftsmanship for a few seconds. Then, with only the meager hurricane glow to guide him, he wrapped his strong arms around the box and slowly, breathlessly, turned it upside down. The bullets rumbled loudly as they avalanched inside the box from its bottom to its top.

Bedros lay still, praying that the clamor wouldn't be noticed. Fortunately the woodshop was distant enough from most of the other quarters that his luck might hold out until dawn. He leaned his aching back up against the upside-down box to rest and then proceeded to the next difficult task. He lifted the hurricane lamp from the floor and placed it on the ammunition box, which was in fact its bottom. Like investigating a complex maze, Bedros eyed every line, every joint that brought the pieces of wood together to form the base of the box. He had made it and now he would have to unmake it, at least enough to allow the bullets to fall through an opening and slide down into the hole in the flooring.

Screwdriver in hand, using it like a prying tool, Bedros found difficulty in lifting the first minute piece of wood. His every move had to be slight, for if he should chip the wood or create the tiniest gash in the bottom, even an undiscerning eye would pick it up. He worked for close to an hour, at last perfectly removing a few small sections from the bottom of the box.

He couldn't wait to rest. The muscles in his hands twisted in pain, and his eyes burned like fire. Wrapping his sore arms around the box once again, he shimmied backward as close as possible to the floor opening. He estimated the proper place to begin turning the box back to its right-side-up position so that the opening in the box's base would almost perfectly coincide with the opening in the floor. Squinting and straining, Bedros at last properly positioned the box.

Bedros glanced around; fearing someone might be watching, but the silence told him no one was there. He overturned the box so that the openings were one on top of the other. In delight, he listened as the bullets sped out through the opening he had just allowed and down into the hole in the floor. They rambled, rolled, and swooshed on their illustrious journey. The bullets fell into the clandestine opening, to be lost forever under the flooring of the woodshop.

He allowed himself a brief moment of relaxation. Bedros closed his eyes in gratitude to his God for his assistance in this painstaking task. It was nearly finished. There was something else, one more thing, and it bothered him.

If he were the binbashi, how would he take the news? How would he react? If indeed Ismael thought the yuze-bashi and his treacherous companions were lethal, he certainly didn't think them idiots. They might be mistaken about what exactly was in the box, but it was ludicrous to believe they could be mistaken about whether the box was filled with anything at all. Surely a man like the binbashi would immediately know the box had been emptied. The only way was to fill the box with something else, something similar to rifle shells in every way—weight, color, and size. Then the buffoons would be viewed as fools who hadn't taken the time to examine the evidence brought before them.

Bedros leaned his head back, searching the ceiling for an answer, and it came quickly. It was so easy, so close. He would go to the barrel which held carpenter's nails. It was right there in the back closet of the room. It was filled to overflowing; the missing nails would not be noticed.

Now he had only to compete with time and the revealing dawn, which would bring with it the pacing of the morning guards up and down the corridor. He didn't know; perhaps they were patrolling at this very moment, and they would see his flickering lamp. They would come in, ending his work, ending his life. He didn't allow himself to dwell in fear, for it would encumber him. He returned to his belly crawl and made his way across from the floor and into the near closet, clutching his hurricane lamp. On the floor, piled up next to the nail barrel, were several smaller wooden boxes. These would save him more uncomfortable trips back and forth. He chose the largest one and began using it like a shovel to scoop out the nails from the barrel.

It took him six trips to the closet to fill the ammunition box. After slowly spreading out the nails uniformly in the box, he returned the smaller box to its original place. On his way back, the crawling snake felt all around the floor, hoping to find any nails that may have fallen during his maneuvers. There were none, or so he hoped.

With the ammunition box now filled with nails, the final phase had to be performed. Bedros Vartanian began replacing the wooden sections of the box, which he had removed. He progressively remade the bottom of the ammunition box exactly as he remembered building it. The placement had to be flawless. The new nails needed to fit perfectly into the original holes. He wasn't dealing with imbeciles here but clever, discerning men, who could immediately determine the slightest sign of tampering.

At long last the base was reconstructed. To Bedros's weary eyes, it appeared untouched. He rubbed his hands affectionately over the finished work and gently turned the ammunition box back to its proper side. The nails swooshed within the box, but they were quieter than the bullets would have been.

He could smell success. The end was so preciously close. But there was one more thing, perhaps the most important of all. He had to close up the hole in the flooring, replace the removed boards, and return everything to its original position—again without notice and without error.

The final phase proved to be easier than the earlier procedures. The slats in the flooring were much larger and less delicate than those of the ammunition box. Bedros was able to work much more quickly but with no less skill and precaution. The floor was at last remade, the hole closed, and the bullets finally rested in eternal oblivion. He sighed and threw his arms and legs out in a stretch of comfort and achievement. His time was limited, and celebration was far too premature. He had to turn out the hurricane lamp and get himself out of there quickly and quietly.

In moments he was back in the dormitory, his head resting exactly as it had been several hours before, but now his tired arms agonized with the spasms of pain and exertion. The soldiers were still soundly asleep, but Bedros couldn't reach the point of total slumber. His mind surged, his brain retraced every step, every maneuver of the past few hours. By the time his body was ready to allow him sleep, the harsh voice of the gendarme awakening the troops startled him.

The new day had begun. Bedros rose, acting casual but suffering over many thoughts. Had he acted too soon? Would the enemy find out what he had accomplished before the day of reckoning? Had he made an error in the multifaceted operation of the evening before? He was sure but not sure enough to stake his life, and that was exactly what he was doing. As he labored through the endless day, his only prayer was that Binbashi Ismael would return quickly and that it would all be over soon.

At dinner Bedros shared his excitement with Hirair, who was astounded with his friend's bravery. It was a source of great comfort to his belabored soul. Hirair was in a glorious state. He had very briefly seen Sonia that day, and he expounded on her cheerful nature and beautiful appearance. It was a good meal, a hearty one, which Bedros sorely needed. There were thick kebobs of beef, a pilaf with pine nuts, and okra in a tomato broth. While eating the less-than-epicurean attempts of the military chef, a messenger waved at Bedros and motioned him out of the mess hall. Hirair and Bedros gave each other a concerned glance, and the latter left his plate, experiencing a sudden loss of appetite.

Bedros didn't know this particular soldier, but the Turk seemed unfriendly. He told him that the binbashi's daughter was awaiting him in the visitors' lobby. He was obviously infuriated that this Armenian nefer should be receiving such an illustrious guest.

Sheida was pacing and wringing her delicate, white hands when Bedros came into the lobby. Fortunately, since it was mealtime, they were the only two present in the room. Upon sight of Bedros, Sheida rushed to him, her lithe arms outstretched in lace.

"Bedo, I was told about your house arrest. I am so sorry, so frightened for you!"

Bedros held her shivering body tightly. His heart sank in awareness of the deep, unreturned love this girl felt for him.

"Sheida," he said, holding her solidly out from the embrace and glaring into her eyes with his mighty stare. "You do not think that they can hurt me, do you? And how did you find out so quickly?"

"I have many friends here at the complex, my love. I know these madmen better than you. They hate anything that is good and strong and right. And especially they hate Armenians; you must know that."

Terror made her lovelier, even more desirable, and briefly he almost felt love for her. Or could it have been pity, perhaps gratitude?

"Sheida, none of them are any match for Bedros Vartanian. I am surprised at you. I have already taken care of the entire matter. It will be solved soon."

"How? You are being constantly watched, are you not?" she whispered.

He was ready to tell her, to boast of his prolific magic and the now harmless ammunition box. But as the words formed, something inside him told him not to continue. It was a new feeling to Bedros; it was a feeling of wariness—even of Sheida—of whom he had been so completely confident.

"Never mind! I assure you, dear Sheida that I will come through this crisis in good health." He laughed, but she didn't.

She took out a handkerchief from her leather purse and blew her upturned, un-Turkish nose. She warmed Bedros's heart. "I sent our driver for Father this morning. I told him to get father home to me immediately. I told him it was a matter of my life."

Bedros was overcome. He drew her close once again and kissed the tears away from her troubled face. Holding her face in his engulfing hands, he lightly chuckled.

"Your life, Sheida? Is that not a bit dramatic?"

She thrust her captivating eyes deeply into his. He felt a tug on the lining of his heart. "That is the way I feel, Bedo—exactly the way I feel."

The room began to gradually fill with wandering soldiers and wives and babies calling to their fathers. It was time for Sheida to leave him. Their meeting here wasn't safe; nothing was until the binbashi returned. They parted—she turning back to bid him an amorous farewell with her dancing eyes; he waving, his face bland and expressionless for benefit of the audience around them.

The next morning the yuze-bashi came to the dormitory to rouse the soldiers, and everyone was wondering why it was he and not the usual private. But Bedros knew, even before the gleaming monster made his pompous way over to his bed. The yuze-bashi stood, legs spread apart, hands on hips, hell mapped out on his leathery forehead.

"It seems you will not have to wait as long as we thought for your trial, nefer. The binbashi returned early this morning and has graced us with his presence."

The captain searched the room with his delighted eyes, hoping for a large gathering in his moment of triumph, but the other soldiers had wisely disappeared. Bedros didn't respond, and the yuze-bashi went on in glory.

"At breakfast this morning I shared our good news with him. After all, we would not want the general to make a serious mistake in befriending a criminal like you. Worse yet, we would not want him to bring such a man into his very family, now would we Nefer Vartanian?"

Bedros didn't answer. His stomach turned upside down; his entrails flipped and rolled about like the nails and bullets had. His head was pounding.

"Come then, suddenly silent Bedros. Your binbashi awaits us in the woodshop."

A worried Hirair, who had been pretending to dress in disinterest, heard everything. He gave his friend a supportive nod as the two left the room.

The woodshop had been transformed into a sullen court of law. The vigilantes stood around, puffing and grinning in the assurance of their success. The yuze-bashi entered with Bedros at his side. Bedros didn't respond to the searching stares of Sebouh, Vahak, and Stepan, who were huddled in the corner, fenced in by five stalwart guards. The ammunition boxes looked the same as when he left them. Binbashi Ismael had been bending over the heavily bolted box when they entered the room. He rose and turned to see Bedros and the captain. Bedros felt a terrible sadness when he saw the look of betrayal on the binbashi's face.

"Now, sir, I informed you earlier of the details of the apprehension of these three at the very scene of the crime." The yuze-bashi strutted about, pointing at the three prisoners. "As you are aware, Bedros Vartanian was seen leaving this room at the very same time; we will not reiterate."

"Get on with it, captain," groaned the disgusted Ismael.

"Of course, sir. We do not want to belabor this issue!"

"Open it immediately!" the binbashi ordered Nooredeen, who had been standing by the ammunition box through the entire discourse.

Nooredeen gave each of the accused a smug look of satisfaction. Then methodically, as slowly as he could manage, he began to remove the iron brackets with a heavy crowbar. Now and then he looked up at Bedros and grinned. He dramatically exaggerated his every motion.

As Nooredeen approached the end of his task and the last bracket was removed, a thick silence shrouded the air. The binbashi froze staunchly. The defendants felt their lives coming to an end.

Nooredeen got up and modestly motioned to the yuze-bashi to do the honors of removing the lid of the box. The captain paced over to the waiting ammunition box with a look so childishly foolish that Bedros felt the sudden urge to laugh —an urge he immediately suppressed. It wouldn't have helped the captain's mood. The yuze-bashi gave his audience one last triumphant smirk and then thrust the lid of the box up into the air, his arms held high like a champion boxer. His hands were still holding the lid up when the entire room, except Nooredeen, burst into boisterous laughter. The dumbfounded captain dropped the lid and looked down to see the box filled with harmless nails.

The yuze-bashi was dumb-struck, his face still contorted in a half smile. The binbashi walked over to the box of nails, and a relieved smile overtook his troubled face. He looked up at the comical yuze-bashi and strained his mouth to keep it from grinning defiantly at the pathetic captain.

"So, my captain, this is your incriminating evidence? Here are your bullets, your traitors, your infidels!" Ismael pointed one by one at the subjects around the room as he spoke. "It grieves me greatly that my soldiers are so poorly trained as to not know a nail from a rifle shell."

"Sir," the yuze-bashi blubbered, "we have been duped. There is treachery here! The bullets have been hidden. The nails have been put in their place!"

"I see," said Ismael. "Then perhaps there is a magician among us who can take things in and out of boxes without opening them?"

The yuze-bashi kicked the box, trying to turn it over, and the pain in his foot was evident. He screamed at the gendarmes to turn the box over. Bedros held his breath.

Two of the guards quickly stepped over to the box and flung it on its side, the nails falling all over the floor. The yuze-bashi got down on his hands and knees like a dog sifting in a can of garbage and began turning the box over and over, his hands scanning the perimeter frantically for some clue. Bedros was terrified but had to appear unmoved.

At last giving up, the yuze-bashi looked around as if for help from anyone in the room, but there was none. He shook his head in defeat and ordered the nails cleaned up. Binbashi Ismael ordered the prisoners immediately released. He walked over to Bedros and merely squeezed his arm, but in his eyes there was an embrace—a look of such joy that Bedros's heart felt warmed by a mighty, roaring fire within.

"So, captain, you were about to execute four young Armenian soldiers for a box of nails!"

Ismael left the room in disgust and ordered that Nooredeen and the yuze-bashi report to his office.

That evening Bedros procured a clarinet. He had not played one since his orphanage days, but the talent had not left him. There was a party in the dormitory, which no guard, no captain, no Turk dared to handicap. The floors shook with the prancing boots of the jubilant soldiers. Bedros embraced his clarinet like a fine, thin woman, and he brought forth music of untold mastery.

The cook had sent fruit, choeregg, cheese, and olives. Momentarily, bigotry had been defeated. Momentarily, the Armenian soldiers had cause to rejoice, to look forward, and to foresee their futures with optimism and self-esteem.

The following evening the binbashi had arranged a gala party at his home. The glittering, magnificent Sheida was the capable hostess.

Ismael's resplendent home was matched only by the pompous, medal-bedecked officials and their fussy, overdressed wives in festive attendance. Though he wasn't sure why, Bedros Vartanian appeared to be the guest of honor.

Though the Turkish bureaucrats abounded here, Bedros felt them to be kinder, more intelligent men than the yuze-bashi. If they were Ismael's friends, they had to be above the kind of treachery the other Turks had shown. Those in the grand living room of the binbashi's residence may have been the last remaining core of sanity and decency left in turn-of-the-century Turkey. Bedros at least felt comfortable, if not at home, among them.

During the evening Ismael secretly reported to Bedros that the yuze-bashi along with Nooredeen and his companions had been transferred to duty in the dismal, dusty training center of Erenkeuy. Ismael was assured that, at least in the Pera center, the bad Turks had been weeded out.

Sheida didn't leave Bedros's side the entire evening. They danced, dined, and drank fine champagne imported from France as all eyes followed Cinderella and her slightly tarnished Armenian prince. Bedros couldn't withdraw. She and her father had captured him. If he didn't feel poetic love for Sheida, his allegiance and gratitude to her couldn't be disputed, nor could the physical loveliness of this fine, gracious young woman. Cheek to cheek, they danced into the night.

Near the end of the gala affair, Binbashi Ismael stood celestially on the stand, where a small quartet had been entertaining, and called for attention from his guests. Bedros stood and listened curiously, with Sheida tight on his arm. The binbashi announced the decision, made by him and a group of several other acclaimed officers, to raise Bedros Vartanian to the status of a high, noncommissioned officer in the Royal Turkish Army.

Chapter 5

CONSTANTINOPLE, 1914

As Officer Bedros Vartanian gained popularity and acclaim, the environment in which he progressed was slowly deteriorating. There was no question that he was held in highest esteem, but this wasn't the case for many of his Armenian peers. Most of them were assigned menial jobs; these were nonmilitary jobs, and they were degrading.

It soon became evident that Bedros Vartanian was living in a curious state of limbo, lacking a true identity. Granted, he was safe from the growing turbulence between the Turkish government and the Armenian people, but it was an unrewarding safety. Bedros wore the uniform of a Turk, lived among the Turks, was betrothed to a Turkish woman, and lived protectively nestled under the wings of a prominent Turkish officer. Yet one significant fact would ever remain unchanged—Bedros Vartanian was an Armenian. It was a fact his fellow officers ignored and one not mentioned among himself, Sheida, and Ismael. It would not go away and could never be any other way. He was an Armenian.

In the changing years since 1909, the storm clouds began to accumulate in black abundance. The air carried with it the smell of incumbent horror. One didn't have to be a scholar to read the signs. They pointed to serious trouble for anyone who had the misfortune of not being a Turk in the Turkish Empire of 1914.

Bedros reluctantly persevered as the deadly winter of 1914 set in rather early. He had the warmth of Sheida and Ismael's devotion and unparalleled hospitality on which to fall back. He had at last succumbed to the unspoken demands of the binbashi and proposed marriage to Sheida. The wedding was to take place in the spring.

Resting in his new bed in his nicely decorated bedroom, designated only for officers in the Pera center, Bedros considered his future more decisively. He was a fool by any man's standards to cause trouble in paradise. It would have been so easy to discount the atmosphere of terror slowly gaining in strength. He could have comfortably slipped his heritage into a back drawer until safe to bring it out into the daylight. But he and his God knew that neither could settle for things as they were evolving. One evening during prayer, Bedros was conscious of God speaking to him.

Bedros, I am your God. I have taken you through much. I have never failed you, and now you cannot fail me. You rest in sequestered peace while the world around you quakes. Can it be that you, my son, will settle for this pseudo prosperity and masked tranquility, thus denying your very heritage?

The answer to his God was immediate and without hesitation.

No, my blessed Father. I shall not disappoint you or myself. I could not live with myself any other way. I wear a costume, but I am me on the inside.

One blustering night near Christmas 1913, as Sheida knelt by him in the posh parlor of her home with a roaring fire as the perfect backdrop, she could see the old look of discontent on Bedros's darkly handsome face. Sheida had matured over the past five years. She had reached the state of womanhood early in her life. But Bedros was now also a man, and at twenty-two years old was a man of such magnificence and power that one wondered how much more beautiful he could become.

Ismael, still the prolific general, still profoundly compassionate and rigidly moral, had several dozen more white hairs on his head. His noble but wrinkled brow displayed the tolls of the past years. The binbashi had never deluded himself into believing Bedros Vartanian loved his precious daughter, and he was most grateful that the handsome Armenian had agreed to marry her and honor her. Eventually love could come. This was the custom in those days, when men and women were said to be backward in their sexual and social endeavors.

On this early winter's evening Bedros asked to be alone with Ismael, and as always Sheida respected his wishes. The would-be father-in-law and his adopted son stood pensively by the comforting fire. Another fire raged in the eyes of Bedros, and Ismael braced himself for what was to come. He knew material comforts didn't impress Bedros as they did most men. He knew too well that Bedros Vartanian was an Armenian—a fact that might not manifest itself at the moment but would gradually boil, like molten lava, and at last erupt in fury from this mountain of a man.

"Sir, before the spring and the wedding, I wish to make a request of you."

Ismael admired Bedros's commanding voice, now deep and heavy.

"Yes, Bedo. I see you are troubled."

"Sir, I feel like I am useless here in Pera. At night I am living in your kind comfort but reduced during the day to nothing more than a teacher of nefers." He drew a breath, preparing himself for the rest. "Sir, I wish to be transferred, perhaps to Maltepe, where I can be of real use and have the physical activity I so crave."

Ismael scowled. He knew that the soldier's request had a dual purpose- to give him a respite from himself and Sheida. He didn't want to grant Bedros the time or distance that might cause him to change his mind, perhaps even leave the country entirely. "Bedo, I understand your reasoning, but I have sources who are warning of impending war with Russia. If this is the case, I want you here with us, where you will not see battle."

"All the more reason, sir. I am a soldier. On the battlefield is where I belong. Would you and Sheida want me any other way?" Bedros's eyes enraptured Ismael with a long, tenacious glare. The binbashi knew he had been conquered.

Ismael was tempted to say, "Yes, Bedo, at all costs, even your pride, we want you here safe with us." But the soldier inside him wouldn't let the words come out.

"Well then, let it be. I will sign the transfer in the morning. I will send Hirair along with you. I know how you feel about each other, and he will keep a watch on you for us."

"Thank you, sir." Bedros embraced Ismael, who fought the urge to cry.

"Now be gone; you have much to prepare. Remember to keep away from those veiled ladies. They are not of the best quality in those desolate, uncivilized areas."

"Sir, I am engaged now." Bedros displayed ardent disapproval of his general's humor.

"Permit me my foolish joking, Bedo. As it is, Sheida will probably not speak to me for the entire time you are gone."

They laughed together, and Bedros decided to walk rather than be chauffeured down to the tramway, which tottered him back to Pera.

Maltepe was more dismal and backward than Hirair or Bedros imagined. It looked like pictures of the American western ghost towns they had seen in their world study classes. The officers' quarters were modest and merely adequate, while Hirair found the living area of the regular soldiers to be squalid and foul smelling.

"This is what you wanted," scolded Hirair while the two ate a terrible dinner.

"It will just be a short while, Hirair. We need to be here. We need to find out just what is going on outside the perfect, little world we lived in Pera."

During their time in Maltepe neither was involved in any productive activity as they had hoped. Hirair, as were all Armenian soldiers, was relegated to road-building chores, which tormented his back, dirtied his face, and reduced him to a mere laborer.

Bedros found his daily duties consisting of nothing more than bellowing orders to young soldiers, who hated him for his position. Bedros found that in Maltepe all Armenian soldiers were completely segregated. They had their own quarters and lived out their daily routines with one another. Even he had been separated from the Turkish officers and shared quarters with three other Armenian officers. There were no officers' meetings, no consultations, no expected war preparations. He didn't like the feeling. While matters of significance were obviously taking place, he was safely shoved into the background. To add to this, no Armenian soldiers possessed arms or ammunition.

However, Bedros, Hirair and the other Armenian soldiers had learned from letters and mess hall gossip that there was growing unrest among the scattered Armenians in the Turkish Empire. Some said the Armenian people had made an appeal to the great powers of Russia and her Western allies to protect them in the event of war. They feared that the Turks, under duress of a possible war, might resort to their old ways of general massacres.

Bedros and Hirair lived out the cruel winter in disgust. The growing hatred of the Turkish soldiers for the Armenians became as obvious as the unyielding, blinding winter winds, the frostbite on their toes from insufficiently warm clothing, and the meager meals in the mess hall.

Spring came and left, and no one was the wiser. Bedros and Sheida's wedding was postponed. Summer came, lessening the physical discomforts at the camp but doing nothing about the fact that the Armenian soldiers had been discriminated against so terribly that many had defected; some had gone to Russian borders. Others simply gave up and settled for slave-like labor in the camp. Bedros had considered protesting but decided this wasn't the place to create trouble. He was without alliance. He would actively defend the rights of his people back in Pera in the fall.

On October 22, 1914, Enver Pasha, the Turkish minister of war, decided to grab the encroaching Russian bull by its fierce horns. He ordered the Turkish fleet to attack several Russian ports on the Black Sea. Even the Armenian soldiers in Maltepe rejoiced, for they believed their time of glory in battle was forthcoming. On November 4, the Russian army declared war. The general Armenian population was trapped relentlessly in the middle. Some felt that supporting the Russians would eventually gain them their freedom from the historic Turkish yoke. Others professed neutrality, fearing the yoke of Russia might be even tighter around their necks. As rumors began to run rampant, the Turks believed that many Armenians were fighting among the Russian soldiers. Immediately, all Armenian soldiers in the Turkish army were placed under austere scrutiny and suspicion.

It was only because of the binbashi's watchful informants that Bedros and Hirair were immediately transferred back to Pera before the madness increased. Once more a powerful and respected Turkish general had ironically delivered the two Armenian soldiers from the grasp of Turkish terror.

Pera seemed like paradise more than ever before. Hirair returned to his normal activities in the woodshop. Bedros reclined once again in his plump and satiny bed, made and maintained by the servants of Binbashi Ismael and Sheida. In Constantinople, at least, Armenians were still held in tolerance. In Constantinople, at least, they were safe to walk the streets, enter the shops, and live relatively normal lives. In Constantinople—at least.

Winter, which was somewhat less ferocious than the previous one, slowly left her station and made way for the spring of 1915. It was March, but the usually blustery lady was incongruously mellow and soft-spoken. Bedros realized that with his forthcoming wedding, his fate would be sealed in protective comfort. He wrote to Ara that the family might attend the wedding, and he sent them money. He suggested that he and Yughaper plan to stay in Bolis from then on.

Across a barren wasteland, two brothers' letters passed each other at identical times. One told of nuptial joy, the other of incredulous horror. When Ara's note arrived in Pera, Bedros had been confined to bed with influenza. The journey back from Maltepe and the grueling winter had taken its toll on his health. The mail carrier brought the note to his bedside and the weary, unsuspecting soldier opened it.

March 15, 1915

Dearest Bedros,

This letter is written in blood, the blood of our neighbors. I am alive to write it with our mother beside me only because the mutessarif, in a moment of humaneness, saw fit to leave our home untouched. As I stand by our window and look out on what was Malatia, I almost wish he had not spared us.

Yesterday we awoke to the strong smell of smoke, and Mother and I both thought the new *furoon* had caught fire. But the fire was outdoors and it was everywhere. We ran outside in our nightclothes to see such madness that it seemed a nightmare, a vision of hell itself.

The streets were overrun with madmen. I cannot say they were Turkish gendarmes. They were dressed in shabby clothes. They looked like nomadic Kurds. They were drunken, sword-wielding horsemen. They screeched in delight as their horses trampled many of the youngsters trying to reach the arms of their terrified mothers.

We watched helplessly from our home. We felt sick and faint with a terror no man could ever describe!

The attackers were going from door to door, drawing out all the Armenian people into the streets. The Kurds, as I still believe they were, entered the homes, taking over some, burning the others to the ground.

After they had finished with the house searches, they returned to the streets, where the helpless men and their families were corralled like cattle encircled by the hollering, insane horsemen. The women and children were stripped completely naked and separated from their men. I can still see them in my sleeplessness, huddled over in shame, while the drunken men laughed loudly at them. Their pathetic husbands were watching! They were heavily guarded and helpless. Once or twice a man would break free and attempt to reach for his wife or child, but they would cut him down in his tracks.

The women and children were taken, some by wagonload, some on foot, and forced out of town north toward the plains. Now and then I could see a young girl being lifted up onto the horse of one of the attackers.

Our men were then lined up and slowly marched two abreast down the center road, our poor Katchadour was among them! He looked back often toward our house. I opened the door, holding my breath for fear of losing my head to a sword and was able, to motion to Khatchig that we were in the house alive. He smiled grimly and waved. Suddenly the men stopped marching and hundreds of shots rang out. Our brother fell to the ground. All of them did. Every young Armenian man in Malatia except myself lay dead.

The town was like a cemetery; bodies were strewn everywhere. Most of the women and children were gone. A few daring Turks and Greeks came from their homes and wandered about the carnage in shock. Shortly afterward, several wagons came. The bodies were removed, but the nauseating smell still lingers.

I went to Khatchig's home, hoping to find Anna and the boys. The house had been ransacked; there was nothing of value left, nor were she and the children anywhere to be found. It grieves me to realize that they were among those humiliated, stripped women and children led out of town. They could never survive the desert; this I know. We heard that many of the women and their children were shoved into the Tigris on the journey north. They were left them screaming for help, drowning in the treacherous waters. Some of them, it was rumored, had actually thrown themselves and their babies into the water for fear of a worse fate.

Can you believe the words you read, beloved brother? How can you, when I myself cannot believe it actually happened? The words I write burn holes in my heart. I shall never be healed. Mother, by some miracle, is calm and sadly strong. She seems to have blocked it all from her memory. She still smokes the cigarettes, now nearly three packages of them each day. At night, I hear her crying, talking to Father from her lonely bed.

You must be wondering about Hovsep and Sahag. So far as I know, they are still alive. They joined the army sometime after I mentioned to you that they would. I believe they are stationed in Nakrkeuy, though how long they will remain safe, I cannot imagine.

Mother and I begin the gathering of our belongings. We will journey to Bolis in a few days. The mutessarif has promised us safe passage, and Mother has a letter from him in case we are captured along the way. I only hope the mad dogs take the time to read it before killing us.

I have told you enough for your poor mind to absorb, brother dear. We shall let you know when we arrive. Farewell. Take care of yourself. Our family is dwindling, with only a few of us left.

My love and my soul,
Ara

Like a tornado the words tore through Bedros's brain, destroying cells and nerves in their wake. His heart palpitated faster than the rolling rifle shells on the woodshop floor. His blood surged violently through his veins. He sat up and tried to jump from his bed but he fell over, his head crashing down with considerable force. Bedros Vartanian lay like death by his empty bed on the cold, wooden floor.

A mighty star dropped from the sky. In Italy a tower bent over to its side in pain. In America a ferocious deluge created a magnificent falling wall of white waves. In Africa the largest coconut in the lushest palm fell clumsily to the ground. All things fine and wonderful would never be the same. At least for Bedros Vartanian, they wouldn't be.

A battle raged inside the young soldier's body. The heart was weary, struggling through each faint pound. The limbs were still and lifeless with not enough blood to feed them the power they once had. The eyes, the immortal eyes, couldn't force their heavy, burning lids to lift up and allow them light with which to see. The ears rang with the bells of death tolls and incessantly howling words of murder. The mouth was dry, his lips pasted together, unable to move, to eat, to kiss, to smile. All these fought against one persistent opponent. It was a spirit that wouldn't be harmed. It was a soul that couldn't die.

When the battle was at last won, a battle that took ten days, Bedros Vartanian opened his eyes. They had lost their fiery sparkle, but their depth and hypnotic, beckoning powers were stronger than ever before. Though still too weak to speak, he was alert enough to recognize two burdened faces hovering over him. One was Binbashi Ismael, looking tired and old. The other was Sheida, looking frightened like a little girl.

"Bedo, at last! You are back with us." This time Ismael didn't care about appearances, and he cried.

"Darling," Sheida wept, squeezing his numb hand, "I thought I had lost you. Allah be praised!"

"And God be praised," interjected Ismael, aware that Bedros's emotions were like a cocked trigger now.

Bedros slowly focused his eyes on them. He could clearly make out their faces. They looked the same, yet somehow different to him. Ismael, whom he had once considered virile and fine looking in his aging years, now seemed pale and drawn, lacking the countenance of a fine general.

Sheida looked older too, much older than she was. She has on too much makeup, he thought. She is not pretty anymore. Perhaps, he considered, they had always looked like this, but now he saw them for what they really were. They were Turks. There was something ugly about that to him now. He knew there always would be.

"Do not try to talk," the binbashi went on kindly. "You need all the strength you can muster. Ara's letter was clutched in your hands when they found you. We took the liberty to read it."

"We are so very sorry, darling. We have wept for you and your family for many nights," Sheida swiftly interrupted her father.

Bedros stared at her blankly, and she could feel the chill radiating from within him. You wept? Bedros thought. Turks do not know what it is to mourn. They do not know suffering. They cannot fathom it; they can only administer it quite liberally.

Sheida went on, considering his coldness as merely the remnants of all he had endured.

"Father has made sure that on their arrival, your family will be brought directly to our home. We shall care for them as our own darling, until you are well. And then"—she gave a sidewise glance and loving smile to her father—"and then we shall be married and put all this horror behind us."

"Bedo," Ismael continued, knowing what must be running through this young man's thoughts, "I want you to know that our officers here in Constantinople are doing all we can to stop these atrocities. Memorandums are being sent daily to all parts of the empire, promising swift punishment for any more barbaric raids."

Even as the binbashi spoke, Armenian blood was being shed in Van and Harput and Sivas. As Sheida caressed her lover's hand, babies were being impaled on swords and churches burned while filled to capacity with praying Armenians. As Bedros stared dumbly back into their pleading faces, he knew the horrors, murders, rapes, and degradations were only just beginning. Father and daughter talked on, but Bedros listened only to his heart. It told him that these two, even though they could offer him and his family safety from the physical harm of these times, could never offer them the pride and freedom to which all human beings are entitled.

Ismael began to speak louder now, aware of Bedros's preoccupation.

"Bedo, you must listen to me. These things that have happened—it is not solely our Turkish soldiers who commit them. We have discovered that most of our soldiers have refused to take part in these massacres, and so these devious officers in the outlying villages have employed the nomadic Kurds to do their bidding. Further, we know for a fact that these same men have emptied prison cells in the more remote areas, allowing the *bashi-bazouks*, the criminally insane, to run rampant on the unarmed Armenians."

Bedros was listening intently now, but the words didn't make any sense to him. No officer—no army—takes this upon himself to commit such atrocious crimes. There were orders, orders from somewhere. He frowned, questioning Ismael's excuses. The binbashi immediately knew that Bedros didn't believe him. The general looked uncomfortably around the room. Then he bent down low, his mouth virtually pressed into Bedros's ear.

"My son, you see through me. We know the orders have come from the top. It is the madman, the minister of the interior, Talaat Pasha, who has issued them."

Bedros's eyes filled with tears and widened in horror. This meant such procedures were now matters of national policy. He closed his stinging eyes. From this there was no hope. But Ismael insistently went on.

"I know what you are thinking," he whispered. "But steps have already been taken to overthrow this pig who calls himself a man. I assure you, Bedo that at this very moment forces of which I am a part, are at work to dethrone him. Even now, the Western missionaries are pounding on the doors of the kaimakam's offices and demanding an end to it all. Even if we Turks cannot bridle him, be assured the rest of the world will."

Bedros felt he was about to vomit and desperately tried to control himself, but he couldn't. His head fell over the side of his bed, and the fowl-smelling liquid splattered on the floor and partially on the fine alligator shoes with brass buckles adorning Sheida's tiny feet. She calmly cleansed herself, undeterred. Bedros flung himself back into his prone position, wondering in agony how many Armenians would die before these promises transpired. And if he had been told that one and a half million would perish in a massive genocide, would he have been able to recuperate?

"Bedo"—Ismael bent over him again—"do you understand what I am saying, my son?"

Bedros nodded faintly, and then motioned for some water, which waited in a dewy pitcher by his bed. Sheida helped him to drink it, holding his cumbersome head in her heavily perfumed arm. He then cleared his throat to finally speak.

"Sir." He coughed, and his normally powerful voice strained. "Tell me, where am I?"

Sheida and her father smiled at such an innocent question in the midst of this grisly conversation. Ismael answered lovingly.

"You are in the hospital, right here in Pera. It is not far from the training center. The doctors say you are exhausted and may have contracted pneumonia. They assured us you will be out very soon, maybe within two or three weeks. Well, we had better leave you to your needed rest, my boy."

As the two turned to leave him, Bedros, even in his delirium, decided that he would be out much sooner than that. Then he fell into a troubled but deep sleep.

When he awoke the next morning, he found several giggling, young nurses fussing over him and obviously enamored with this mysterious and handsome patient. He laughed to himself as they nearly fell over one another, trying to attend to his comforts, and fed him from a meager breakfast tray.

"Good morning, lovely ladies!"

They unanimously greeted him, bustling about like little, white-capped pixies.

"And who will do the honors of my bath today?" he roared as their delicate cheeks turned varying shades of red.

In two days Bedros felt his strength slowly returning. He took leisurely walks, assisted by too many nurses, up and down the hospital corridors. Sheida came to see him twice each day. The fear of losing him showed in deep seams under her tired eyes. The nurses, the doctors, and the orderlies all fussed over Bedros, as did Sheida. Everyone fell instantly in love with this large, massive-looking man, in whose veins lustful blood ran abundantly.

It was no wonder that one week after he regained consciousness; the morning nurse came to wake him and responded with a piercing screech, which brought aid from all ends of the ward. The entire hospital was in an uproar, but the din was all in vain. Even the summoned binbashi and his fretful daughter were of no use. Bedros Vartanian was gone.

•   •   •

The March morning was misty cool, escorting a hooting wind characteristic of this fickle month, which couldn't decide if she were winter or spring. Bedros was still feverish and fighting weakness as he made his way from the hospital out into the Pera streets. Fortunately it was very early, and human beings had not yet taken over the natural serenity of the place. Along with the Armenian, a stray cat and a skinny dog would occasionally scamper by. Bedros didn't know where he was going or whether he would get there alive. He was now a criminal—a deserter. He was a very sick and very marked man.

It was the salty smell of the Sea of Marmora that opened up his stuffy nostrils and brought to his mind the Galata Port, which Hirair had pointed out on their first evening together. It was close to the port toward the water in a brick row house where Garabed Hamparian and his wards lived. His fuzzy mind remembered, at first with difficulty, that his lucky number was seven, like that of Garabed's house.

Nearly ready to collapse, Bedros lumbered on toward his destination. The way reappeared before him as fresh as Hirair's words—past the veiled ladies, past the fish market, then a turn on this cluttered street and on and on toward the water. If he forgot a turn, the increasingly strong smell of the fishy waters drew his discriminating nose closer and closer to the Galata Port.

He sat down suddenly on the damp, icy road, fearing he might faint. He couldn't afford anyone to come to his aid and in turn discover who he was. For a few precious moments he rested. His breathing was heavy and irregular, his vision severely blurred. But the sights and sounds of the now gradually awakening city spurred him to rise up and get to his sanctuary as quickly as he could.

At last he came to the long, narrow road lined with plain brick houses all stuck together one after the other in endless array. A few concrete steps led from each doorway down to the street. As Bedros perused the houses one by one, he at last found number seven. He stood, foolishly gaping at the home. Its curtains were drawn tightly. He hesitated, wondering what kind of welcome he would receive. Would they accept him? And if they did, would they keep his secret and harbor a criminal? He immediately dispelled the thoughts from his head. Regardless of whether this was Garabed's home or whether they immediately remembered him, one thing was certain. If they were Armenians, they would help him. Allaying his own misgivings and stumbling up the steps, he leaned his heavy body against the front door and pounded with his last remaining ounce of strength.

For a long time there was no response. They were no doubt all asleep. He drew a painful breath and punched the door louder and more impatiently. It flew open so quickly that he lost his already shaky balance and fell—like a great human parcel—to the floor at the feet of the astonished, young girl.

The frightened child wanted to scream but instinctively covered her mouth, for she was frugal with her emotions. The Turkish uniform immediately signified trouble and fear to her, but when she further examined the fine-looking young man who lay unconscious at her feet, she somehow felt calm, assured that his mission wasn't harmful. Besides, in his present condition, it was clear he could do little harm to anyone.

She knelt down by the massive body and turned his head to one side. He was solidly still, but his warm breath proved he wasn't a cadaver. With compassionate scrutiny, the girl examined the fascinating face. Thick, bushy eyebrows bowed low over a large but beautifully shaped nose. His lips were thick, carved by a master. She guessed that when those heavy, black lashes opened, they would reveal a pair of breathtaking eyes. But more than his handsomeness, there was something else about this stranger. The face was like an image from a recurring dream. Incredible as it was to her, she felt that she knew this startling young man from somewhere.

As she gently stroked his brow, the girl considered getting a pail of cool water and some towels to revive him. But it wasn't necessary, for Bedros quickly roused. He shakily sat up on his elbows and opened his eyes, proving her right about her prediction. They were magnificent eyes. There they sat—she, curiously looking down at him; he, woozily looking up at her. There was silence for several minutes, and then the soldier smiled.

"You must be Syrvart," he said groggily.

Her eyes widened in amazement. She had been right. He knew her, and from sometime, someplace, she had known him.

"Yes, that is right. How do you know me, soldier?"

"I met you many years ago. I am Bedros Vartanian." He paused. "Remember the carpenter who worked on your house back in Malatia?"

She remembered him well now but wouldn't dare let him know it. She had thought of him many times in her little, girlish daydreams. At the time he had been the most beautiful young man she had ever seen. He still was.

"I am not sure," she lied. "How long ago was our meeting, soldier?"

"Bedros," he corrected her with annoyance. "Oh, I think it was nearly five years ago. You were about seven at the time."

"Well, then, it must have been that long. I am twelve now."

With her frail assistance, Bedros slowly stood up. She helped him over to a bumpy, velvet couch propped against a wall in the living room of the small house. He was still very wobbly and tripped several times along the few short steps from the front door into the parlor.

The soft, sinking couch felt warm and comfortable against his aching bones. He happily let his pounding head flip back against the crimson velour.

"I will fetch my mother and make you some tea. My cousin, Garabed, is not at home yet."

The words trickled through his slowly clearing mind. Cousin Garabed. Where was the unfriendly fellow? Had he left these two women unattended through the long night? There went Bedros again, reverting to the old fancy of tearing apart the miserable man and questioning his every intention. Why did he dislike him so? Even he himself couldn't say.

In his heavy thinking, he tired and dozed off. When he awakened, he saw little Syrvart clad in a long, fleece robe and sitting by his side. She showed great concern on her pretty, delicately appointed face. Standing in front of him was an attractive woman in her middle years with a compassionate and pleasing smile. She held a trembling cup of steaming tea in her hands and gently lowered it down to him.

"I am Mariam," she volunteered, "Syrvart's mother. We are old neighbors, Bedros."

Her words carried with them a soothing, relaxing tone. They settled peacefully in his ringing ears. She looked like an angel of mercy. Her long gingham nightgown covered her so completely that only a pair of hands showed dangling from the bottom of its puffy sleeves. Her slightly lined face emerged like a turtle's head from the heavily ruffled neckline, which ran all the way up her neck to the very base of her chin. The lavish collar gave her head the stiff, upright appearance of regality, but her manner was modest and hospitable.

"I know, madam. I remember you and your daughter from the days when I helped expand your cousin's house."

"Yes, I remember those days well, Bedros. It is hard to believe that little Hagop is five years old and that we live here in this fine home with all these modern conveniences." She motioned about the room.

Bedros looked around, thinking to himself that this home was impoverished compared to the extravagances of the binbashi's palace. But its true worth was right there before him in these two lovely ladies. He felt safe and at home with them. He let himself sob at last. Mariam sat next to him and put her sweet-smelling arm around his shoulders, her eyes flooded with sympathy.

"We have been hearing many rumors of slaughter, Bedros. I didn't want to believe them. I am so very sorry for you. We have heard through neighbors how you have lost a father and a brother by the terror of our times. I am truly sorry."

"That is why I am here. I got very sick back at the training center. When I received the news from my brother, Ara, I collapsed. And when I woke up, I was in the Pera Hospital. But I ran away!"

Mariam showed obvious alarm and clutched Syrvart's hand. She shook her head morosely.

"So, you are a fugitive, are you not?"

Bedros nodded, afraid of what consequences his answer would bring.

Mariam gave him a mischievous smile, trying to assuage his fears of rejection. Giving Syrvart a wink, she turned back to the exhausted soldier and softly brushed his unruly hair from his forehead.

"Bedros, this home is your home as long as you need it. We are your family."

"Syrvart will help you to a small bedroom we have next to ours. It is a fairly sizable room but you will have to share it with Hagop. I think you will find my son most placid. Right now, you must rest. I will prepare your breakfast."

Bedros felt a lump swell up in his sore throat. His eyes followed this incredible woman in awe as she quickly rose to leave the room. Before leaving, she turned, directing her attentions to her daughter.

"Syrvart will find you something of Garabed's to wear, perhaps a nightshirt. She will show you to the bath." Then the angel fluttered away.

Bedros wasn't delighted with the thought of wearing anything of Garabed's but thought better of protesting. He was able to get up now. He followed the bashful, silent, little guide through a short hallway and into a bathroom, which had a toilet with a long pull chain by its side and a modest-but-working sink. While he washed his unshaven face, Syrvart, with a gentle knock on the door, brought him his clothes—an old, green flannel nightshirt, which looked exactly like Garabed Hamparian. He made himself as clean and presentable as his strength would allow, then reluctantly placed the scratchy nightshirt on his body and made his way to the bedroom Syrvart had previously pointed out to him. Sleeping in a rickety crib by the bed was a curled-up little boy he knew was Hagop.

The child didn't stir at all as Bedros carefully pulled down the hand-knitted coverlet and crawled into the invitingly fresh linen cocoon. Just as he was about to fall into blissful slumber, he was aroused by Syrvart, who peeked her curious head through the doorway.

"*Parev!*" he called, shocking her, since she had expected to find him asleep.

"Hello," she answered shyly. "I am sorry, but I wanted to make sure you were all right."

"Thank you, Syrvart. I am just fine now that I am here."

"Good." She started to leave.

"Wait!" he called to her, noticing Hagop as he flipped over restlessly but quickly settled back to sleep. "I want to ask you something." He whispered, trying not to awaken the child.

"What?" she said quietly, daring to venture to his bedside.

"Where is Garabed?"

A pale discontent suddenly showed on her face and she looked nervously back at him.

"He works nights in a bakery. He comes home very tired, very angry."

"I see." And Bedros said no more. It was obvious the young girl didn't wish to discuss her cousin further. "You can go now. Thank you so much for everything."

"I will see you at breakfast," she said, her back already toward him as she sped from the bedroom.

Bedros didn't know how long he slept; only that it wasn't long enough. But something shattered his dreams. He opened his eyes, annoyed. He realized someone was shouting, screaming, banging, and someone else was crying, and pleading in some sort of squabble. He lay quietly for a moment, trying to make out the voices. It didn't take long. The hollering, crude-sounding voice was that of Garabed Hamparian, and the pathetic crier was Mariam.

The noise caused the peacefully sleeping Hagop to awaken abruptly. The sounds of his mother crying inspired her little son to imitate her. Bedros, his head still ringing, feeling like a bleak fog had settled tenaciously around his brain, struggled to get up. He made his way to the little boy's crib and introduced himself groggily. The terrified, little child screamed even louder at the sight of this large strange man looming over his bed. Patience not being one of his assets, Bedros quickly left the room and the screaming Hagop and rushed down the corridor toward the ever-increasing shouts of anger.

In such a small home, it wasn't difficult to discover that the hassling was coming from the kitchen. Garabed was cursing and using crude Turkish expressions with Mariam, whose crying was reduced to a subdued whimpering. Bedros didn't immediately enter the room but waited a few steps away in the hallway, trying to determine the cause of this fury. It was soon evident that Bedros Vartanian was the reason.

"Foolish woman!" Garabed growled, his voice comically high pitched as he screamed. "You let him in here, without consulting me, in my own home?"

"Garabed, I tried to tell you. He is in trouble. He needs our help."

"What help do we owe a fugitive? His presence here can mean our death if the Turks find out. You know that!" His tone had settled somewhat from fury to exasperation.

Mariam sniffed, sobbed, and then Bedros could hear her gently blow her nose. The sound made him feel heartbroken for this fine woman.

"He is an Armenian from Malatia, an old friend and neighbor. What are we if we turn our own out to the wolves?"

Back and forth went the slurs and pleadings, and Bedros had had enough. He was about to make his presence known, but a tug on the back of his robe halted his forward step. There, standing behind him, was Syrvart. He had been so engrossed in the battle in the kitchen that he hadn't noticed she was there. His troubled, ebony eyes questioned her. He was about to speak, but she immediately put a finger up to her mouth, motioning him to remain silent. The hollering continued.

"Spoken like a true woman!" Garabed howled in sarcasm, and Bedros thought he heard Mariam moan in pain of some sort. "We look after ourselves now, no one else. Bedros goes! Today he goes from this house."

Bedros looked over at Syrvart, and there was genuine fear combined with sadness on her tiny face.

"You forget, Garabed," Mariam retorted. Her tone was surprisingly defiant. "This home is half mine and my children's. If it were not for my mending and my meager savings, we would not have survived long on your great fortune."

No sooner had the words left her mouth when Bedros and Syrvart heard a loud slap, and Mariam yelled out in pain. Bedros could bear it no longer; he bounded into the kitchen.

There he found Garabed, his hands grasping Mariam's shoulders like a wrench. Mariam held her head down. She was crying, and her hand covered her cheek. Garabed, surprised by Bedros's intrusion, quickly released Mariam. Bedros walked gently over to Mariam and lifted her hand from her cheek. Her skin was bruised.

Without a word, needing no explanation, Bedros Vartanian turned around to face the dumbfounded Garabed. The soldier had a crazed fury swirling around and around in his glowering eyes. He marched over to the terrified, frozen Garabed, staring incredulously at him.

With a short last look at the Mariam, who sobbed helplessly in pain, a side glance at Syrvart, who ran weeping to her mother's side and with the incessant wails of Hagop whining in the background, Bedros's long-term hatred and disgust for this poor man culminated. He turned, mustered up what little strength was left in his body, and threw a walloping punch squarely at the beard-stubbled jaw of Garabed Hamparian. Not realizing his own power, Bedros was surprised when Garabed's head flew back, hitting the kitchen wall. The pathetic man, his face petrified in an expression of disbelief, fell to the floor.

Mariam and Syrvart let out a simultaneous scream. Hagop was hysterical in the bedroom. Garabed Hamparian was mortified and humiliated. And Bedros Vartanian felt better than he had felt in a very long time. Quickly composing herself, Mariam asked Syrvart to fetch her brother and then walked to her sink and washed her bleeding face. She prepared a moist, cool towel and walked over to Garabed. She gently knelt by the stricken man's side and proceeded to wash his face and puffy jaw. Mariam showed a surprising compassion for the man who had just struck her so cruelly. Bedros walked angrily out of the kitchen but stopped short of the doorway as Mariam called to him in her usual angelic voice. He turned to find her following him out into the hall.

"Bedros," she said very quietly, "that was most kind of you to consider my honor in such a valiant way. You are a proud and fine young man. But we must remember, Garabed does not mean to hurt. It is just that he is a sad, tortured man. I have learned to live with his moods."

Bedros didn't answer her; he only shook his tired head and made his way to the bedroom, where he found Syrvart faithfully dressing her squirming little brother.

Syrvart, embarrassed by the recent incident, ignored his entry into the room and his heavy collapse on the bed. She pulled a pair of muslin knickers up Hagop's swinging legs to his tiny waist and fumbled with the fasteners. She didn't turn around when Bedros spoke to her in a disgusted tone of voice.

"Does this sort of thing go on often around here?" he asked. She shyly shook her head no.

"Then why is it that you always look scared at the mere mention of his name?"

Syrvart tugged on her brother's stiff shirt sleeve and then tucked the crisp, white top securely into Hagop's pants. She didn't answer.

"You do not talk much, do you little girl? Not only that, you are rude!" He got up from his bed and nervously paced around the room.

Syrvart looked up at him, a little frightened of what he might do after what she had just seen. She patted her little brother on his behind and sent him from the room to find his mother. For a few moments, she eyed the large bull, who roamed about the room like a caged animal.

He did everything with gusto and determination. She was enamored in little-girl fashion. She wanted at that moment to tell him everything Garabed had ever said or done. But there were some things too personal, too humiliating for a little girl to share with an overpowering soldier, who was ten years her elder.

"Garabed works long hours every night, Bedros. He comes home tired, and I can tell he is afraid of...of what is happening. They say the Turks are killing all the Armenians everywhere."

Bedros at last stopped his pacing. "So that gives him the right to harass women and frighten little girls?" he growled.

"No, I did not say that. It is just that Mother, Hagop, and I have no one else to care for us. If we could, if we had the money, we would all get out of Turkey."

Bedros frowned at her but finally settled back, reclining comfortably on his bed. Syrvart watched him as he nestled his mighty head on top of his arms under his neck. He stared silently at the ceiling, and she wondered what he could be thinking. He was pondering what she had just said. She had mentioned money. It was the second time he had heard reference to it in a few short minutes. He thought back to his days in Malatia and the sight of Garabed crouched over his treasure chest which was filled with *piastres*. At the time it had seemed like all the money in the world to Bedros. But, of course, now he realized that Garabed's meager fortune must have long since been exhausted. This was why Garabed worked nights in a bakery, why Mariam did mending, why he hadn't left Bolis with his wards as quickly and mysteriously as he had left Malatia many years before. His thoughts finally crystallizing, he looked over at Syrvart. There was a glimmer in her eyes that begged for more conversation.

"Well, little flower," he laughed, trying to relax her troubled brow, "I guess we have all had enough excitement for one morning. I am sorry if I frightened you. I think I embarrassed you with too many grown-up questions."

"You did not, Bedo," she responded meekly, her head drooping down.

He considered her for a moment and then dared to ask her one more thing. It was the one question—the one burning misgiving—he had harbored from the very beginning when he had learned that Garabed had come back to Malatia adopt this needy family.

"Syrvart," he called gently as she started to leave, "can you answer me one more thing? It is a difficult question, but you need not answer me with words—just a nod, yes or no."

Her eyes agreed.

"I am concerned that Garabed has done other things to hurt you or your mother."

The little girl's face turned ghostly white, and she stared at him in horror.

"I see you understand what I am saying. I am sorry. I just had to know. After all, he is the only man alone here in a house with two defenseless women. I feel I must know, Syrvart, if I am to help you and your mother. I must know. Has he ever...?"

Terror seized her face. For that second she was transformed into a worn woman of the world as she threw a distasteful glance out the bedroom window toward some distance somewhere.

"No!" She said the word clearly and without pain.

Bedros drew closer to her. He wanted to embrace her in this most difficult, embarrassing encounter. She was merely a child.

Syrvart slowly walked out of the room. Enough had been said. She hoped they would speak no more about it.

After the young girl left, Bedros dressed himself quickly as Mariam called melodiously from the kitchen that breakfast was ready.

When Bedros entered the aromatic kitchen, he found Garabed sullen and still, Hagop curious and wiggly, and Syrvart gracefully poised—all sitting around a wooden table on mismatched chairs. Mariam called a cheerful greeting to him as she fussed over a tiny, black, gas-fired stove, which was squashed against a white sink in a corner of the small room.

"Sit down, Bedros while I prepare your eggs." Mariam sang out to him as he fumbled for an empty chair and sat among the unresponsive eaters.

Garabed wisely refused to look at Bedros who perused the abundance on the table before him. The memories of home overtook him.

It was as it had been in Malatia. It was the way his mother would have prepared her table of plenty, even when there was virtually no bounty with which to create such delights. Mariam, who had the time and a little money to assist her, had appropriately used it all to her tribute. She was an accomplished cook.

In a basket, encased in a clean, white towel, there was warm, golden, sesame-seed choeregg resting side by side with softly brittle *parag hatz,* which was as thin and bubbly as his mother used to prepare it. In another tray was an array of cheeses encircled by a dewy display of tomatoes—ripe and red; cucumbers—pale green with thin, dark green skins; leafy green mint leaves; thinly sliced reddish peppers; and raw, white squash cubes. Together the multitude of epicurean splendors sang out to him, each in a different alluring tune, and he felt his mouth salivating. He tried to fill his plate slowly and in a gentlemanly fashion, though his desire was to grab everything in one sweep and devour it in one mouthful.

"It seems spring has decided to arrive at last, Bedros." Mariam made her announcement while placing two perfectly fried, golden eggs before Bedros.

"I didn't notice." Bedros was busily sampling all the delicious food; though his answer seemed curt, it was rather a polite, fast way of getting on with his eating.

Mariam knew that and laughed at his boyish delight in her cooking. "After you finish eating, you can get some fresh air and enjoy the warmth of this beautiful day."

Garabed finally looked up from his half-eaten plate and grunted. "You should not walk outside. It is not safe. Just open up your bedroom window. It will have the same effect."

Mariam gave him a look of disgust for ruining such a pleasant moment.

"I cannot argue with that, Garabed," Bedros responded, undaunted and savoring his luscious breakfast.

Garabed, looking as though he wanted to say much more but considering it twice, got up hastily and announced that he would be taking his morning walk, after which, as usual, he would sleep until lunch.

Everyone in the kitchen silently rejoiced in his leaving. It was as though a chilling wind had suddenly ceased blowing, and a warm healing sun permeated the room.

"*Tserkerit tallah!*" raved Bedros in traditional response to a perfectly prepared meal.

"I am glad you enjoyed it. *Anoush allah,*" Mariam pleasantly answered as she poured him a fresh cup of steaming coffee and then sat by him with her own coffee cupped in her talented hands.

"Garabed is right, Bedros, though I realize he never says anything in a pleasant tone of voice. I am sorry I mentioned the beautiful day. I forgot that you really cannot walk about freely."

"Do not think of it, Mariam. I will find a way out of this. And"—he placed his hand on hers—"I will find a way to save all of us."

Syrvart gazed at him in admiration. She was beginning to believe that this wonderful man who had dropped at her feet the evening before would save all of them one day. Hagop tossed aside his fork and slid down out of his chair and toddled off to another room to play.

Mariam gathered up her dirty dishes and pondered the words the young soldier had spoken. She had admired him from the start. Even in the old days in Malatia, she had marveled at his good looks, jovial nature, and skilled craftsmanship. She knew Bedros Vartanian was the kind of man who sought out, struggled with, and at last conquered the precipices of life—goals Garabed Hamparian could only dream of doing.

"You had best get yourself back into bed, or you will not be saving anyone from anything," Mariam teased.

Syrvart began to help her mother as Bedros excused himself, still complimenting Mariam lavishly.

But Bedros didn't sleep. He couldn't because he knew that the most precarious turning point in his life was upon him. His mind was in turmoil. Shortly, when Garabed returned home from his morning walk and entered his bedroom, he found to his fury that Bedros Vartanian was sitting on the edge of his bed, waiting for him.

Garabed looked as though the angel of death had swooped down on him as he faced this incorrigible soldier.

"*Asdvadz, chem havadar!* Is there no sacredness to a man's bedroom? What are you doing in here?" He spoke angrily but cautiously, remembering his sore jawbone.

"It seems the sacredness of bedrooms is not of importance to you either, my old friend!" Bedros glowered at him, speaking his bold words with sarcastic hyperbole.

"What does that mean, fool?" Garabed pretended disinterest as he busied himself in preparation for his day's rest.

"Garabed, sit down and listen to me. I think you know what I am referring to. It is time we talked like men."

"You pride yourself in that, do you not, Bedros—being a strong, virile man with blind, bullish pride? You dislike me for my polish, my manners, and of course my inheritance!"

"No, Garabed, I wish I had some of the sophistication, but I know I never will. I do not begrudge you that." Bedros found himself softening.

"Then what is it? Why do you torment me? You look nauseated at the sight of me. Now you accuse me of indecent actions!"

Bedros got up from the bed and circled the room. It was a fair question, one he had asked himself a thousand times. If he could answer it for Garabed, perhaps he could answer it for himself. He looked long and silently out a window into the bustle of Pera's morning streets, and then, in the fluttering sunbeam rays, he found his answer.

"Garabed," Bedros began; his usual glare of contempt had been somewhat transformed into a look of sympathy and understanding. "I think what I hate about you is that you constantly relive—in fact, wallow—in your misfortune. I know too well the way your father was killed. It was exceptionally disgusting and degrading. I know that you saw it and that you live with it to this day." Garabed turned pallid. He grasped his stomach in pain, and his intestines cringed, and then tied themselves into knots. He couldn't speak.

"We Armenians, all of us, go into our lives with these kinds of hideous, incredible memories. They are stories people will not believe many years from now. But we must cast those memories behind us. We must go on and live out our lives, remembering the good things, the proud things about our ancestors. I do not wish to tell my children that their grandparents were slaughtered like pigs! I want to tell them that they were brave and proud and productive!"

"So, you say, let them die in vain? Let us forget?" Garabed was growing livid.

"No, Garabed." Bedros's voice mellowed. "We and our children and theirs—we will never forget. But we cannot dwell on these things. What kind of heritage do we offer our nationality if all we consider ourselves is a mass of murdered sheep? There is no pride in that!" Bedros had tears in his eyes.

Garabed considered his words with a frown of impending agreement, though he would never verbally do so.

"And," Garabed said, returning to his usual condescending voice, "you think that I live in self-pity and morbid memories?"

"Not only do you, but you drag everyone else down with you. You are a miserable, unhappy man, Garabed, and for that I am very sorry."

Bedros watched Garabed for a long time. The back of his head was toward him. It was tilted down as though he were gazing at his shoes. But shortly Bedros heard him sob. Garabed was crying, whimpering, like a little boy. It took him a while to compose himself, but he refused to capitulate without a few last remarks.

"And now, Bedros," Garabed retorted, his head held strenuously high, his nose red, his eyes still stained from crying. "Now you come into my home to woo my precious family away from me? Is that how you show your sorrow for Garabed Hamparian?"

"There, you are at it again! I am not the enemy, my friend. I come here as a fugitive, true, but my plans are to help you and these women."

"Help? Well, thank you, but we are doing just fine. We have been until now."

"I know, Garabed. I know everything." Bedros glared at him, utilizing the magical powers in his flashing, hypnotic eyes—the commanding beams that wouldn't permit anyone to look away or ignore what they had to say. "Your inheritance has been spent long ago. That is why you have to work and Mariam must take in sewing."

Garabed could offer no argument. He stood, foolishly enthralled in Bedros's bold discoveries.

"I know that you came to Malatia, not to help a family in need, but to help yourself. You must have been so lonely, so desperate, that you decided by coming to Mariam's home and financially settling them, you would automatically obligate them to accept you."

Garabed flung a weak arm into the air. "How dare you accuse—"

"Garabed," Bedros went on, undaunted. He had at last found the words. He at last understood why he felt the way he did about this pathetic man. It was important to both of them that he finish. "You have made them accept you. You have made them feel obligation to you. But you cannot make them love you. Not until you change your cruel ways."

"They do love me, Bedros. They love me in their way. And one day, you will see, I shall even come to marry—"

"Yes, marry who? A woman older than you? Or will you wait patiently for Syrvart to grow up? That is the plan, is it not? Has it not been your plan all along?"

Garabed had been conquered. This young man had read him, delving into the innermost depths of his secret soul. He felt coldly naked and unassailably ashamed.

"Now that you have this all figured out, Bedros, I presume you will do all in your power to prevent me from my terrible task." In his surrender, Garabed was still eloquently biting.

"No, my miserable friend. I have no desire to do that. If either Mariam or Syrvart decides to marry you one day, that is their decision. But I will not stand by and allow them to be bullied into such a decision either."

"I see," Garabed retorted, sounding almost relieved.

"Right now you and I have more serious matters to consider." Bedros walked over to the window and pointed symbolically outside. "In a few weeks the madness that is sweeping through the scattered villages is going to spread everywhere. I assure you, Garabed, we Armenians are all dead men if we stay in this country. We must now—all of us— methodically plan our escape."

"Easy to say, Bedros, but I have no money as you have discovered I am not the brave warrior that you think you are. I think I will take my chances here." Garabed slumped weakly down on his bed.

"You are gambling with more than one life here, Garabed, or did you forget your family?" The last word was blasted out with angry exaggeration.

"No, I have not!" Garabed had been forced into facing a gruesome eventuality—one he had for several months tried to sweep under the dead folds of his encumbered memory.

"All right now, let us sit straight and talk sharply. You have not enough money to get out of here and start a new life elsewhere. You are basically afraid. We both know that. And I am a fugitive. I am of no use to you here. In fact, I present a danger to all of you."

"This is all very true, my bullheaded friend." It was a sign of incongruous humor—a glimmer of affection. Bedros felt he had struck a chord.

"It is obvious I must get out of here—to a free land where I can raise enough money to get all of you safely evacuated."

Garabed went into an uncontrollable fit of laughter. "Oh, I do not believe you! And what other miracles do you have up your sleeves, almighty Bedros?"

Bedros stared back at him, unmoved. "My plans may seem impossible to you, but to me they are a simple matter of survival. They are another step up my climb through life, and I must take the step or not move at all."

"Oh, incredible, you are!"

Bedros could endure this fool no longer. He grabbed Garabed's arms like two vices. He squeezed until the pain showed clearly on his victim's face.

"Now you listen and listen well! You and I are about to make a deal. And if you are nothing else, I believe you are a man who will keep a gentleman's agreement. Are you ready? Or do you plan to giggle the rest of your life away?"

Garabed suddenly became serious. "I am ready, Bedros."

"All right then, this is it. I do not know yet where I will escape to, but I know I soon will. I must. Then soon I will let you know where I am. I will raise as much money as I can in as short a time as possible. On my word, I will send you half."

Garabed's thin, pale eyebrows rose in wonder, but he dared not dispute this man again.

"Yes, you heard me. I will use my half to get myself to America, and you shall do the same. We will meet there—in America—and make our plans from that point on."

"I am to take your word for all of this, Bedros?" Garabed asked.

"You have my word, my friend—a most valuable possession. I, in turn, ask but one promise from you."

"Aha!" laughed the still-incredulous Garabed.

"Shut up and listen, you fool! You will promise me that you will not suggest marriage to either Mariam or Syrvart."

"That seems an odd request. At this point I cannot help wondering if you yourself do not have some amorous designs of your own!"

"Shall we agree on this? I can go on my own, you know, and leave you and your family to your own devices. I do not have to offer you anything." With that he held out a determined hand.

Garabed thought only a few seconds, but the eyes of Bedros couldn't be denied. He at last offered his hand and the two men—not quite friends yet too enmeshed in each other's lives to be enemies—made a pact that would alter both of their lives more critically than they themselves could have even imagined.

"Bedros, where will you go? How, and with what?"

"I do not know. I do have enough military pay saved to afford some sort of transportation. The real problem is getting out of here safely, unnoticed. But I will find the answer; I always do." He beamed impishly.

With these final words of self-assurance, Bedros Vartanian flashed a victorious smile and left Garabed to his needed rest. He himself was exhausted and had to recuperate to begin his task of escape. His sleep came slowly as he discussed with his God the dangerous journey ahead. Assured of God's assistance, Bedros fell into a beautiful sleep. He slept through lunch, until Mariam finally awakened him for a delicious meal of cabbage dolma and lentil soup. He then fell quickly asleep for the night. He slept undisturbed until the next morning. He was again awakened by Mariam's sweet voice, apologizing for disturbing his sleep but announcing that he had a most upset visitor. His name, she said, was Hirair and he had to see Bedros immediately.

"I knew he was from Malatia, so I thought it was all right to let him in. Did I make a mistake?"

But Bedros was already scurrying down the hallway in his nightshirt and didn't turn around to answer her.

Hirair stood nervously inside the doorway of the tiny home with a look of torment on his face. But that was only until he saw his friend bounding toward him in the silly nightshirt, his hairy legs protruding like two muscular, pirouetting pistons as he flopped into Hirair's outstretched arms. The two, as they had always before, fell over onto the floor in boyish romp and unabashed delight in their reunion.

Mariam walked in on the scene and gently giggled at their pranks. She finally coaxed them to have a seat, since their present position wasn't conducive to casual conversation. But when they had at last risen and untangled, it was clear from Hirair's face that his mission there was hardly casual.

"My dear old friend, you knew where to find me?" Bedros slapped him on the back as he always did—a little too hard.

"I had a feeling you would come here. Remember, your lucky number—seven?" Hirair smiled but sadly.

"Ah, yes." Bedros threw his head back in laughter.

"Bedo, the binbashi sent me to find you. He begged me—he and Sheida—of course. All last night over a fine dinner, they coaxed me to bring you back at all costs."

The smile left Bedros's face, and for a moment he glared suspiciously at his friend.

"I know what you are thinking, but I had to come and see for myself if you were all right. I told them I didn't know where you went."

"Of course, Hirair." This time Bedros patted the back of his friend more gently. "I know my secret is safe with you."

"Now I must relate to you all that I have promised. First, the binbashi assures you that if you return within the week, you will not be prosecuted. He will attest to the fact that he gave you a sick leave."

"I see." Bedros scowled, looking over at Mariam, who rose and excused herself on the pretense of preparing some tea.

"Bedo, it is not my place to persuade you one way or the other. Of all people, I know you are your own man, but I must say that those two really love you. If you could have seen the sadness in their faces—the worry. Sheida is deeply in love with you. I know they will take care of you. There is nothing they would not do for you."

"Go on, Hirair; there is more. I can see it in your eyes. There is more news."

The two friends had been through so much that by now one could read the other without the need of words. Hirair wished that at this particular moment such were not the case. He looked sadly down at a letter he was holding in his shaking hand.

"I must give you this letter. I feel you have to read it before making your decision. I confiscated it yesterday from the mail carrier. I just told him I was in charge of collecting all your mail until your return. Thank God, the fool didn't ask any more questions. "

"Let me see it. It is my mail, you know." Bedros scowled.

Hirair looked nauseated and limp. "Before I do, let me tell you I have read it, and it is terrible, terrible news." Tears were streaming down his face as he passed the letter to his impatient friend. Bedros voraciously grabbed it.

"It will not be the first time," he growled, tearing open the envelope written in his brother's hand.

At first Bedros only stared at the paper. Then he held the letter tightly against his chest as though drawing strength enough to read it. His bright countenance had fallen gray. He knew too well that letters written in these times, from one Armenian to another, were most often written in splattered human blood.

March 20, 1915

My dearest Bedros,

Though it has only been five days since my last letter—as if there could ever be more to this tale from hell—I must tell

Irene Vosbikian

you that there is more to report. Mother and I were preparing to leave this morning when a letter came from Garo in Aleppo.

He is still working with the Tashnaks there, and he tells us that the Armenian resistance there is strong. Little bloodshed is coming from the Turks at the moment. But he has learned from friends in the army near Nakrkeuy that a horrible and devious scheme was undertaken there.

Under the pretense of segregating and deporting Armenian soldiers from the training centers, all Armenians in the Nakrkeuy center were placed under arrest. There were 1,500 of them at Nakrkeuy. I do not have to remind you that our brothers, Hovsep and Sahag, were among them.

These soldiers were banded together and sent off at night under the escort of gendarmes.

On route, though the Turks deny this, the soldiers were attacked by other Turkish gendarmes. They were accompanied by bandits, whom they called *"chattiest."* In a regular series of such night raids, thousands of Armenian soldiers were brutally slaughtered with axes and hammers. They were then dismembered, decapitated—there was no indignity left undone!

Garo tells us that the corpses are methodically buried in ravines and gullies leading from the training center all along the roads toward Bolis and other major cities.

So my dearest, only surviving, true brother, we have now lost the two babies—and they were only babies when these madmen ended their precious lives.

To say Mother and I are tormented is a mild explanation of our frenzy. Upon closing this letter, we will board the waiting carriage to be escorted to you in Constantinople. We have only the mutessarif's letter and two gendarmes as drivers to take us on our way. Only God knows if we shall ever reach your loving embrace.

We have decided to go directly to your binbashi for aid, as you have suggested him to be a trustworthy man. I pray that this letter finds you safe and well until I can look into your beautiful eyes once again.

I am yours with what heart is left me.

Ara

• • •

Bedros fell silent, morosely staring off into nothingness. Only the torrent of water spilling from his lifeless eyes proved him to be among the living.

Respectfully, Hirair silently waited. He too was weeping in pain with his lifetime companion. At last he spoke, fearful that Bedros might slip into a catatonia from the precipitating anguish.

"Bedros, please, what can I do for you? If I had the power to spare you from the pain I know you are feeling..."

Bedros forced a smile for his sad friend. "All any of us can do now is get out of this hellhole so there will be no more death, no more destruction! If we are to survive as a nationality, it cannot be here!"

"I know this, Bedros, and I must tell you even more, as I knew this would be your reaction. Binbashi Ismael told me more in confidence when Sheida wasn't present."

Hirair and Bedros curtailed their conversation a moment when they heard the sounds of talking and laughter coming from the kitchen. The family had awakened and was obviously having their breakfast.

"So"—Bedros sighed wearily—"go on."

"The binbashi realizes the kind of pain you have gone through, and he does not yet know about your two younger brothers. Still he understands. He confided in me that if you choose to flee, as he fears you will, he promises his prayers will be with you. He further swears that your mother and brother will be protected under his roof until you send for them."

"God in heaven, he is a wonderful and loving man, Hirair! If it were not for all of this...Oh, how I would consider staying here with him and marrying Sheida." Bedros shook his head and paced pensively around the room.

"I thought it was a generous gesture on his part, too, Bedo. He is an unusual man, for a Turk."

"Or perhaps," Bedros mused, "it is the mad murderers who are the unusual Turks, my friend."

"Perhaps," said Hirair, not believing this to be the case.

Bedros sat up rigidly, slapping his hands on his thick thighs. "What else?"

Hirair gave him a sly grin. "Your old friend has some plans in the fire too."

"Bravo! Let me hear them and then we will end all this heavy talk with one of Mariam's delectable breakfasts."

"Well, my friend, tomorrow at dusk a French pleasure liner will be leaving from the Galata Port. It is carrying a load of wealthy vacationers to Marseilles, France."

"Where did you obtain this knowledge, oh wise one?" Bedros asked, pretending cheerfulness but filled with the agony of his lost brothers.

"Sonia told me. She works with a French girl who will be going to Marseilles on the vessel with her boyfriend—a rather notorious general who happens to be Turkish, married and with ten children."

Despite his pain, Bedros laughed, "I suppose he could really use a trip to France!"

"I can imagine. Well, at any rate—I do not know how—the girl procured another ticket for Sonia."

"Why does she not use it herself?"

Hirair flashed a look of dismay as he shook his head. "It is strange Bedo, but she refuses to leave. It is as though some mysterious bind draws her. She is, believe it or not, happy and comfortable here."

"You cannot ask for more than that, Hirair," Bedros insisted, still thinking of the French liner.

"I know, Bedo, so I have been telling myself. But believe me, I know as you know that we must get out any way we can."

Hirair paused and cautiously looked around the room, but Bedros waved his hand to allay any fear that there was treachery in this home.

"It happens that tomorrow evening is my night off. Immediately after dinner I will go to my room, dress in civilian clothes presumably for a night in Pera. Then I will make my way to the ship. And damn it, I am getting on that vessel, and I am getting myself the hell out of here!" Hirair was defiant and determined in his every word.

"I am proud of you, my dear friend. Only I beg you to remember the danger. We are living in times when we are regarded as no more than dogs lying in a gutter."

"Bedros—my dearest, most precious friend—my only fear, my only sorrow, is in leaving you behind. I cannot bear the thought of it."

Bedros strongly protested, "Think no more of that! These are treacherous times, Hirair! Times of war and famine. Our people are being slowly massacred. I would say, as did our professors, that these are extenuating circumstances."

The two laughed uncomfortably but Hirair saw there was sorrow in his friend's eyes. At that moment, he knew Bedros would have given anything for access to that French ship. They both knew it.

Hirair at last broke the silence and the forlorn gazing of his friend's normally vivacious eyes.

"Do you know? I am really hungry. Talking about all these exciting plans has made my stomach growl. Am I invited to breakfast?"

Before Bedros could reply, an angelic voice filtered out from the kitchen. "Is that any kind of question for a young Armenian boy to ask an Armenian mother?"

It was just the three of them in the kitchen now—Mariam, Bedros, and Hirair. Garabed was off for his morning walk. Hagop was never where he was supposed to be, and little Syrvart had gone off to school, which she attended three days a week.

"Bedo," Mariam said while fussing over the two boys as if they were royalty, "I couldn't help overhearing about your brothers' deaths. I cannot say how..."

Bedros calmly interrupted her trying to spare the fine woman the words of grief which are never adequate. "Please, Mariam, don't say anything. We have all had enough of this horror. We must turn our heads toward the sky—our thoughts toward the future."

"I for one am turning my thoughts toward this beautiful *parag hatz*. It is excellent, Digin Hamparian."

As if normal Armenian hospitality were not enough, Mariam went even further in lavishing these two young men with her graciousness and fabulous foods. If they protested that they had had enough, she would pile on even more. When the coffee cup was just emptied, it was that quickly refilled. When it seemed that one of them needed to reach more than two inches to obtain an item on the table, she would scurry to the rescue and bring the dish over to them. On and on it went, to the point of being delightfully amusing to the two guests, who desperately tried to control their laughter.

When at last their stomachs were bursting from fulfillment with vegetables and cheese, fruit, homemade breads, and fresh Armenian sausage and sweet rolls, the mood turned uncomfortably somber. With no more eating to do and a workday ahead of them, Hirair and Bedros realized they would soon be parting, perhaps for the very last time. Neither could bear to look into the other's eyes. The conversation grew short and belabored, and Hirair at last decided to excuse himself and leave. He would hurry away before they both cried.

Standing together at the front entry, they ached inside. The two gazed long and silently into each other's eyes. Instantaneously they embraced and kissed on both cheeks, as was the way, even among the most masculine of men. Hirair spoke through a lump that felt as if it would burst from his throat.

"Bedo, what will you have me tell Binbashi Ismael?"

Bedros thought, then gave his friend a peaceful smile.

"Tell him that instead of waiting for an answer, he should consider the person to whom the question was asked."

They both laughed heartily and hugged quickly for one last time. Hirair turned abruptly to flee from this scene of pain. Bedros called out to him.

"Perhaps you are not rid of me yet, my friend. Remember—have no fear when Bedros is here!"

Hirair heard but ran even faster toward the Pera Training Center. He didn't care that bystanders stared at the soldier running by, sobbing, and sniffling like a little boy. For in actuality, that was what he was.

When Bedros returned to the parlor, he found Mariam picking up the letter he had forgotten about and left crumpled in a ball on the floor. It was an appropriate way to leave the past, he thought.

"You may read it if you like, Mariam. I will not be offended. I must warn you it is not very pleasant."

"Well, I do not think I care to at the moment, Bedo," she said, busying herself in cleaning up the parlor.

"It does not matter. Just, if you will, please burn it when you are finished. It is not a fact of my family's past that I would like to leave for posterity."

"I understand, Bedo."

"Yes, and Digin Mariam, your breakfast was so fine. I cannot thank you enough. Really you are putting yourself out much too much for the likes of me."

"Do not be silly, Bedo. It is my pleasure. You are a fine addition to our household."

"Thank you so much. And now this latest news has taken its toll on me. I think I will go to my room and rest."

"Please do, my son." Mariam watched him with sadness and fondness as he disappeared. He did grace their home and their lives with greatness, and inside she knew he wouldn't be with them for very much longer.

Again, after sleeping through lunch, Mariam woke up Bedros for dinner. He found everyone seated, politely waiting for him, and he felt ashamed to have slept so soundly. He was now keeping a very hungry family waiting for their dinner.

"Excuse my lateness, everyone. I am afraid I am weaker than I care to believe."

"It is no problem, Bedros. We all just sat down," insisted Mariam. Garabed didn't encourage her, nor did the thumping of Hagop's legs under the table or the cool silence of Syrvart.

Bedros was glad when the meal was finished and he could retire to the parlor for some reflection and relaxation. Garabed went off to dress for his evening's work at the bakery, and Mariam was busy cleaning up the kitchen. Soon she would be preparing Hagop for bed. Bedros was blessedly alone for a few precious minutes. Then Syrvart entered the parlor and sat by him in a nearby chair.

He didn't acknowledge her at first, only looked amused at her thick, long, brown hair all done up like a young woman's in a chic bun. She wore a ruffled ecru blouse and a long, blue flannel skirt. Her features were not totally delicate; the nose was a little flat and a little wide. Her face was too round and a bit heavy. Her eyes were a pleasant hazel with black but thin lashes. Yet though each individual feature wasn't indicative to a raving beauty, when put together, a lovely, delicate young woman emerged. At least she was pleasant to look at and a soft-spoken, most feminine sort of girl. Too young for me, he thought, amused at his wistful mind, but a fine Armenian girl.

"Bedros, I read the letter from your brother, Ara. I am so sorry. Why are these terrible things happening to us? Will it be our family next? I am so afraid. I do not even want to leave the house for school anymore."

Bedros ached for her, understanding the terror she must be feeling—so young with no father to protect her.

"Oh, little lady, no one can tell why God has let this thing happen to his people. I have no answers for the past or the present. Only I promise you, as I did your cousin and your mother, that I will find a way to get you away from here."

She looked up at his strong, deeply lined brow, under which two thick, bushy eyebrows nearly met perfectly in the middle. If he says it, I believe it must happen, her young mind thought.

"Bedros, if you could see—every day I am in school, new children come in. Many of them are staying with relatives. Their parents are dead. They are so skinny, so yellow skinned and sickly looking that sometimes I am afraid to sit next to them."

"Syrvart, they are the lucky ones. Right now thousands more children in much worse condition are being sent to the Christian orphanages and hospitals all over Bolis. I lived through it when I was a child. Only now it is worse than anyone can imagine."

"I do not believe I will ever leave here. I do not believe I will ever grow into a woman. Oh, Bedo, I know I am going to die—I know it!"

In a display of uncharacteristic emotion, the little stoic threw herself into the soldier's dumbfounded embrace and sobbed so violently that her whole body trembled. Bedros held her as tightly as he could—his one arm around her shoulders, his other caressing her soft, brown hair.

"Do not be afraid of anything ever again, little Syrvart. Remember, Bedros is with you always."

Mariam finally came into the parlor. She had at last finished her evening chores. By this time, Syrvart was calmer, and the two young people were sitting next to each other in serene conversation.

"Ah, this is a fine scene." she announced, sitting respectfully away from both of them.

"Yes, it is a peaceful evening. I feel as though there are no more tears left in me—as though no new pain could ever grieve me again. Nothing worse in this world could ever happen to me, so from now on, I must go upward." Bedros spoke with strength and the warmth of an inner blind faith.

"May God hear your words, Bedo." Mariam said in prayer like chiming.

There was silence for a while. But in the eyes of Bedros there was a loud conversation, as though his mind was whispering to his heart and his heart was shouting back to his mind, and his eyes were the mediators between the two. Though his face was unflinching, his eyes fluttered back and forth, and then suddenly stopped and beamed in shining, black magnificence.

"Mariam, tomorrow is Saturday, is it not?" The question seemed to come from out of nowhere.

"Hmm, I had almost lost track of the days since you came, Bedo, but yes, it is." Mariam answered, wondering about his impulsive question.

"Good, then I propose an outing."

"An outing? Bedo, you know you are not free to go sight-seeing—especially now. It is too dangerous!"

"Yes, I know that, Digin Mariam, but I have this insatiable desire to take a small boat ride on the Marmora. They must rent pleasure boats at the Galata Port." Bedros jumped up and began to pace.

"Why, yes they do, Bedo." Syrvart volunteered, much to her mother's annoyance. "We have taken Sunday strolls there many times and watched the people rowing around in the water."

"Bedo, please, it is one of the busiest places in all of Pera. It would be suicide—"

"Dear Mariam, bear with me. I have a plan. Will Garabed be able to join us?" Bedros was pacing faster now.

"No. He works every evening." Mariam said, still wondering about Bedros's sudden, nervous excitement.

"Fine! Well then, what do you say? Shall we give it a try?"

"Would it make any difference if I said no?" Mariam smiled sadly.

"None whatsoever," laughed the daring young Armenian.

"Then I am sure Garabed could keep Hagop at home with him while we are gone. I would not trust that little wiggler in a boat!"

Then Bedros bent down and bid mother and daughter good-night with a kiss.

"*Keesher pari*, Bedo. We will see you at breakfast." Syrvart called to him.

"*Pari keesher*, my two little ladies." And he left them to their dreams—dreams of Bedros Vartanian and what an enduring mark he had made upon their lives.

The following morning Mariam rose early, as did Syrvart, each taking careful pains with her personal appearance. It was as though they were both going on a first date—Sunday shoes, ruffled blouses, golden barrettes, a little rose water, and of course a touch of what the Western ladies called lipstick. They both entered the kitchen at the same time, each complimenting the other on her finery.

When Garabed arrived home, he frowned distastefully at such frivolity, especially so early in the day. "What is this all about?" he growled.

The two women looked at each other and giggled like schoolgirls with a very special secret. Their foolishness made Garabed even more furious.

"Is anyone going to answer me around this madhouse?" he ranted.

Mariam, feeling sorry for the poor, left-out man, sat by his side and told him of Bedros's plans for the day. Garabed was wild.

"Now I know he is insane! He will get us all slaughtered!"

"Garabed." Mariam calmed him while preparing some coffee. "Bedros says he has a plan, and whatever it is, I know he would not endanger Syrvart and me."

"Well, thank you for the vote of confidence, Digin Hamparian!" a burly voice called out as if attempting the high pitch of a woman's voice.

The three people seated around the kitchen table looked up, and when they saw Bedros, a roar of laughter went up so loudly that little Hagop woke up screaming in his crib. Incredible as it was, even Garabed had himself a short but good laugh.

Standing in the doorway of the kitchen was Bedros Vartanian. He had on a long, patchwork skirt, out from which his shabby military shoes peeked. Around his massive shoulders he had wrapped a beige crocheted shawl, and around his large head, completely hiding his hair and both ears, was a grayish plaid scarf, tied tightly under his chin. There was no question he was a vigorously handsome man, but he made a most clumsy, unfeminine-looking woman. They couldn't control their laughter at the sight of him.

"I took the liberty of borrowing some of your things, Mariam. I hope none of them are very important to you," he said in a high-pitched female voice.

"Oh, no, of course not," answered Mariam, still choking from her now-diminishing laughter. "As a matter of fact, I think you look much better in them than I ever did."

"Ridiculous!" growled Garabed, the humor eluding him as usual. "You are all ridiculous. I am going to fetch Hagop. Do not think about breakfasts, Mariam. I would rather prepare it myself after you fools are gone."

He shuffled away, pretending disgust. But somewhere in his painful, belabored soul there was a tiny opening allowing in a glimmer of light. His scowl gave way to a pleasant, understanding smile knowing Bedros had begun to keep his part of their bargain.

So it was that the two well-dressed ladies, with all their modest trimmings, emerged from the doorway of the tiny brick row house, accompanied by a rather dreary-looking, cumbersome, woman, whom most might presume was their poor unfortunate aunt from the backward interiors of Turkey. In part at least, the onlookers would be right. Bedros stood for a moment and breathed in the fresh spring air of April.

They strolled three abreast down the bustling street, which came up to the main road leading to the Galata Port. There was a tramway station right there on the corner and the ladies had a seat, awaiting their transportation. The busy corner slowly began to fill up with such an array of people that Bedros sat back in awe, amused at the different sizes and styles—fat, skinny, young, old, mostly common, everyday people, for whom the impending holocaust still had no meaning. Shortly, two young, fiendish-looking Turkish soldiers marched over to the tramway stop and suspiciously eyed everyone about them. The chattering and cheerfulness of the waiting people quickly stopped, for the gendarmes as always had brought with them fear and mistrust. Bedros lowered his head, and Mariam froze in terror as one of the glowering men turned to peruse the three of them sitting there. He gave Mariam a suggestive grin, and then wickedly eyed Syrvart. When his stare turned to Bedros, the chill of death ran through their bodies. But instead of showing any recognition, the soldier just wrinkled up his nose in disapproval at what he thought to be a squalid-looking old woman.

At last the tramway arrived. Everyone piled on. The gendarmes pushed their way on first with no regard for the women or the elderly. Bedros and his female companions took front seats, keeping their gazes distant and their composures cool as the trolley rolled along its way to the port.

After getting off the tramway, Bedros took an even more bent-over position and faked the wobbling unsteadiness of an arthritic cripple. Mariam and Syrvart obligingly took his arms and assisted him off the train. They stepped safely aside as the trolley nearly emptied, and the passengers scurried in various directions. The gendarmes got off last, again looking ominously around them but finally starting on their way.

Assured that the gendarmes were safely out of range, the three slowly made their way down a cobblestone road which led in a snakelike trail toward the water. The vast, very placid water stretched out like a silky thrust of flowing fabric, bustling out from a regal wedding gown. The air was crisp, wet, and lavish with the smell of fish and the oily aromas of passing and harbored vessels. The boats, like the people of Bolis, were as varied as the animals of the earth, from the tiniest most simple canoe types to huge and aristocratic ocean liners. As in life, each had its place in accordance with its stature. The entire Galata Port was a U-shaped joining of hundreds of different moorings, which jutted in and out, either harboring a boat or awaiting the arrival or departure of one.

Here in this lively, refreshing environment, the world rotated in splendor and excitement. It was a world oblivious to the screams of the maimed children, the howls of the insane mothers, the wails of the starving, the splattering of the blood, the sickening smells of burned flesh and rotting corpses. Even if this world were aware of the other, it was doubtful that it would have done anything about these horrors, for the Western world was busy with its own war and it wouldn't be until its culmination that she would turn her weary eyes to the deprivation and savagery that had deluged the pathetic Armenians in the East.

Bedros realized all of this, and his feelings of helplessness in this godforsaken country grew ever more intense. The three made their cautious way to the small dock, where a sign for boat rentals was on display.

The proprietor was a grizzly, old, bearded Greek with squinting eyes. There were no other customers, and it seemed to be one of the safest areas in which to acquire a boat. The old man walked with a pronounced limp, and he wore a beret-type hat that rested to one side over his comically balding head. In Greek, he asked if they wished to rent a boat. Mariam was the self-appointed speaker. She attempted speaking Armenian, hoping he would understand, as most Greek merchants did of necessity.

"Yes, sir. We would like to rent a small rowboat for about an hour or two." Her voice was even more sweet than usual, though tinged with a slight quiver of nervousness.

"It is by the hour, madam—one *piastre*." He spoke horrid but understandable Armenian.

Mariam looked over at Bedros, who motioned two hours with his fingers. The arrangement was agreed upon, and the Greek led the three ladies over to a very small, wooden rowboat which had been freshly painted and seemed fairly sea worthy. Bedros nodded his head in approval of the boat, and the three shakily got in. The old Greek eyed them curiously for a moment and before untying the rope, he decided to ask them a question.

"Does one of you at least know how to handle a boat?" he asked apprehensively.

"Oh, yes, sir," Syrvart volunteered. "My mother and my auntie do this all the time!"

Bedros and Mariam gave each other a smile of surprise and admiration for the little lady's sharpness.

"All right then," said the old Greek, shaking his head, "but stay right here in the harbor area. I do not want my boat floating out to sea."

The three sailors started out on their morning boat ride, and the Greek called out to them one more time.

"If you head toward the northern docks, you will see the *Napolean* loading up for its journey back to Marseilles. It is a large, dark-green vessel. You will not believe the rich vacationers—all their hundreds of trunks and fancy belongings are being loaded about now. They must be taking half of Constantinople back home with them!"

Bedros felt his heart flip. In his mind he was already lifting himself up into the mighty vessel of salvation. Syrvart and Mariam were too involved with the bustle all around them to take notice of the drifting look in Bedros's usually attentive eyes. They didn't realize they had at that moment lost him, though he sat so close to them.

The gulls swooped down for fish, now and then landing on the edge of the rocking boat, bobbing their curious heads for some food. Bedros continued rowing with fervor which was easy on this mirror-smooth bay. The conversation was excited and cheerful, but the two enthralled women didn't notice that Bedros wasn't speaking. They didn't see the dilation of his pitch-black pupils as the *Napolean* grew greater—more foreboding and nearer with each swoosh of the oars. They didn't know that the body of Bedros was with them but that his spirit, his very life, had fled from the tiny boat upon first sight of the French pleasure liner. She was hoisting trunk after laden trunk up to her protruding bow.

Suddenly there was a loud splash. Mariam turned, startled, as Syrvart pointed and gasped. Bedros Vartanian had jumped into the blue, beckoning waters of the Marmora Harbor. Mariam begged him to come back. Syrvart wept and wrung her tiny hands in hysterical frenzy. He kept on swimming—didn't turn; he just labored on and on in the direction of the waiting *Napolean*. In Bedros's wake, Mariam's shawl and patchwork skirt comically returned to the rowboat. It was all they would have left of Bedros.

"*Mayrig, Mayrig,* what shall we do? What will happen to us without him?" Syrvart wept like the frightened child she still was.

But Mariam Hamparian didn't immediately answer her pleading daughter. Her sad eyes just stared hypnotically off at the swimmer as he made his way to the northern docks and then jumped on top of a waiting trunk. In a few moments the creaking hoist lumbered its way down and hooked onto the fasteners on the trunk, taking it and Bedros Vartanian up to the bow of the ship. Mariam's eyes, straining from the tears and the sea breezes, then lost sight of him. She sat in the row-boat with her sobbing daughter until she believed Bedros was safe and wouldn't be put ashore. She then blotted her stained cheeks with her kerchief and looked sympathetically and lovingly over at her child.

"We must hurry home now, Syrvart. Do not worry. Our Bedros will survive."

"Mommy," cried the incredulous Syrvart, "how do you know?"

Mariam looked at her with an all-knowing, ageless shining in her eyes. "I know, darling. I just know."

Chapter 6
MARSEILLES, 1915

She lay like a serpent—her long, tantalizing tongue outstretched into the frolicking waters of the Mediterranean. Into her ravenous belly she captured the wanderers of the Eastern Hemisphere. She was Marseilles, France. Her commanding artery was the mighty Rhone River, which profusely emptied itself through her veins, out into her placid and most secluded harbor. Up until the merciless Nazi invasion of World War II, she remained peacefully serene and protected in the confines of her most infamous coastal boudoir, the Côte d'Azur. Marseilles began the parade of coastal cities on this luxurious and breathtakingly beautiful stretch of beach, at the end of which trailed Menton.

Marseilles was an old lady—in years at least—being the eldest city in all of France. She was also France's largest and most productive seaport. Yet amid all the commercial activity, her beaches drew the wealthy—those who lay lazily and without care on her Riviera, which was boasted as one of the most beautiful resorts in the world. To immigrants from the East, however, Marseilles was something else. She was a safe resting place, a sort of halfway breathing spot where they could gather their weary senses, fill their empty pockets, and then move on. In most cases this was to America, which, though less captivating, offered the opportunity of true assimilation—something the French lady only pretended. France, after all, was for the French, and America was for everyone.

After one week the *Napolean* made its lumbering way into the peaceful waters of the Old Port. To most of the passengers, Marseilles represented a jovial, refreshing holiday on the shores of the Côte d'Azur. Marseilles was a respite in the Western world. Her guests could bask in the notoriety of her elegance and frolic along her sparkling beaches and clear, blue waters. To most of her guests, she was shallow and frivolous.

But to Bedros Vartanian, Marseilles couldn't be what she would have liked to be—what he would have liked her to be. She was a boulder—a great stepping stone. She was to serve but one purpose in his life. She was to grant him the time and the opportunity to make some money as quickly as he could. As the luxurious liner at last docked, the young Armenian was still unsure how he was going to go about this task. He didn't even know how he was going to get into the city through her lines of customs and port authority personnel. It was incredible to him, in fact, that he had been allowed to remain on the *Napolean* at all.

When a young Armenian mate who had been helping to fasten the cargo onto the hoist of the French ship turned and saw Bedros, he had grabbed his arm in anger. But upon seeing the eyes of his countryman— one who dared to seek freedom-, the sailor saw a chance to free a fellow Armenian by merely turning his head the other way. That was how it had happened. Then Bedros Vartanian, like so much baggage, found himself flopped onto a wet, slimy deck with the *Napolean's* captain and an assistant—both Frenchmen—looking down at him in anger.

"Sir, please," he begged. "If you can understand me, let me stay on board. I must get out. They are murdering my people! I will work, gladly—anything you ask—if you will let me stay."

"*Continuez Armenian,*" the captain responded, and Bedros could see from the compassion in the man's eyes that he wouldn't turn him away.

"*Merci bien,*" he said, nearly bent over in gratitude, using one of the few French expressions he had ever heard in his life. Without need of words, Bedros ran over to a stringy deck mop, perched sloppily in a corner of the bow. He embraced it, pretending to dance with it, and began a clumsy waltz around the deck. Bedros and his mop. The Frenchmen laughed appreciatively. He had been hired. At least he will make it to Marseilles. After that, only God could predict.

During his time on the ship Bedros slept, worked, and ate either on the deck or in the galley below. He had not caught sight of Hirair; nor was he sure whether his dear friend was aboard the fancy liner at all. If he were, Bedros was hoping that his friend was spending his time in more tasteful accommodations than he. But the work and the filth and the lack of communication were all tiny pebbles under his toes compared to the boulders over which he had just leaped.

The Napolean had at last reached Marseilles. Bedros waited impatiently and watched as the puffy, old, moustached gentlemen and their gilded, fur-enveloped ladies disembarked in royal pomp. He stood back, unwashed and exhausted, with other miserable young men, many runaways like himself. He felt ashamed, dirty, and belittled as the regal parade of passengers continued down the plank. As he watched them, he vowed this was the last time he would be held inferior to any man. Bedros Vartanian knew what he was and who he was. All of those travelers with all their finery possessed nothing of his exuberance for life and zealous penchant for achievement. I, Bedros, he thought, am greater and richer than all of you. He glared at them and then smiled in embarrassment as he caught sight of Hirair, who was dressed in a fine, vested suit, all neatly polished, as he paraded down the ramp with the others.

It was all Bedros could do to stop himself from racing after his friend. He ached to see the surprise on Hirair's face when he realized that Bedros Vartanian was one step behind him. He felt disappointment overcome him as he lost sight of Hirair amid hoards of people, who now waited to pass through the gates of protocol into Marseilles.

As Bedros watched this procession, the captain came to the deck and motioned to all hands that they could leave. Bedros wanted to get off the boat quickly, but slowed his pace when he noticed the many police and customs officials, who were checking the less prominent voyagers as they departed from the ship. How in God's name was he to be let through with no identification and no knowledge of French?

Bedros gulped, braced himself, tugged on God's sleeve, and started down the ramp. He was flanked by several other young men, all of whom had no more identification on them than he did. In a solemn line the slovenly brigade made their way toward the gates. As they passed through, looming before them was a huge metal door leading to customs. The line abruptly stopped as one by one these frightened unfortunates were led through the doors. Bedros began forming a plan, a good story, and a plot of charismatic salesmanship— anything that would get him through this red tape and into Marseilles. The shouting voice of the French captain interrupted his contrivance.

"Armenian! You, Armenian! Come here quickly!"

In terror Bedros turned back to see the *Napolean's* captain. He motioned for Bedros to come to him. Bedros froze at first, and then reconsidered his fate, realizing that anything was better than facing an ice-blooded customs official who might very well send him back to the land of the dead. He moved from the line of startled refugees over to the French captain. Another naval officer stood next to the captain. He wore a fine uniform of blue with white-and-green stripes and a display of many brass buttons and silvery bands. What made him even more appealing was that he turned to Bedros and spoke, though with some foreign accent, in acceptable, delicious-sounding Armenian.

"You are an Armenian, I understand?" he asked Bedros gruffly but with a glimmer of a smile.

Bedros timidly nodded, wishing he would soon answer that question in pride rather than under the shroud of intimidation and duress.

"Good, good!" The officer brightened. "Young man, I need your help. I have a ship full of Armenians from Trebizond brought here by a British Protestant missionary group. As you can hear, my Armenian is horrendous. Most of the missionaries are having similar difficulty communicating with the frightened refugees. Can you come with me to help, please?"

"Of course, sir," Bedros responded without hesitation, though thoughts of what he might find tightened the muscles in his stomach.

"Good. Thank you. And thank you, captain." The two men saluted each other in cooperative naval fashion, and Bedros respectfully followed the impatient officer as he hurried along toward the awaiting British vessel.

"This way, please. What is your name, son?" It was a disinterested try at kindness, but Bedros understood and answered him.

"That is a strong name. It means Peter. It translates to mean 'rock.' Did you know that?""No, sir," responded Bedros. "I didn't know that. But I shall remember it."

"Good," remarked the fast-pacing officer, "because when you see the state of your poor countrymen, you will need the fortitude of a rock. I must give you fair warning."

From then on there was silence until at last they came upon the large British vessel, a mammoth ship painted a dull, blackish gray. They bounded together up the plank and onto the deck, and the captain opened the door to the galley, motioning Bedros to go down. Apparently the officer didn't intend to go below himself. He simply closed the door behind Bedros who, having reached the bottom of the stairs, began to reel in dizziness from the stench. He quickly turned around and started back up the dark stairwell to the deck but stopped when he heard the crying, moaning, and mumbled prayers of his people in the darkness below. He knew he had to face whatever was down there.

Bedros once again descended into the galley. There he found a scene that would be forever marked upon his memory. Lying under the hull of the ship, piled upon each other, slumped in corners, and huddled against cold walls were his countrymen—the fortunate ones, he morbidly reflected—the ones who had escaped with their meager lives.

The disgusting smell overcame him once again. It wouldn't let up. What was it? What mixture of deadly things could be so offensive that even a man as powerful as he became so sick? He nearly collapsed and then vomited onto the algae-stained floor.

"Please, you man, this way."

Bedros looked up to see a young woman, pale and drawn, wearing very modest, very masculine clothing. She spoke Armenian with a British accent.

"What can I do here?" begged Bedros, still faint from the odors.

"Please talk to them. Explain to them where they are and that we will help them here in France. We have hospitals. We have refuge-relief centers. Just try to calm them, take away some of their pain. We have only three missionaries in here and as you can see, there are well over two hundred Armenians strewn about this ungodly room." The woman was obviously exhausted. Red circles rimmed her swollen eyes.

"I will try. I do not know what to say. But I will try."

"Thank you," she replied in genuine gratitude and disappeared into the pathetic assortment of emaciated bodies doused in blood and urine and dried feces.

"*Aman, aman Asdvadz, asi inch eh? Inch shuni bes yem!*" An old voice was weeping. Bedros stepped down, responding to the cries of an elderly, shriveled-up woman lying just near the base of the galley steps. She grabbed his leg, and he instinctively wanted to pull away. Her sunken face and mucous-filled voice terrified him. But then, allowing himself to adjust to the hideous situation about him, Bedros softened. These were not animals, though they had been reduced to living as such. These were Armenians like him. He looked painfully with ardent torment into the shallow eyes of the ailing, frightened old woman, and he finally knelt by her side. He began to stroke the bug-infested scarf matted against her oily, wet hair.

"What is your name, woman?" Bedros asked her softly, though he wanted to scream it out—so intense was his fury over her miserable state.

"I? I have no name anymore. I am no one. My sons are dead! My daughters are stolen! I have seen my firstborn grandson slain, still in his mother's arms, right before my eyes. "She wept on and on uncontrollably until at last she stopped, more from exhaustion than from regained composure. "No, I am no one."

"Dear lady," Bedros began, not believing his own words but staunch in his attempt, "you are someone because you are here. You are alive. You are in France. The people who brought you here are English missionaries. They have the means to help you. They will make you strong so you can live here, free and safe."

She looked up at him in shocked horror as though he had just told her some hideous joke.

"Me? An old, penniless Armenian woman without a family, with no relatives? I am to live here?"

She broke into a raspy laughter, filled with choking and coughing. Bedros held her trembling head in his arms to try to allay her madness. At last, he burst into weeping as he held the woman's head in his limp arms. The two rocked together in a rhythmic medley of anguished moanings.

It seemed as though he held her for hours. Bedros found himself eyeing one by one all the people he had to help, and he didn't realize the old woman had ceased her crying. Finally, he looked down at her. In horror he released her. She fell heavy to the floor and her body made a thumping sound on the wooden planks.

He wondered for how long he had been embracing and rocking her cold body. The old woman was dead. He was able to bear the terror of the moment only by consoling himself that this unfortunate woman was far better off now than she had been only moments before.

Bedros found himself gradually hardening to the reality of this morbid experience, though the pain he felt drilling into his heart was no less intense. Like some stupefied, mindless wanderer in a graveyard, he went from one begging, sobbing, crushed body to the next—talking, dressing wounds, offering water, and changing diapers that had been worn for weeks without attention. Often, even under the most grotesque situations, he would force himself to make jokes. He assured a blind old man that he was lucky not to see the surroundings in which he lay. Then he came upon a young woman, whom five drunken bashi-bazouks had raped continually and left to die in a pile of garbage. One of the missionaries had found her weeping, naked, and huddled under filthy rags and kitchen waste.

"Once you get yourself cleaned up," laughed the handsome jester to the young girl, who looked more like an old woman, "I will take you out to dinner!"

Morning thrust itself into evening, and Bedros didn't realize the ship had grown dark and that his belly was cringing from hunger and fatigue. He had become enmeshed in these sickly surroundings. He was crazed, undauntedly going on and on, knowing that all he could do here would never be enough. It was the soft hand of the English lady who had first spoken to him that brought him back into consciousness.

"Young man, you have done more than enough here. They will sleep now, and in the morning, after our medical team comes in to assess them, they will be transferred to the city hospital. You should go home."

Bedros fought the urge to laugh sarcastically at the word 'home', but realized this kindly lady had no knowledge of his position. Still he didn't feel comfortable in leaving his people.

"I cannot go. I cannot leave them this way."

"I assure you, they will be well cared for. We will find their relatives, or if need be, we will find homes for them. That is our job."

Bedros stared into the tired, bloodshot eyes of this sharp-featured Englishwoman, who was more foreign looking than any woman he had ever seen before. She wasn't of his world, yet she was sacrificing her very life for these desperate people—his people. She deeply moved him.

"Who exactly are your people? What is your business in our trouble?" he asked her limply.

She smiled, understanding his confusion. She had often wondered herself just what prompts a missionary to carry on with these thankless, often dangerous, endeavors.

"We are missionaries from England. We are members of the Archbishop of Canterbury's Assyrian mission. There are many hundreds of us, and we have been assigned to various villages throughout Turkey. Our particular group went by ship to Trebizond several weeks ago. It had been rumored that in the early part of summer, a general edict would be coming from the Turkish government that would encourage— perhaps I should say demand—the deportation of all Armenian women and children and the total extermination of all the men."

Bedros's head fell forward in grief. He had seen it and lived through it, but the fact that these deeds were matters of edicts and proclamations was beyond even his widening realm of horror.

"How can the world let it happen? How are they getting away with this?" he sobbed, knowing this woman could give him no answer.

"You see, we are at war. Under these conditions most of the Western nations are afraid to get seriously involved. So it is up to nonpolitical groups like us to go to these towns. We try to help those stricken and get the others out before they are hurt."

"Who are these groups?" Bedros was astounded at this fascinating foreign involvement in the troubles of the Armenians.

"Mostly it is our Protestant missionaries," she answered. "There is also the American Committee for Armenian and Syrian Relief."

"Thank God for all of you!" Bedros responded, tears filling his tired eyes, his ears still ringing from the tormented chanting around him.

"We can do very little. No sooner had we pulled into Trebizond harbor, then to our chagrin the Armenians were waiting on the shore. When they saw our ship, they began jumping into the water, many with babies in their arms, wading through the cold waters to reach us. We were soon so filled that there was no need to go ashore, so we simply turned around and came back here to Marseilles. In a week or so, we will be going back to another suffering village somewhere in Turkey."

"It is madness!" Bedros shouted. "The world is inhabited by madmen! But then I see people like you, and I feel encouraged. With your help and through our own determination, they will not succeed in exterminating us. They will not!"

Bedros rose abruptly. Fire was raging in his eyes.

"No, my young friend, I think not. Not with people like you- with your courage. Your people will survive." She put a soft arm around his waist and escorted him to the steps. "Now, so that you can help them survive, you had better get on your way and start caring for yourself. We thank you." She gave him a kiss on the side of his cheek.

Bedros started up the steps wearily. He couldn't look back. The voice of the proper English lady called up to him one last time.

"By the way, young man, what is your name?"

Bedros looked down at her with a feeling of sudden freedom and a thrust of renewed self-esteem. "Rock," he said with an exhausted smile. He lifted the galley door and breathed in the cool, sweet night air of Marseilles, leaving the *Napolean* behind him.

• • •

As he walked from the ship he noticed that no one was around. The customs gates were unmanned. The Old Port was silent and sleeping, and he was free to walk from the huge, horseshoe-shaped harbor and through the steel-meshed gateways out past the ancient, looming buildings of fine, chiseled French architecture and into the nighttime streets of Marseilles. Bedros wandered around in circles and finally found himself a wooden bench away from the main thoroughfare in what was known as the popular Pharo Park. He fell instantly and fastidiously asleep.

As nighttime fell, the streets of Marseilles entertained a different population. The workers, the common people, the professors, the shopping mothers were all nestled in their respectable beds. Now, tumbling, rolling, and sneaking into the alleys, the backstreets, and the cabarets came the night people. There were the ladies, all painted and gaudy; the gamblers, bold and smartly dressed; the thieves, cunning and swift; and the tourists, precariously attempting to partake of it all yet never really grasping the inner tempo of the city as did the indigenous celebrants.

In similar manner Bedros Vartanian's dreams evolved into misty, rambling tales of now-appearing, now-fading faces. Syrvart called to him from the tiny rowboat in Bolis. He saw her face, tear stained and horror stricken, among those huddled in the foul-smelling British ship. He heard his mother, Yughaper, calling to him from afar. Malatia was burning all around her. And then Ara—he could see him fighting off gleaming, bloodstained swords; then crawling on his belly through the desert; then galloping through the streets on a mighty horse. And all the time Bedros was there, sitting on a golden throne right in the middle of the horror. Though he called, reached out to them, begged them to come to him, they didn't see him, couldn't hear him. He screamed, wanting them to know he was there, that he loved them, that he hadn't abandoned them. He jolted awake, eyes wide, sweat pouring from his head. He was breathless and grateful that it had all been a dream.

Marseilles had ignored the screaming young man crouched on the bench. She had seen so many, heard so many, that she couldn't run to their aid. One by one the tormented, the lonely, the sick—they would have to find their own way, just as this young man would have to. Bedros was aware of his aloneness in this massive city. He was astutely aware of something else, something he had never really realized before this moment. He was starving, ravenously so, and he had no money to buy food. He had left the money in his hasty escape from Constantinople. A feeling of panic seized him, but he squelched it, holding his arms tightly around his middle as he solidly rose up to meet the beautiful April morning.

He would walk, he decided—walk and walk until he found a job, a place to live, and some food. At this moment the latter was the most important. Stumbling at first, he steadied himself to meet Marseilles head on. He found his way up to a heavily populated road, which was diversified and replete with humanity, sidewalk stands, cafés, shops, and restaurants. Here, he felt sure, there would be something for him. He had come upon a fabled street, on which there was definitely something for everyone. It was the famed Canebière—the Bourbon Street of New Orleans, the Fifth Avenue of New York. The Canebière was Marseilles. From this lively avenue, the heartbeat of the city originated. From it her blood flowed. From it her reputation was indelibly stamped.

"Armenian? Excuse me, are you Armenian?" he asked the question again and again to chosen passersby. They stared at him and shrugged. He was undaunted; sooner or later he would find one, and he or she would tell him where to go and what to do.

Finally, it happened. "Excuse me, *Hye es*? Are you Armenian?"

The woman stared at him, flabbergasted at first but answering instinctively, just as birds will respond unquestioningly to distinct chirping of their own kind.

"*Ayo, deras, Hye em!*" She smiled at him, and her eyes twinkled in warmth.

"Thank God! Dear lady, please, I am new here in Marseilles. Is there an Armenian home or restaurant or hotel—somewhere I might find?"

The tiny woman with the sparkling eyes looked like an angel dropped from the clouds as she responded. "Oh, yes, my son. There is the Sebouh Hotel. It is that way," and she pointed a bent finger down the Canebière toward the south. "It is a little old, but a nice place."

"*Shonorhalgal yem, digin.*" He thanked her and started in the direction of her pointed finger.

As the lady had promised, the hotel soon appeared. Bedros blinked his weary eyes at the sight of the narrow but tall brick building with a feeble front door, above which someone had hand-painted the words:

SEBOUH HOTEL

ARMENIAN PROPRIETOR

It was a squalid-looking, old building that seemed far too narrow to be so high. But if the outside appeared morbidly dull and inferior, Bedros knew it would be warm on the inside. There would be food and comfort and companionship. For inside, there would be only Armenians.

Bedros opened the door and came upon a dark alcove with another door. Upon opening this one, an endless array of steps confronted him, leading up to yet another door. As he puffed his way up, he laughed at this typically laborious road to heaven. At last, he opened the final door and entered a dark, modestly decorated lobby. There was a long, mahogany front desk, behind which was a mail board brimming with white letters and brown packages. An old man lumbered past him and bade him good morning and then he disappeared through another doorway. The furnishings consisted of an antiquated, burgundy velveteen sofa adorned with beautifully carved ebony wood. Two stuffy and mildew-smelling, brown tapestry chairs flanked a rickety, old table, upon which a lamp of questionable origin sat. They formed a comical grouping across from the old sofa. In the center of this tiny conversation area lay a fine-looking Oriental rug, one of the things Armenians always had access to. The rest of the lobby was cold and barren with a hard wooden floor and pale-gray-painted plaster walls, but to Bedros it was a haven.

He walked up to the front desk and banged impatiently on a miniature bell. Immediately a door behind the desk opened, and a man emerged, wearing a gray flannel suit that was twice his size, a red wool shirt, and a floppy, black felt beret. He was a leathery, dark man, whose deep tan had a sallow tinge to it. He sported a moustache, which was so long and curled and heavily greased that it seemed as though it would fall from under his ample nose. His voice was deeper than anything Bedros had ever heard, and he wanted to chuckle at the sight of this amusing gentleman.

"*Pari luis, baron!*" It was the first time Bedros had been referred to as a sir. "A fine French morning, is it not?"

"Yes, it is, sir." Bedros replied.

"And what can I do for you?" The proprietor leaned over the desk and peered curiously into Bedros's gleaming eyes.

"I am Bedros Vartanian; I wish to rent a room."

"Fine, fine, Bedros. And I am Sebouh, Sebouh Kaloustian, the owner of this grand hotel." He comically waved his arms around the meager room and grinned through a mouth with many missing teeth.

"Yes, sir, but I must tell you. I am nearly out of money. I certainly don't have enough to pay you."

"No money!" Sebouh roared and slammed his fist down on the desk so hard, Bedros thought it would break. His growl reverberated through the echoing emptiness of the lobby. It wasn't until the demonic scowl on the man's face turned mischievously into a broad smile that Bedros realized the proprietor was toying with him.

"Young man"—Sebouh's voice had mellowed into a gruff whisper—"when do we Armenians ever have any money in these times? Half the people who come to me are penniless at first. I rent them their rooms, and in time I always get paid. Such is our way, right, my boy?"

"Yes, sir, such is our way." Bedros found himself immediately liking this odd but lovable man. If on the exterior he appeared disheveled, on the inside he was a wise gentleman.

"Well, now, we have room number seventeen available as well as thirty-two, eight, fifteen…"

Bedros thought he might go on all day. "Ah, seventeen will be fine, sir."

"Seventeen it is, Bedros. Here is your key." Sebouh tossed it up into the air, and it plopped down into Bedros's waiting palm.

"Thank you, sir. I shall go out to find work first thing this morning as soon as I am settled in."

"No hurry, my boy." Sebouh fluttered his two hairy hands back and forth in front of his face. He used his hands prolifically in exaggerated fashion, and it made the man enjoyable to watch.

Bedros started down the hallway leading to his room then abruptly turned back and confronted the owner again.

"Excuse me. I forgot to ask you. Are there many Armenians staying here?"

Sebouh threw his head back in jest, banging his hand against his forehead in astonishment at the question. Then he let out a grisly sound, which was his laugh.

"Many? I have one hundred rooms here. Only fifteen are empty; the rest are filled with Armenians. I do not know of an Armenian who comes to Marseilles and does not grace my hotel - except, of course, the rich ones!" And he roared at his own feeble joke.

"Then perhaps Hirair Plebian is staying here?"

"Hirair? To be sure he is here. He is a friend of yours?"

"You could say so." Bedros smiled at the inadequacy of such a word for what Hirair was to him.

"Yes? Good. Well, you can use a friend here. It takes time for these lost Armenians to warm up to each other these days. Everyone is so cautious, so nervous. But then, you cannot blame them."

"No, you cannot, Sebouh. But we will rise again. We will be the loving, crazy, laughing people we once were. I believe that."

Sebouh stared affectionately into the dancing and defiant eyes of Bedros.

"It is a good thought, Bedros. I pray you are right."

"I am right, my friend. Now can you tell me in which room Hirair is staying?"

Sebouh gave him a suspicious glare. "You are sure he is your friend?"

Bedros glared. "He is more like a brother."

He needed to say no more. Sebouh softened. "Room number seven. I remember; he said that seven was his lucky number."

Bedros laughed softly, thanked Sebouh once more, and made his way down the hallway again. But before reaching room seventeen, he would make a stop at room seven.

It was a musty-smelling corridor, painted light brown with a green rug running crookedly along it. He came to Hirair's room and peered at the difficult-to-read, faded number on the dark-green, chipped wooden door. He drew a long, excited breath and knocked.

"I'm coming!" called the voice from within as Bedros's heart leaped in recognition that it was indeed Hirair.

Impatiently, and to rile Hirair, Bedros began to pound in thunderous rapidity.

"All right, do not break the door down! I am coming!"

Hirair flung open the door with a look of anger and concern on his face. He stood frozen in disbelief for a few short minutes. Astonishment was in his eyes.

"Excuse me, *baron*, I am lost in this big place. Do you think you can tell me where room number seventeen is?" Bedros had mimicked the face of a drunk and had contorted his body into a twisted, half-bent-over position as he squinted up at the paralyzed Hirair.

"You? It is you! I do not believe my eyes!" Hirair immediately flung out his arms and impatiently pulled his friend into his room. Once again the two young men dove on top of one another, hugging and wrestling all over the tiny floor. A table fell over, and an oil lamp went crashing down. The smashing sound quickly brought them both to their feet.

They stood for several minutes, catching their breath and playfully patting each other on their broad shoulders. Finally, they looked around; accounting for what damage had been done. They tidied up the room. Bedros perused the shabby apartment.

"So this is the Sebouh Hotel," he remarked, taking in the closet-sized room with a single, uncovered bed, an ancient nightstand, a frail wooden bench, and a hole of a window with no curtains. The floor was bare, as were the walls.

"This is it," smiled Hirair, holding out his arms in mocking presentation. "It is not much, but it is home, my friend."

"Not for long, my friend," Bedros retorted.

"Now, do not start that mind rolling again with your giant schemes. Not until we have had a little drink, and you tell me everything about how you got here."

Hirair walked over to a trunk-style chest sitting under the tiny window. He opened it and fussed around inside, pulling out a few pieces of clothing and at last coming up with his find -a bottle of French cognac.

"Here it is! I bought it yesterday. I decided that clothes and food could wait for a while."

Bedros's eyes gleamed in desire at the fine golden liquid in the bottle, but a pang in his stomach warned him that he'd better tend to filling it with some solid food before celebrating with his friend.

"Hirair, you know I am the last person to deny myself a drink, but I am famished. I have not eaten since leaving the boat yesterday."

"Yesterday! Boat? What boat? Do not tell me! The *Napolean*! Why you old..." Hirair was in a hysterical fit of laughter.

"Please, please. My friend, believe me. I do not even have the strength to begin telling you everything until I get some food into me."

Hirair really looked at Bedros for the first time since their riotous reunion, his friend was pale and sallow looking. The poor man was really starving, and foolish Hirair was trying to talk him to death and pour liquor down his throat.

"I am sorry, Bedo! Here, you sit down on that fancy bed, and I will prepare something for you."

Hirair went over to a small, cast-iron, coal-burning stove. It was a miniature model, sitting on a round table and surrounded by two chairs. He bent down to retrieve a brown paper bag sitting on the floor under the table, and from it he pulled out a loaf of sourdough bread, some golden-yellow cheddar cheese, and a jar of black Greek olives. Then, from three wobbly shelves above the stove, he took down one of only two dishes and proceeded to tear apart the bread and place the cheese and olives on the dish along with the large chunks of bread. His utensils were kept in a small cabinet just next to the table. He also had a frying pan, some silverware, a porcelain pot, a coffee pot, and a large pottery urn.

"Here you are, sir," said Hirair proudly, offering his ravenous friend the plate which held the precious food. "Now I shall prepare you some eggs." Hirair was beaming like an excited child.

Bedros took a seat on the uncomfortable, ladder-back chair.

"This is the way you eat here?" asked Bedros, his mouth so brimming with food that he was barely coherent.

"This is it. Each room has its own small oven and the kitchen facilities you see."

"Are there no restaurants? Not even in the hotel itself?"

Hirair laughed. "Bedo, these people do not have the money to go to those fine restaurants along the Canebière and in the Old Port area. So it is best, I suppose, that Sebouh set up the place this way. Now, how do you want me to fix your eggs? They are fresh. I bought them at the chicken stand early this morning."

"Well, all right then. If it is not too much trouble, I will have them *vosgee*, sunny side."

Hirair prepared them quickly, comically tossing the two eggs up into the air and then down and finally presented his friend with the meal.

Bedros ate voraciously, thinking nothing had ever tasted so good to him in his entire life, though he knew his mother wouldn't have appreciated such a thought. Then he sat back, rubbing his belly from the pain of eating too quickly. It was one of his worst habits. He let his tired head fall back, and he took in a long, deep breath. He thanked Hirair and walked over to the bed. He flopped down, feeling totally at ease and at home with his dearest friend.

After cleaning up using a pitcher of water he had to bring in from a bathroom down the hall, Hirair took a seat by the bed and dearly pondered his prone friend, whose eyes were making love with the ceiling.

"What goes through that whirling mind of yours, Bedo? Can you never let yourself relax?"

"To relax is to die, Hirair. There is no relaxation for us. Not yet. First we must work, work until we ache. The time will come for relaxation. The rewards will be plentiful."

Hirair tried to get his friend out of his somber mood. It wasn't like Bedros. Today Hirair could see he was downtrodden, no doubt from exhaustion. He would let him relax and then get him to talk, to open up, to become what Hirair knew him to be.

"Well, Bedo, I hope that does not mean that while we are working ourselves to death, we cannot have a good time."

"What?" Bedros sat up stiffly on the bed. "You say that to me, Bedros Vartanian? That we cannot have a good time? We will have such good times that the ceilings will fall in, the floors will break open. People will nail the furniture into the floors when we walk into a room!"

"Is that so?" Hirair taunted him.

"That is so. God damn it! Now where is that whiskey?" Bedros impishly growled.

"Correction, Bedo. It is cognac." Hirair said the latter, adding a stuffy nasal haughtiness in his tone.

"Whiskey is whiskey, my friend. Now bring it out! Bedros is ready!"

As the lusciously warm April morning burst into maturity, illuminating Marseilles with golden-red sunbeams and the vibrant rainbow colors of frilly ladies, spring flowers, skipping children, and stumbling old men, Bedros and Hirair became slowly, deliberately, and fabulously drunk. This would not be the last of such inebriated moments between these friends.

When Bedros awoke, he found himself in his own room, laid out neatly in his scratchy, hard bed. His room was a perfect replica of Hirair's, much to Bedros's dismay. Groggily he got up. It seemed to be midafternoon, judging from the fading glare of the softened sun. He would have to go down to the corridor bath to get some water for cleaning himself up. Then somehow he had to find work. He was nearly out of money. In fact, he didn't even own any clothing but the shabby, filthy things on his back.

He looked around his bedroom and discovered a note. It was folded into a tiny square and rested on the table next to the little, black stove. Curiously he unfolded it, and his heart caught slowly on fire as he read the message scribbled upon it.

Dear Bedo,

Here are a few francs. Do not argue with me. You must accept them! It is merely a loan. You cannot find a job in those awful clothes. I expect to be immediately paid back.

Your friend,
Hirair

Bedros shook his head in earnest gratitude. He dared not argue with his friend, knowing well that if the situation were reversed, he would have done the very same thing. Taking the money, he hastened to the street to buy some clothing.

Upon his return to the hotel, he was anxious to clean himself up. He found that the hall bath wasn't too terrible. There was a pull-chain toilet, a sink, and a tub that hadn't seen a good cleaning in some time. Bedros filled the tub and lay back in the water to bathe. Finally feeling refreshed, he dressed in his new clothes and decided to face the streets and find work. It wouldn't just be a job for his own needs but something substantial enough so that he could quickly raise considerable funds. Mariam, Syrvart, Garabed, his mother and Ara—they were all waiting. He prayed they were all safe. They all depended on him. It was an awesome challenge.

As he made his confused way along the streets, which were laden with pushing, rushing people, Bedros realized he was nothing more than a refugee, a man without a country living in a land that wasn't his. He walked among the crowds, listening to the flowing French, watching all the people who knew exactly where they were going and why. And he, Bedros, this impoverished Armenian, was going to walk into some fine place and seek employment. He suddenly stopped his meandering and stood still, allowing the shoving crowd to make its way around him. He laughed loudly, not minding the ensuing stares. It occurred to him at last that he had no idea where he was going or what he would do when he got there.

At last he came upon a small restaurant. Above the stained-glass door were the words LE TARGUI, and a menu was taped to one of the multicolored panes of glass. Bedros drew close to read the dishes and realized they were familiar names. There was pilaf; there was lamb, *tebuleh*, *baklava* and there was even dolma. He opened the door and heard two of the waiters conversing. He recognized that they were speaking Arabic. It was probable that they would understand Armenian. It was worth a try.

The dining area was very small with only ten tables, each having four wrought-iron chairs. The tablecloths were plaid and very well starched. On each cloth there was a flickering candle encased in a tiny, red glass globe. The waiters—only two of them, from what he would see—wore red velvet fezzes with floppy, black tassels. They had white napkins flung over their shoulders, and they looked at him curiously as he approached them.

"Do any of you speak Armenian?" he boldly asked.

One of the waiters, after a long pause, condescended to answer him. He spoke in flawless Armenian.

"Yes. What can I do for you? I own Le Targui as well as serve tables."

"I need work very badly. I will take anything if you will give me the chance."

The tall string bean of an owner/waiter, with tawny, sunken cheeks and outlandishly large ears, turned to his partner and gave him a wary frown.

"Sir," Bedros continued, hating himself for being in the subservient position of a beggar. "I am a good, hard worker. I am not lazy, and I will gladly accept as payment anything you think fair."

His words seemed to strike a penetrating note to the lithe Arab, and he and his partner responded to each other with sly smiles.

"Very well, Armenian. You may begin right now."

Bedros was overcome with joy but held it in reserve, not daring to sublimate himself to these two men any further than he already had.

"Thank you very much," he responded coolly, thankful that they couldn't hear the thunderous pounding noises his heart was making.

"This way, Armenian." The tall man led Bedros through a door and into the kitchen.

It was a good-sized room, which reeked from the mingling smells of garlic, olive oil, and human perspiration. An obese chef was bending over a large stove, shaking his head in frustration over some sizzling concoction. He didn't look up, nor acknowledge Bedros in any way.

The owner brusquely handed Bedros a long white apron and led him to a huge, double-sided porcelain sink. There was a bucket of sponges under the sink, and piled high on a shelf above him was a pyramid of brown soap bars.

"You will be our dishwasher. There is nothing to do right now, but soon the dinner patrons will arrive, and you will have plenty to keep you busy. Wash in this side of the sink, rinse in the other. Put the clean dishes over there."

He pointed a bobbing finger toward a long, metal counter a few feet from the sink. Then he patted Bedros sharply on the back and sped away. Bedros looked over at the fat cook for some sign of comradeship, but seeing the old fool dripping with sweat and frantically juggling himself between stove and icebox, he thought better of it. He also thought better of staying there at all but decided to at least give the job a chance.

Within a half hour, Bedros found himself in a battlefield, he being the enemy—he the target of so many flying dishes, catapulting spoons, rocketing forks, and bombarding pots and pans. His hands couldn't move quickly enough to clear the sink before it was refilled with greasy, food-encrusted platters. On and on it went—dishes going from the soapy water to the clean, then drying everything with thin towels, then rushing them over to the long metal counter, then rushing back to find another overflowing sink full of work.

He labored twelve hours, well into the early morning. At last it was over. His face was beet red, his hair a wet mass plastered to his aching head. He was exhausted. His feet throbbed from the long hours standing on the concrete floor. He turned around to see how the round chef had fared through the grueling night and found he was gone. Slowly, he lumbered into the dining room to find that the two Arabs had gone as well. The restaurant was empty.

As he made his way to the door, he found a note, tied to a string and hanging like a condemned man from the doorknob. On the envelope was written the word "Armenian." Hastily Bedros tore open the small, white parcel and read the sloppily written note.

Armenian,
    Here are your day's wages. You did a fine job, the best dishwasher I have ever employed. Report tomorrow night at dusk.

Tucked into the envelope, were three meager francs.

Humiliated, infuriated, exhausted, Bedros made his weary way back to the Sebouh Hotel. If he had the strength and if at that moment he should encounter the hateful Arab, he would have left him crushed on the sidewalk, his blood rushing down the gutters into the sewers. If he had the strength and if he had the knowledge of French, he would have bought a newspaper from the blind boy who held it out to him with pleading arms. If he had read it, he would have seen a front-page picture showing emaciated children squatting in nakedness, looking like human skeletons. And if he could have understood it, the caption would have said, "Armenians Slaughtered, Maimed and Tortured En Masse in Turkey."

It was nearly dawn by the time he closed his burning eyes. His thoughts tottered, sizzled, pulsated about in his head. He was too tired even to talk to his God. He was afraid of what he might say. Wondering how much food he could buy with three francs. Wishing he didn't have to cook his own breakfast on the ridiculous, little stove. Wishing there was a restaurant right there in the Sebouh Hotel. Wishing, wondering, dreaming, tossing, and twisting. During the short sleep, half-dreaming, half-scheming, Bedros Vartanian got an idea. A good one. And he couldn't wait to begin.

He ran down to Hirair's room, banging wildly on his door. Hirair, just awakening, was somewhat angry but immediately complied with his frantic friend's request for a fresh cup of coffee and some conversation. He prepared the coffee and some flaky croissants and watched Bedros pace around the room like a caged animal. The young man was pulsating as if his whole body might suddenly explode. It was no use asking him to calm down. Hirair knew Bedros well enough to see that he had come up with something wondrous, and he wouldn't rest until it was undertaken.

Hirair finally persuaded Bedros to sit down and enjoy his coffee and croissant. The two friends sat across from each other, and silent stares were tossed back and forth across the tiny wooden table. The sounds of gulped coffee and munching pastries were the only conversation between them. At last Hirair could bear it no more.

"All right, now what is it? What is whirling around in that head of yours, Bedo?" He frowned.

Bedros didn't immediately answer; he just gazed a long, pensive stare out the window. And then, as though suddenly revived, he turned abruptly to confront his patiently waiting friend and pounded on the feeble table, shaking the cups, spilling the too-strong coffee.

"Hirair!" Bedros's face was aglow. His eyes radiated an almost supernatural power. "We, my friend, are going to open a restaurant!"

Hirair knew better than to laugh, though it was his first instinct. But the eyes of Bedros couldn't be denied. His friend was indefinably serious, and Hirair decided he had better sit back and listen.

"All right, we are opening a restaurant. And may I ask how you propose to do that with no money, no connections?"

"Hirair, if the imbecile I worked for last night could make a go of something like that, just think what two great minds like yours and mine can do."

"Bedo, I am not questioning the minds or the desire. I am questioning the money!" Hirair snickered sarcastically.

"You are just like my brother, Ara. You think too much. You worry too much instead of doing too much." With that Bedros picked himself up, ordered Hirair not to move, and sped out the door. The room still resounded with the echoes of his booming voice, and Hirair obediently waited for his companion to return.

In a few minutes the door to Hirair's bedroom flew open, and there stood the broadly smiling Bedros holding on to the proprietor, Sebouh, as though he were a large fish he had just caught and wasn't about to release.

"Your friend here is a little crazy, I think, Hirair! He comes down to the desk, grabs me like this, and drags me up the hall, babbling something about opening a restaurant."

Sebouh looked like he had slept the night in yesterday's suit. His floppy beret was still sitting on his unwashed mop of hair. Scanty prickles appeared all over his face in accompaniment to his bountiful moustache.

"Take it from me. Sebouh, you had better let him tell you what he has in mind, or you will not sleep very well. My friend does not dissuade easily."

Bedros lugged the cumbersome Sebouh into the room and set him down across from Hirair, who immediately rose to prepare fresh coffee and set out more of the croissants. But Bedros put his heavy hand on Hirair's shoulder and gently shoved him down in his chair.

"Not now, no food now. This is business. Serious business. We eat after we produce!"

Hirair sat like a trained puppy, and Sebouh held his chin up with a dirty hand crowned with even dirtier fingernails. A look of boredom was plastered all over his face, and he shook his head over the folly of this whole meeting.

"All right, Bedros, get on with it," he grumbled.

"I will, my friend. And you better wipe that look off your face, because what I propose will not only make money for me and my friend here, but it will make you famous as well."

Sebouh liked that and swapped a foolish grin for his disinterested scowl.

"Now, listen to me. This hotel of yours sorely inadequate!" Sebouh was overcome with anger. Bedros continued. "I am sorry, but it is true."

"You can always find some other place to stay," said the now sad looking owner.

"Come now, Sebouh. I am not talking about the rooms." Bedros softened. "Actually you have done very well here, all things considered. But your biggest mistake was these silly coal-burning stoves in the bedrooms."

"What? And how else do you suggest my patrons eat?" Sebouh replied.

"Exactly my point, Sebouh. Let them eat in the Sebouh Hotel's own restaurant!"

Sebouh and Hirair shared dumbfounded stares as Bedros went rapidly on.

"First of all, it is dangerous to allow cooking in a bedroom. Imagine what could happen! *Asdvadz*, I am surprised nothing has happened yet."

Sebouh slid slightly down in his chair with a guilty look on his face, which suggested to the two young men that perhaps some fires had already occurred, but neither of them pursued the issue.

"Now," Sebouh asked, trying to change this uncomfortable subject, "how do we go about this? With whose money, or need I ask?"

"Listen, Sebouh." Bedros smiled, knowing the proprietor felt he was about to be drawn into an unwanted partnership. "You will need very little money!"

This brought a unanimous roar of disbelief from both Sebouh and Hirair, who considered that this overconfident optimist had gone a bit too far.

"No, I am serious," Bedros Vartanian went on, undaunted, assured, not letting anyone, anything deter him. "Look, you have one hundred stoves here now. They are in good condition. Fairly new, I suppose?" Sebouh nodded affirmatively, but Bedros took no notice. "So, you sell them and in return buy yourself one very large, oven, a good-sized ice-box, and a large sink. Surely you have space for a kitchen."

"Just like that?" retorted Sebouh.

"Yes, just like that. Surely one hundred ovens will more than pay for these other items and some food. Even if you have to dip into your precious wallet, my friend, you will be reimbursed the very first day. I promise you!" Bedros spoke with confidence. He excelled in salesmanship.

"You are very sure of yourself, Bedo," Hirair said cautiously.

"Sure? Of course I am sure. Where else are these Armenians going to eat? The prices will be modest. The food will be home-cooked Armenian style. We cannot lose."

There were a few minutes of awkward silence. Bedros paced the room furiously, not waiting for a response. "All right, so we begin. Sebouh, sell the stoves, and acquire your supplies. We must do this quickly. You must rush. I will get my recipes straight in my memory. Yes, that is right. I will be your chef. And you Hirair, you will help serve, prepare, purchase." His exuberance was effectively contagious.

They all laughed together now, finally agreeable, finally convinced they couldn't go wrong with this wheeling, dealing entrepreneur in their midst. They decided to forego the coffee and seal their pact with a stronger beverage, which Sebouh volunteered to quickly procure. And so, in the tiny bedroom, over a fine bottle of bourbon, three heads bent low over a small table began what was to become the Sebouh Hotel

Restaurant. In ten days the restaurant opened in the formerly barren lobby of the hotel. Bedros and Hirair spent each day preparing the food in the makeshift kitchen, which was hidden behind a wooden, folding screen. Breakfasts were a simple, offering of eggs, fresh bakery items, coffee, and cheeses. Lunch was usually light platters consisting of cold meats and leftovers from the evening before. Clientele at both of these times was spare but enough to require modest labors. The guests generally sat on the lobby furniture or the two sets of tables and chairs Sebouh had purchased.

It was in the evening that the brilliant, magnetic Bedros Vartanian truly excelled. He prepared mounds of buttery, soft pilaf in giant pots. There were shish kebab, fresh vegetables, and fine Armenian desserts such as *baklava* and *bourma*. Bedros made mistakes at first and his dishes were prepared rather amateurishly, but it didn't take him long to prove himself to be not only an acute businessman but also a splendidly talented cook. The food and the clientele increased in quality and quantity.

The reputation of the Sebouh Hotel Restaurant spread. Soon it catered not just to the patrons of the hotel but also to non-Armenians. It was the latter that seemed to appreciate the luscious, painstakingly prepared cuisine. The menu expanded to include the more difficult dishes such as *kufta*, dolmas, and *media-* a delectable appetizer Bedros created using the abundant mussels from the waterfront. Daily routines soon became a well-oiled procedure that produced fast, delicious foods to hundreds of appreciative, knowledgeable patrons.

In six months Bedros, Hirair, and Sebouh enjoyed abundant profits. The restaurant was a wondrous success. To Sebouh, even Hirair, it all might have been the beginning of a lucrative future, but to Bedros it was only an end to a beginning. It had served its purpose. What Hirair might have wanted to do from that point on would have to be his decision. If Sebouh wished to continue on in the profitable business, for which Bedros's mastery alone was responsible, well, that too wouldn't bother him. None of it mattered to Bedros. His money was made. His course was predetermined.

He quickly wrote two letters, one to Ara, whom he prayed would receive it in the safety of the binbashi's home, and the other to Garabed, whom he earnestly hoped had also fared well through the terror of the times. In each letter he sent enough money to ensure a trip from Constantinople to America for all of them. Bedros smiled sadly as he sealed the two envelopes. He thought to himself how ironic life was that the six months of cooking Armenian foods to people who delighted in it should allow him the money to save his family and friends from a world that would have happily exterminated them.

Bedros impatiently waited to hear from his brother and Garabed. He couldn't consider his own exodus until he knew for certain that they had received the money and were getting out of Constantinople immediately. At last a letter arrived. Bedros felt like he had waited a lifetime.

October 11, 1916

My dearest brother,

I rushed to write to you immediately. Your precious letter just arrived, and my eyes couldn't believe the money you sent. You must have performed some great robbery over there! But I do not care; you can tell me everything when we meet in America.

Binbashi Ismael has been absolutely wonderful to Mother and me. Both he and his daughter are beside themselves trying to make us comfortable. It is as though by their kindness they are trying to make up for all the hideous things their countrymen have done to our people. I believe in my heart also that they hoped my letter to you would convince you to return here.

The latest reports say that half of our three million people are dead. The old towns, like Malatia and Sivas, have been flattened, burned. Many of our surviving children have been taken into Turkish homes and converted to Islam. There have been many missionaries trying to help, and the Red Cross is still trying to find homes for all the refugees. The hospitals are filled with our battered and dying. There is nothing left here for any of us! And so, within a week, we shall gather ourselves together and leave for America.

I am sure that you will arrive there before us, so please let us know where we can find you. Would it not be horrible to lose each other in that huge country after all we have been through? I pray that does not happen.

Garabed, by the way, has asked me to write to you and tell you he received the money and is most grateful. He says that Syrvart and Mariam are doing well but living them has been unbearable since all they do is talk about you and how they miss you. How he must hate that! He says they will leave for America very soon.

Mother is fine, growing stronger and more optimistic every day with thoughts of America. Praise God there have been no incidents with the Turks for us here in Bolis.

Enough writing. It is time to start packing. I cannot wait to see you! Can you believe in a short while we will all be together again? That will be some reunion, will it not, my dear brother?

With all my heart,
Ara

It was all Bedros needed—the letter, the hope, the words that meant it had all not been in vain. It meant that his God had not forsaken him. It meant that in free conscience he could now leave Marseilles and go on to the land where he would make his home, the land that had been waiting for him since the days he had been introduced to her, back during the dreary afternoons at his desk in the orphanage. Even if the road from Armenia was paved with blood and bones and bodies, he believed the roads in America had to be paved with gold and along the way, he could bend down and pick up the golden pieces one by one.

The next day Bedros Vartanian was on an American tanker leaving Marseilles harbor. It wouldn't be a luxurious journey. No pleasure cruise was this. He would sleep on the floor of the hull. He would eat on the deck and find comfort wherever he could. The journey would take over two weeks across an unfriendly ocean with waves that would toss the mighty ship about like a child's toy. And through it all, he didn't care, felt no pain, knew no discomfort. It was the most wondrous, revitalizing ride of his life. With each diving and dipping mile, Bedros grew a little more alive and a little more determined. And to add to his bursting joy and unabashed excitement, there was one thing more, something that made the difficult journey warm in the cold, smooth in the roughness, swift during the delays. For by his side, as it seemed he had always been, there he was—the little, lost boy he had met at Saint Mary's, the friend he called Hirair.

One by one other ships would come - not only from France and Turkey but from all over the world. They brought the hungry, the sick, the poor, and the oppressed. In massive deluges they would come, all with one desire, one lifelong vision—to live in peace and prosperity in the promised paradise that was called America.

Chapter 7
AMERICA 1916

October was rapidly approaching its end as the ship drew close to the reprieving shores of America. For almost their entire journey the travelers had enjoyed summerlike weather, with only the wet, cold nights and the chilling sea air to remind them that winter was soon to arrive. But then, wearing her windswept cloak of frosty white and a sweeping crystalline silver gown, the shimmering, blustering, merciless ice lady arrived; and overnight it was winter.

The refugees huddled together by a makeshift fire in the hull of the ship, where they spent most of their days and nights. Talk was rapid. Teeth chattered. The vessel tossed them about relentlessly, and many became violently ill. Some contracted pneumonia. Others died. Yet the travelers bore it all. There were joyous smiles on their faces and songs from their mouths. For this journey—unlike the others in their varied, mostly pathetic lives—would have a glorious ending. And it would promise them all a new beginning.

Much of their time was spent telling one another where they would be residing and what their aspirations would be once they were settled in the Promised Land of the free. Often the ship would become a floating classroom as they would try to help one another with the difficult English language. The words came out in thick, adulterated garble most of the time. But they tried, practiced, and wouldn't be embarrassed as they forced themselves to learn the words they would soon need in a foreign land.

It was during one such English session that a tumultuous roar suddenly sounded from above. So thunderous was the noise that the deck timbers shuddered from the resonance. And from the reverberating ceiling above them, the Armenians could hear roars and shouts and the sounds of stomping feet. Bedros looked up, concerned, for it seemed as though the entire ceiling was going to crash down on them.

"What is going on up there?" Bedros shouted, jumping up with the others and craning his head upward.

Simultaneously they all bounded up the steps, not bothering to conjecture the answer to Bedros's question. When they reached the deck, the wind nearly blew them from their places, and the sky was black with threatening clouds gathering like so many billowing pillows, about to burst open and shed their feathers all over humanity. But more fascinating than the ominous weather or the pitch and roll of the ship was the cluster of passengers huddled together on the slick deck—some leaning over the railing, all pointing and jumping and screaming in jubilant unison. Bedros and Hirair looked at each other in astonishment, wondering what the ecstatic passengers were seeing. Curiously they pushed their way to the bow rails and peered out into the heavy mist.

It didn't take long to know why such hysterical exuberance had overcome these fellow travelers. In an instant, when they caught sight of her, the hearts of Bedros and Hirair leaped in acrobatic folly, flipping and spinning and somersaulting high up into the air and finally flopping back solidly into their respective bodies. For there—faintly through the fog, tall and stately, long and lean, stood the elegant, bronze lady holding her torch of freedom high into the air. And though they had read about her, been told about her, and seen pictures of her, they still couldn't believe how magnificent and wondrous she really was. In all their lives, none of them had ever seen any sight so majestic and so mighty!

She was like a mother beckoning to her lost children. She was like the Virgin, placating the fears of a young girl in her evening prayers. She was like Juno—assured, authoritative, austere in her queen's stance, holding her hand high in her own self-esteem, gloating in the adoration of her subjects.

New York and New Jersey claimed her, but neither was right. For all of America and her thousands of emerging children owned the Lady of Liberty. They were arriving every day, seeking the security of her bosom—children like those now dancing and hugging and crying on the bow of the freighter, children like Bedros and his friend.

When the frenzy finally subsided, the voyagers settled into a peaceful apprehension. Their minds wandered, fleeting like the passing gulls. Their worries dove down to the deepest depths of the ocean. Their hopes flew high into the sky like the puffing vapors of the great ship. One by one they gathered their few belongings, wiped their brows, rechecked tiny, crumpled notes with addresses of relatives and friends they had never seen in a country they had never known.

The ship finally docked. The passengers disembarked, parading like awestruck, wide-eyed ring bearers as they made their way down aisles and through gates into the mayhem that was Ellis Island.

Bedros couldn't speak. He was overcome with a euphoric joy while taking his first step onto the ground that was America. He felt his toes tingle and his feet wiggle in a sort of electrifying tremor when his holey and torn shoes first landed on the concrete platform under the exit ramp of the ship. Hirair grabbed Bedros's arm and squeezed it in fright and fascination. They looked around them, looked at each other, and laughed at the tears flowing shamelessly from one another's blushing cheeks. Their bodies shook; their skin turned into a veritable mass of bumpy, little pimples. A surging warmth—as though they had each been injected with a needle filled with liquid fire—flooded in torrents through their pulsating veins.

"You know," Bedros reflected to his friend, still crying without reserve, "this must be what it feels like to be born."

Hirair didn't answer. He felt faint. At this moment, in this experiencing of unabashed joy and ecstasy, he knew that his life had finally, truly begun. He knew that at last the pain was over. The horror had been left behind, buried forever where it rightfully belonged. He would never look back.

"Well," Bedros said, shaking him gently, "let us not stand here crying all day. We have work to do. Come, let us get in line."

There were many gates, each handling lines of thirty to fifty waiting immigrants. The people awaiting entry were as varied as the stars, as colorful as the floating leaves of autumn, as overwhelmed as adolescents attending their first dance. There were pregnant women in thin cotton dresses, flimsy sweaters, and open-toed sandals, shivering from the cold. There were bent-over, indelibly wrinkled old men making their shaky way through the slowly moving lines. There were elderly women with leathery, brownish skin, their heads wrapped in plaid babushkas. And there were the children, less enraptured than their parents, taking for granted that they were there, assured that their mothers and fathers wouldn't have led them astray, unaware of the price that had been paid to get them there and the prices yet to come.

Hirair pulled a neatly folded note from his pocket. Bedros looked down at it also, making sure he remembered the address.

Dikran and Anahid Azarian
Vine Street
Philadelphia, Pennsylvania. U.S.A.

Neither Bedros nor Hirair knew this family. They had simply heard through the network of well-connected Armenians that they existed and had an attic apartment for rent in Philadelphia.

Bedros took out another note. It was a list of several other Armenians in Philadelphia, who likewise offered tiny attics, small garages, and meager rooms for rent. If one didn't have a vacancy, certainly another would. They were all Armenians, sacredly but silently sworn to help each other—to feed, clothe, employ when they could, and enjoy each other in this new country. They couldn't allow the serpent of assimilation to swallow them up.

Bedros and Hirair each took out one American dollar from their pockets. They had already exchanged currency at the Old Port in Marseilles. They had heard that if they gave one dollar to the man at the gate, the kindly American would provide them with a bag of goods worth thirty times that amount.

When the two young Armenians came closer to the gate, they discovered that what they had heard was true. They could see ahead of them the grateful people offering their modest dollar bills one by one and walking off with huge burlap bags filled with clothes and canned goods. Finally Bedros and Hirair came up to the gate. Bedros was first. He eyed the uniformed customs worker with cautious impatience and a thumping, jubilant heart.

"Name?" asked the impersonal gate attendant, not looking up.

"Peter Vartanian." It was the first time he used his American name and he shouted it out proudly at the expressionless man, who wasn't the least bit impressed.

"Destination?" the cold man questioned.

"Destination?" Bedros stammered now, embarrassed by his lack of understanding of this new language.

"Where are you going?" the official gruffly explained.

"Where? Well, me and my friend here..." He turned around and pointed proudly at Hirair, who was watching the annoyed man behind the gate and Bedros's deliberate delay of the tedious entry procedure. "Ah, his name is Harvey, we both going to Philadelphia".

Hirair nodded, desperately trying to hold back his swelling laughter.

"All right, all right. Now, may I have one dollar?" Surprisingly, the officer smiled faintly.

"Here is your one dollar, my friend." Bedros gleamed and handed the crinkled green bill over.

So went the exchange. Bedros was handed a bulging bag and told to walk over to gate number five. There he would receive a medical examination. Then he would go to the rear gates, where a huge ferry waited to take the aliens across the Hudson and over to the wagons, on which they would be transported to the train station.

Similarly Hirair passed through the gateway and joined his companion. They were pressed together in a large group of people—all from different countries; all frightened and confused; all clutching tiny pieces of paper on which various addresses had been written. They carried little else except the bulging burlap bag. One by one they were led into a small room, where their teeth and hair and skin were hastily examined.

Then they boarded a ferry, which floated them over the Hudson River to a procession of waiting wagons.

Huddled in small groups they then awaited directions. At last a bony, cadaverous-looking man, whose age was anyone's guess, ordered Bedros's group into one of the wagons as though he were corralling a group of cattle. The driver had a habit of shaking his head in disgust at everyone around him, and Bedros wondered why he had taken such a job if he found these poor immigrants so distasteful. Looking more closely at the man he noticed half of his teeth were missing. His thinning hair was dyed a false-looking, reddish-brown hue; and his eyes were watery and bloodshot. Bedros decided that the contents of the wagon were far superior to the driver.

Fortunately Bedros didn't have to look at this miserable man for long, because the ride was a short one. At the train station, another immigrations man checked their names and notes and directed them to the proper trains. A few of the fortunate ones had relatives and friends waiting. But Bedros and Hirair walked on alone until finally reaching the correct platform, which read PHILADELPHIA—DEPARTURES.

Obligingly the train was punctual. The doors slid open in welcome to the young Armenians. Hirair and Bedros were delighted to spy a double unoccupied seat, to which they quickly flew. Then for two and a half hours, while most of the exhausted travelers slept, Bedros, in his uncontained joy, continually sang. The rolling of the wheels on the tracks provided the rhythm, melodies from old Armenian songs provided the tune, and the hilarious Bedros Vartanian with his assistant made up the rest in makeshift, laughable English.

Here we go, here we go, you and me, you can see.
Here we go, America she is waiting.
She is waiting for you and me.
Don't you worry, don't you hurry.
She will not go away, and I know and you know and she know
That we are here to stay.
Dingle, dingle, dingle, ding, dingle, ding, ding...

They jumped up and stomped their feet, snapping their fingers, clapping their hands, and prancing up and down the aisles, dancing to the beat of their own singing. A few others joined them, feebly attempting the comically distorted English. Some clapped, tapped their feet, and hummed along. Others simply sat back, unaffected by the celebration, still fearful of their futures in this massive country. They shook their heads in disapproval that these dancers and singers took this serious venture with such naïve levity.

The train made several stops along the way until finally the relentlessly swooshing wheels came to a slowly screeching halt. An attendant entered the stopped car and announced to the travelers that they had arrived in Philadelphia. There were spontaneous cheers, pats on the back, handshakes, and hugs. Then the momentarily melodious comrades left the puffing train, all going in different directions, never to see one another again.

Philadelphia awaited Bedros and Hirair with her gas lights burning, twinkling in anticipation of dusk. Her carriages tottered here and there along the streets, their wheels clattering in rhythmic tinkling on the cobblestones. Now and then—to the utter disbelief of the immigrants—there would pass a new wonder of modern man, the horseless carriage. The statue of William Penn, though far less looming than the gigantic Statue of Liberty, was cordial in bidding welcome to his guests. He stood formidably atop the intricately carved City Hall, around which a circle of merry-go-round travelers transpired continually. Philadelphia was an incredible carousel of lights and sounds.

Bedros and Hirair stood gawking at the bustling, modern city. They held nothing but their bags and the little note with the address on it. As in Constantinople, there were horse-drawn trolleys everywhere, forming the main network of transportation throughout the city. Bedros asked directions from passersby. Finally they found the right spot to stand. At last a trolley came along and stopped in front of them. The words VINE STREET were bannered on its side windows.

The Azarian house was like a thousand other row houses in Philadelphia. It was made of brick. It had a living room, which led into a dining room, which led into a kitchen. It was two stories with three bedrooms and one bath. There was an attic apartment.

The Azarians were a simple, childless couple. They had no relatives to complicate their lives, and it was obvious they liked it that way. A round-faced, white-haired woman warily bade Bedros and Hirair welcome. Her husband was still at work at his grocery store. She would have offered them food, but she hadn't yet shopped. The two young friends expected more hospitality from this Armenian lady but conceded that all their women couldn't be like Yughaper and Mariam. They asked to see the apartment for rent.

Mrs. Azarian led them outside to the black, iron fire escape steps. The steps led up to a side door, which was the only entrance. The attic apartment was extremely tiny. There was a worn Oriental carpet on the cracked wood floor; a double bed with a decrepit, old coverlet; a tiny round window; and a potbelly stove. There was an ancient china closet sitting diagonally in a corner. It held a few kitchen articles. Fortunately there was a small, enclosed bathroom with toilet, sink, and tub. The attic was modest, to say the least. But it was warm and comfortable in its minute way and a most welcome abode to the two tired, disoriented men. Most important of all—its owners were Armenians.

After Mrs. Azarian left, Bedros and Hirair unpacked what little belongings they had and placed them in a closet, which wasn't more than two feet wide. They would have to buy a trunk for storage. There were clean sheets on the bed, but the icebox was empty. It was essential that they get some food and of course a bottle with which to celebrate. There would be plenty of time after that to make their plans for the future.

Vine Street was just a few blocks from Broad Street. They decided to walk in that direction. Broad Street was a gigantic thoroughfare that stretched from north to south, covering the entire city. The two immigrants had their pick of bars, shops, and restaurants, though in their particular proximity they were not of the finest caliber. At least most offered decent food, good liquor, and reasonable prices.

They stopped in a small restaurant simply called Joe's Bar. It was a long, very narrow place, but it had booths and warm decor. They enjoyed two scotch and waters and something delightful called a hamburger. They gulped and munched in agreement that everything tasted delicious. The scotch felt so warm and smooth that they decided to have two more. Bellies full. Properly fueled. Now they were ready to begin their lives as Americans.

Back in their room, the young men felt superior of soul and superlative of spirit. They had purchased some food, which they placed in the small icebox, which was crowded in a corner of the room. Next to it was a Formica-and-chrome table with three matching but peeling pink vinyl chairs. Two bottles of scotch and one of bourbon were placed under the bed. They decided they would have just one more drink, some talk, and some sleep.

They crouched together on the floor next to the stove and ceremoniously opened the bourbon. The bottle was passed back and forth along with the conversation. It was a comfortable pleasure to speak in their mother tongue once again.

"The lady said her husband had a grocery store, did she not, Hirair?" Bedros's words were beginning to slur slightly.

"I think so, Pete."

Bedros looked at Hirair, amused at the sound of his Americanized name. His thick eyebrows rose comically high, nearly touching his thick, slick, black hair.

"Yes. Pete. That is what I will call you from now on. It sounds very American. After all, you called me Harvey at Ellis Island." Hirair gently closed his eyes as though he were in a dream. He still couldn't believe he was here.

"So be it. From now on you are Harvey. Oh yes, very American. We are both very American." Bedros simulated sophistication in his tone.

They shared a good laugh together—these two foreign young men with their felt berets, baggy pants, French cardigans, and worn flannel shirts. They laughed and talked about the past. They dreamed about the future. Their heads bobbed up and down in drunkenness. Their eyes fluttered open and shut, on and off, with the slowly incoherent discussion. At last, Hirair's head fell heavily down to his chest, and Bedros roared in delight.

"You are some big drinker, old friend!" With that Hirair's head bobbed up. His eyes, though, remained shut. "Come, let us get some sleep. Tomorrow we will find work."

The morning sun spotlighted through the small attic window and landed warmly on the closed eyes of the two young men. It was persistent, and though they wished it to go away, it wouldn't. Soon they had no choice but to obey its beaming call. They woke up slowly with much difficulty. Their heads were pounding from the evening before. They took turns in the bathroom. Hirair prepared breakfast except for the coffee. Bedros insisted on making it after several disappointing encounters with Hirair's black brew back in Marseilles.

"Today, we go to find Azarian's grocery store. It is a good way to start. I am sure he will give us work." Bedros's deep, black eyes were not opened to their usual round fullness yet, but the brightness shone through with no less vigor and intensity. He was energetic and optimistic.

"Well, we can at least try. I hope he is more receptive to us than his wife was." Hirair sounded lethargic and reserved.

They went downstairs to the entrance of the Azarian home. Bedros rang the bell and Mrs. Azarian opened the door cautiously. She peered through a golden chain lock but wouldn't open it all the way, even though she recognized Bedros.

"Excuse me, digin. We just wanted to know where your husband's grocery is. We thought he could help us with work," Bedros requested.

She thought for a moment, as if unsure whether to tell him. Then she looked into his magnetic eyes. She directed him to Dikran's Grocery, which was just a few blocks away, going north on Broad Street.

It was a small store with large glass windows displaying toilet paper and soap suds. Taped all over the glass in scattered array were posters announcing specials in this and reductions on that. Hirair and Bedros could make out only a few of the words. They boldly entered the store.

Dikran was behind the counter neatly arranging some matchbooks in a small cardboard box by his register. He looked up curiously at the two men lumbering in, wearing their shabby clothing. Bedros didn't give him a chance to question their identity. He pranced right up to him.

His face was aglow. He politely slipped off his hat and bombarded him with a blustering, "*Pari luis*—good morning."

"*Luis pari*," the elderly but healthy-looking man responded, grateful that his patrons were fellow Armenians. It was always easier, more comfortable to speak Armenian even for those like Dikran who spoke English fairly well. "May I help you, gentlemen?"

Bedros—always the spokesman—introduced himself and Hirair, and explained that they were his new tenants. The owner was delighted, coming out from behind his counter and hugging both of them fondly. "Wonderful! Well, welcome to America, to Philadelphia! What do you think of it?"

Bedros and Hirair looked at each other, flashing embarrassed glances and shrugging their shoulders. How did one answer such a question? How could either of them explain their feelings about at last arriving in America, about beginning a new, unencumbered life? How did one describe how they felt about being alive? It was impossible to explain. Dikran laughed warmly, remembering how he had felt after fleeing Turkey only a few years before.

"Never mind, you do not have to answer that. I think I know how you both feel." He grinned through a scattering of decayed teeth.

"Well," Bedros said, smiling smartly, "we both would feel better if we could find some work—and quickly." So saying, Bedros flashed his alluring, mesmerizing gaze upon Dikran, who melted instantly but then reversely pondered the two of them with a worried frown.

"Surely, I can use help here. But I am afraid in this tiny place, I could really only afford one of you. Not to mention, all of us would not fit very well in so crowded an area." He frowned, embarrassed.

Hirair's heart dropped. It was the first blow in this new land. He wondered how many more disappointments there would be until they were at last secure, settled, and in control—instead of on the bottom looking up. But Bedros turned to him instantly, displaying a wide grin. Then he turned back to the old man.

"Well then, here is your man!" Bedros cheerfully announced, pointing to an astonished Hirair. "He is well suited to this kind of work. One thing Hirair knows about is food."

"Oh, no. You are not going to do this, Bedo." Hirair was overcome but determined that he wouldn't allow Bedros to sacrifice this job for him.

Bedros didn't give him the chance to continue. He interrupted vehemently and spoke heartily, grabbing his friend tightly by the shoulders and pulling him into the limpid pools that were his eyes. "Look, Hirair, sooner or later we knew we would have to go our separate ways. We live together. That is enough. We cannot hold each other's hands forever. It is a big city. There is work enough for both of us!"

"I will not," Hirair blubbered foolishly.

"You will! Besides, I would gain too much weight surrounded by all this food. You have much more willpower than I when it comes to eating."

Bedros's strong, tan face was radiant. He was self-assured and determined. He wasn't assuming the role of martyr but rather of a leader, one who could take all that life threw out, grab it securely in both of his mighty hands, then sort it out perfectly and precisely in its proper perspective. Hirair knew there was no arguing with him.

"All right, I will give it a try." Hirair was fighting a lump in his throat, which made him feel weak and helplessly grateful.

"Good. Now let me be on my way. We will see each other at dinner." Bedros was already at the door.

Hirair called out, "Thank you," but Bedros was gone.

In a way, Bedros was glad it had happened. He had worried for a long time that he and Hirair were becoming too dependent on each other. He had thought that sooner or later familiarity might breed ill feelings, jealously, or mistrust. It was better this way. And besides, in his heart- though he would never have said it- Bedros worried that Hirair would become a burden, a hindrance to his quest for dominance of this new world. Now Bedros was totally free, a master of his own future. He basked in the liberated feeling as he wandered about Broad Street. For some reason he headed south and wandered toward the river, his nostrils hitching a ride with the alluring aromas of the waterfront, his eager body was following obediently behind. It was as good a place as any to start.

He walked several miles along Delaware Avenue. He stopped into various factories along the way. Most of the time gruff foremen or matronly women behind desks shook their heads, waving their arms like trained robots, assuring him there was no work. It seemed to him that they went into these negative gestures automatically upon sight of him—any immigrant—not allowing them the chance to open their mouths or show their worth.

Though such was totally against his nature, he was beginning to feel dejected—a victim of social prejudice. He looked questioningly up to the clear sky, asking his God how he was expected to achieve any kind of success in this land of opportunity, which was offering no opportunity at all. It was a short prayer, a genuinely reasonable request. And when he looked down from the clouds, he saw a huge, rusty-red brick building with hundreds of black-trimmed, lead windows, upon which was painted in thick black lettering - PENNSYLVANIA SUGAR COMPANY. He glanced back up into the heavens and thanked God. He walked defiantly through the large, garage-type door; assured that here he would be hired.

A skinny, blanched woman with a long, pointed nose peered snobbishly out from her thick, black glasses. Her nostrils dilated, and her mouth pursed as she curtly asked the young Armenian, "Yes, may I help you?"

Bedros wouldn't be denied. "Yes, ma'am. I am looking for a job."

"I see," she sang out through puckered lips. "I am sorry, but we are not hiring at the moment."

Something seized him. A demon lunged inside him, reaching out through his eyes and manifesting itself in his seething glare. So intense and filled with hatred was his look that the stuffy woman froze for a moment, paralyzed by his stare.

"I have been walking all day to find work. This is supposed to be a country that helps all men, but I am getting no help from anybody here." He was livid, leaning over onto the frightened woman's desk. "What kind of people are you?" His eyes began dueling with hers in avid fury.

She looked around uncomfortably, seeking assistance, but the other office workers pretended not to see, snickering under their breaths. The miserable matron had a remarkable way of scaring away all the poor aliens who came to her again and again, seeking employment, receiving nothing but cold stares and fancy words. But this man was different. He held her invisibly by her bony neck. He wasn't about to let her go.

She nervously cleared her throat. "Well, we don't want you to feel like that, now do we? Let me see. Perhaps Mr. Peterson, our plant foreman, could be of some help to you. Ah, right through that door there." She pointed with a trembling finger, hoping this young man would disappear forever through the door and not trouble her anymore.

Bedros entered the mammoth plant. He was overwhelmed and awestricken at its massive, mechanical wizardry—huge, rotating wheels; systems steel leading up to bridges and balconies and leading down to steaming vats, filled with bubbling brew. His ears nearly burst from the sounds of swooshing, grinding, swirling, and churning. It looked to his immature eyes like a system from out of the future, somewhat like the exterior of a huge locomotive. He became immediately aware of the progress of America compared to her European neighbors. It was no wonder that here was the cradle of invention, the hope of the future. He emphatically realized that in this country alone were the vast choices of vocations, the backup of brilliant technology, and the archives of human achievement. All these would serve to promote even the unsophisticated likes of him.

And then he saw him, the man who had to be Peterson. Just from the man's strapping stride, hands-on-hips stance, and domineering facial expressions, Bedros knew this was the foreman, of whom the skinny woman had spoken. Peterson, watching Bedros wandering about, began a furious forward motion toward the Armenian. But Bedros didn't flinch, didn't step backward. Peterson instinctively didn't like him. He wouldn't tolerate anyone he couldn't subjugate, especially a foreigner. He was, after all, a full-blooded American, a second-generation Irishman; and none of these ignorant aliens were going to get anywhere as long as he had something to do about it. All these things Bedros perceived before the approaching man even began to speak.

"What are you doing in here?" Peterson glowered at him. His blue eyes were wide in astonishment at the boldness of this man, who walked freely about his sugary domain.

"I have come for a job." Bedros stood fast, meeting Peterson's eyes— glimmer for glimmer, blink for blink.

"Sorry, we don't need you here; just go." Peterson turned his back and began to rudely walk away. He had large buttocks, placed comically high above long, slender legs.

"Oh, you do not need me, eh? I think you do, Mr. Peterson. You have some pretty dumb people working here!" Bedros announced, undeterred.

"What?" Peterson pivoted, nearly tripping over his own feet. He paced back to Bedros, glaring in disbelief at his impudence. "What in hell are you talking about, foreigner? And what kind of crazy accent is that you have, anyway?" His sandy-blond hair flopped straight and flat over his well-set ears.

"My accent, is Armenian. I am Bedros, Pete Vartanian. I am a very proud man. I am very strong as you will see. You have weaklings working here. I can do twice the work and I can do it better!"

Peterson watched his listless workers. This outspoken foreigner wasn't telling him anything he didn't know. He simply deplored him for saying it, hated him for observing it.

"They're just tired today. It's hard work here." He shrugged.

"Sure, it is hard work. That is why you need me. I work cheap. I work good!" Bedros stood eagerly before this dumbfounded man, his eyes never once deflecting from their mission. It was all very academic. The eyes of Bedros went into battle alone, fought bravely, masterfully, then in victory took the rest of his body right along with them in glory.

Peterson stood very quietly, staring at Bedros. Admittedly he needed competent help. Admittedly this young bull was strong. He could see rippling, firm muscles bulging from beneath his flannel shirt. It would be to his advantage to hire such a worker, making it appear to be his decision to increase productivity in the plant. But the devious man made a vow to himself. As soon as he was able, as cleverly as possible, he would rid himself of this egotistical immigrant.

"All right, greenhorn," Peterson submitted. "You get yourself over to that wagon and unload the cane. Take it over to the washing vat. Then, when the wagon is unloaded, come to me. I have something else in mind for you."

Bedros didn't thank him. There was immediate, conjugal hatred between the two. But each in his own way needed the other, at least for the time being. He walked briskly, his head held high, over to the wagon. In less than two hours, the overflowing transport was emptied of its bounty of cumbersome, sticky sugar stalks. Peterson was aghast when Bedros confronted him and said the unloading process was completed. It had taken the Armenian less than half the time of any other worker he had ever employed. He wouldn't compliment him and refused to comment. He just glared, conjuring up some arduous task for Bedros to perform next.

Peterson didn't appear to be much over thirty, though he assumed great wisdom and condescension over this young man, who was not much younger than he. His hair was interspersed with pale, ashy colors, and he looked as if he were graying, which, in fact he wasn't. He was an attractive man with small, well-placed features. His skin was a ruddy hue, but when he grew angry, it turned almost purplish, giving him a sickly appearance. What destroyed him and warped an otherwise handsome face was a continual frown and a sulking scowl, which made him look years older than he was. This compelled people to keep their distance from him whenever possible.

Bedros and Mr. Peterson made an incompatible-looking twosome as they stood evaluating one other with wary, distasteful stares. Peterson embodied second-generation America—secure in her heritage, comfortable in her language, taking for granted all she had given him. His clothes, his hair, and the color of his skin all worked to his benefit through no necessary worth of his own. Bedros, on the other hand, was gruff, unsophisticated, and poorly dressed. He could barely put two understandable English words together to form a thought. His happy, frolicking mounds of hair went in whatever direction they so chose. His dark, thick skin and strong, punctuated nose made his face look like a caricature—a person who embodied all people from all nations in his part of the old world. But in one essential way, Bedros was more American than Mr. Peterson, for he was indefatigable, courageous, and ever in search of self-improvement. He would reap the rewards that life had to offer. And no matter what they might have been taught or how they might have evolved together, these two—Vartanian and Peterson—would never learn to accept one another. They would hold in contempt the very favorable characteristics that graced each of them. They were different and for that reason they would each seek out only their own kind. They might live next to each other, but they could never be close to each other. So it would always be—for them and millions like them.

"All right." Peterson blustered through puffy, red cheeks. "There is plenty more to do around here, mister. Don't think you're going to knock off early like the rest of these bums just because you happen to work a little faster."

"Mr. Peterson, before I do anything else, I would like to see how everything works." Bedros had said it more like a demand than a request. His eyes were still tenaciously locked onto Peterson's eyes.

"I guess you think you can figure this all out in a few minutes, eh?" Peterson gave him a demonic smile; his hands perched stiffly on either hip.

"Maybe not in few minutes, but in about an hour or so. "Bedros laughed.

"Oh, boy, I can see it's going to be fun trying to understand you, greenhorn. All right, all right, look around if you want. Look, but don't expect to be paid for it. I want to see you back to work first thing tomorrow morning; plant opens at six thirty." Peterson hustled away, flinging his arms wildly into the air as though Bedros had in some way disrupted his whole life.

Peter Vartanian wasn't a bum, nor was he an ignorant immigrant. As he strolled from one end of the long, clattering, steaming plant to the other, his mind rapidly absorbed all the intricate workings of sugar production. Immediately he perceived what each section of the operation was doing and why. He began to develop his own ideas on improving some of the operations - which he would soon offer to the foolish Irishman.

As Bedros watched in fascination, wagons arrived filled to the brim with stalks of raw sugarcane which had been secured from a ship unloading at the Delaware River. After the unloading process, which was the most elementary of all the procedures, came the washing. It was done by hand in huge vats of cool water. The stalks floated in the water like miniature logs in a giant bucket.

The stalks were then conveyed into the shredder-crusher vat, which took the tough, stringy canes and smashed them into flat, wet masses.

The next process was the most fascinating to Bedros. The flattened and crushed stalks were passed by conveyor belt through a series of very large, heavy rollers with smooth surfaces. There were three sets of these rollers, each made of solid, iron cylinders, which were six feet long and three feet in diameter. The cane stalks were passed through these like a wringer. This step was how the pure sugar juice was extracted from the cane.

The remains of the stalks were discarded, while the juice was sent by pipelines into a huge vat with a slow-burning flame beneath it. Here the juice was heated. Bedros presumed this was a sort of purification process. From there, the heated juice moved into a second vat where an evaporating procedure was performed. The fire underneath was much more intense. The liquid sugar boiled rapidly, giving off steam, which eventually removed most of the liquid content of the juice.

The next process was a form of filtration. The heavy syrup was spilled into a huge, spinning mill called a centrifuging machine. It spun the syrup so rapidly that the molasses content was spun off, leaving just raw sugar crystals. This sugar was sifted into huge burlap sacks, each weighing nearly one hundred pounds.

A large crane precariously lifted the sacks up into the air and plopped them down into a huge pile, which awaited loading onto the shipping wagon. As he watched the crane lift the heavy bags, then drop them onto the pile, what occurred to Bedros was that a far more efficient method would be to transfer the bags directly from their filling right onto the wagon. This step would eliminate the human labor of slow loading.

With the fascinating process still whirling around in his head like the sifting crystals of sparkling sugar, he decided he would leave. He would return early in the morning, refreshed and ready to take on the factory, along with its nasty foreman. As he began walking out, he heard Peterson call out to him loudly above the incessant din of the machinery.

"Hey, just a minute, greenhorn. Where are you going?" he yelled, looking down at Bedros like a demon from above.

"You told me to leave after I looked around, and that is what I am doing."

"Do you think you understand what's going on here?" Peterson glowered at him sarcastically.

"Yes, Mr. Peterson. I understand very well." Bedros proceeded to explain to the astonished foreman just what he had observed and how each process achieved its purpose and how some processes didn't. His English was atrocious, but Peterson had to admit—if only to himself—that this man knew precisely what he was talking about. He possessed natural mechanical intuition. In that instant, Peterson considered Bedros Vartanian as something more than an egotistic alien. Now he looked upon him as a threat, perhaps even to his very own position here at the plant. It was a strange tug-of-war, but his hatred won out over his respect.

"Well, well. You have it all down real good, don't you, greenhorn?"

"My name, I told you, is Pete—Pete Vartanian." Bedros used every ounce of control to keep from killing this pale, impudent man right there on the spot. It wouldn't be a good way to proceed with his ominous plans for a fine future in America.

Peterson shot him a sterile, icy look. "If you don't mind, we'll leave it at greenhorn."

Bedros forced a smile. "Okay boss, that's alright. Good-bye, boss. I'll be back first thing tomorrow."

He left, leaving Peterson gawking, wondering why he tolerated his defiance—why he fought off a growing feeling inside that resembled a liking for the young bull.

Bedros strolled happily up Delaware Avenue. He was inspired by the raging industry, the passing ships, the busy streets, the puttering of an occasional gleaming, black horseless carriage, filled with white-capped gentlemen and feather-bedecked ladies. It was all so beautiful, so magnificent—the sounds and smells and sights of Philadelphia—of America—of prosperity and hope. He stopped in a small café and had some raw oysters on their shell, smothering them with a tangy red sauce, which made his nose run and his eyes tear. He washed them down hastily with two cold spring beers, and then made his way to the trolley which would take him home.

Hirair was already there, exhausted from the emotional strain of such rapid orientation into this confusing society. They spoke little and drank not at all, which proved they were both not themselves. Hirair lightly mentioned that he wanted to work for himself and decided to stay on at the grocery, perhaps one day buying it from Mr. Azarian.

Bedros spoke of the factory, his new job, and the wicked Peterson, who he knew would be his nemesis but only for as long as he had to endure him. They both fell asleep early, and in their dreams arose raging questions. Have we done right? Is this really the land of the free? Where will this freedom take us? The questions came from exhaustion. The fear came from weary bodies and burdened minds. But with the morning and the sunlight, optimism would prevail and foolhardy scheming would commence. And each would reaffirm that he had made the right decision in choosing America for his home.

It was six o'clock in the morning when Bedros arrived at the factory. Peterson was waiting for him. He must have known this aggressive immigrant would arrive even earlier than was necessary, and he was determined to be there before him.

"Listen, greenhorn. Yesterday you mentioned that you had some ideas for improvement here. Would you like to share them with your old, dumb boss?"

"Well, Mr. Peterson, I figured that with that big crane you got over there, why don't you let the crane drop the bags of sugar onto the wagon instead of the floor? That way you do not have to use anybody to load the bags onto the wagon."

"Interesting," Peterson mused, eyeing the now-dormant, looming crane at the far end of the factory.

"Yes, well, the way I figure it, you are going to save time and labor. And it is safer, because nobody is going to be standing underneath those things" he said, while motioning to the heavy bags of sugar.

Peterson stood staunchly still, not speaking, considering the outspoken Armenian. He looked at the crane, back at Bedros, then back at the crane. His eyes lit up as if some delightful plan had just occurred to him. He turned back to Bedros with a crooked grin on his unfriendly face.

"Not a bad idea, greenhorn. But there is one problem, ya know. The crane operator has to be guided from the floor so that he drops those big bags in just the right place. It is much easier to let them fall onto the floor than into a small area like the wagon."

"I do not think so, not if he is careful." Bedros couldn't understand. There didn't seem to be any problem to him—unless of course Peterson had created it to make him look foolish or perhaps for a far more devious reason.

"Well, my craneman is not too bright, ya know. One of those winos. No, I think the only way is to have someone standing on the ground, directing him from the filling area over to the wagon."

"That is dangerous, Mr. Peterson. What if the bag falls? It weighs almost a hundred pounds. If it falls on the man underneath, it could kill him for sure."

Bedros was getting the point quite well. "Oh, it wouldn't be a problem for somebody real smart, somebody real brave. I mean somebody like you, greenhorn."

Bedros glared at him in disgust. So this was where it all was leading.

"Okay, boss." Bedros defied him with undaunted eyes. "How much are you going to pay me to almost get myself killed every day?"

"Oh, I guess you're worth about twelve dollars a week." Peterson was having himself a grand time.

Bedros was overcome with frustration. He needed this ass of a man—for a while anyway. For a while he'd swallow the mockery—only a little while. It was hard. This was the kind of pain Bedros could bear even less than physical inflictions. No amount of money was enough for that suicidal job, but for now any amount would be a blessing to him.

"All right, make it fifteen, and you got a deal." Bedros grinned at him so widely it seemed his cheeks would crack. Inside he loathed him with a vengeance.

Peterson was livid. He had hoped Bedros would renege. He should have known better, though, and decided to let the fool go ahead with it. "All right, you start today as soon as the dago gets in. He'll probably be late. These people always are—you know how it is, don't you, greenhorn?"

"Nope." Bedros laughed, ignoring the needling and feeling victorious in his own way. "Nope, I don't know how it is, Mr. Peterson, sir." In fact, Bedros liked the Italian people, they reminded him of Armenians. They were warm, kind and they liked a good time.

Peterson didn't respond but walked away, not turning back, hoping that his silence had somehow saved his face.

Soon, the short, pleasant-looking Italian named Vincenzo arrived. Through a hilarious form of sign language, Bedros explained to him the new plans for loading the wagon. The dark, curly-haired man looked frightened. He shook his head frantically, motioning with flinging, juggling hands what might happen to Bedros. But Bedros reassured him that he would be very careful. Thus, the treacherous routine began.

For the next two weeks, Bedros spent each day standing precariously under the hovering crane, which held in its shaky mouth a bag weighing nearly as much as a man. His neck ached from continually looking up. His eyes were burning and bloodshot from the strain. His arms and back were throbbing and sore from the distorted positions he had to assume in guiding the sack of sugar from its filling area to the appropriate spot on the wagon. But the money was good, at least to Bedros. He was able to pay his share of the rent and buy some food, a new pair of shoes, and a shabby, used winter coat. He knew all along that his time at the sugar plant would be short. Life had too much to offer him. And he had much more to offer—more than working for a demagogue like Peterson and risking his life every day for a peon's pay. He never worried. He diligently persevered; assured that sooner or later something would happen to change his plans for the better.

It was almost quitting time on a Friday afternoon. The plant workers were getting lazy and loquacious in anticipation of the weekend. Peterson had stepped out for a while, and everyone took the opportunity to relax in their duties. But Bedros didn't, he couldn't; he knew only that above him hung one hundred pounds of raw sugar, which had to be carefully guided over to the now-piled-high wagon. This would be the last sack it would take. He held his breath as he always did when he found himself under the sway of the bag of death.

And then it happened—just as it had ten times or more in his restless dreams. Vincenzo let out a helpless scream. The crane creaked and groaned like an aging invalid, and the huge bag of sugar came hurling to the ground. Bedros stood terror stricken, his feet frozen to the floor beneath it. Then at the very last moment, as though God Himself had shoved him out of the way, he jumped aside. He fell to the floor just inches from where he had stood. Simultaneously, the mammoth bag crashed down onto the floor, a half foot away from Bedros's trembling body. Sugar splattered everywhere, covering Bedros in sticky, white snow.

Vincenzo, along with many other workers, French, Irish, Ukrainian, Greek, and Indian, circled around Bedros in hysteria. They knew what had almost happened to Bedros might have happened to any of them. In an unspoken comradeship, they became aware that the Armenian, sprawled out on the floor, was each of them and all of them.

Peterson marched onto the scene, looking like a schoolteacher who had just caught his students engrossed in cheating during an examination. The workers scattered. Only Vincenzo remained to help Bedros. He brushed him off. Then the infuriated Italian gave Peterson a hateful glare and walked out of the plant without a word. Peterson was about to speak. He thought of so many amusing things he could say to Bedros at this moment. But when he saw the seething black eyes, shooting bullets and daggers out from underneath their sugar-laden lashes, he thought better of it. He turned away abruptly, saying nothing.

Bedros rushed home, bathed, and ate a sandwich accompanied by a few straight shots of bourbon. Hirair wasn't home yet. Wearily, Bedros Vartanian flopped into bed and conspired with his God. On Monday he was sure he would quit the job at the sugar refinery. The thought helped him to sleep.

His dreams were incongruous medleys of people he knew and loved—all coming together, and then floating away from each other. The hazy actors looked like wistful cherubs frivolously prancing about in the clouds. He dreamed of Syrvart. In his dream she was a young woman, lovelier than he had ever remembered her, and she called to him. He saw Mariam holding out a tray with so much food that it all fell, rolling helter-skelter about the floor. He tried to chase it, wanted to bend and pick it up, but could never quite grasp any of it. Then Garabed appeared in a fog, grinning at him as though he harbored some fantastic secret. Interspersed throughout the dream—coming in and out like figures appearing, then disappearing on a cuckoo clock—was Yughaper and Ara. They looked exactly as he remembered them. He reached out to grab them—embrace them—but they disappeared.

It was the most mystical sleep he had ever experienced. In his half-way slumber, he could feel Hirair in the room, wandering about. Bedros was so lifelessly tired; he could neither open his eyes nor respond to his friend. He didn't care. He knew Hirair would understand.

In the morning, he could feel the bright, playful sun fondling his eyelids, and he wished it would go away. He wished it might be a bleak, dark day so that he could blame his oversleeping on the weather. But the dusty, gold-sprinkled rays of infiltrating sunbeams were insistent. They landed on his eyes and reluctantly the huge, sparkling, black eyes opened wide. Bedros looked over at his sleeping friend. Hirair didn't stir. He snored gently. Quietly Bedros slipped from the bed. He bathed at the sink, dressed quickly, put some coffee on, and sat back, pondering the day, the sunlight, and his future.

His thoughts were interrupted by voices from below. They sounded like voices from the past. He closed his eyes, trying to visualize the persons who were speaking. A few moments went by and he was aroused by the sounds of footsteps climbing the stairs leading to the apartment. The iron stairway shook in a murmuring vibration with the footsteps as they gradually progressed higher and louder. He heard the haunting voices again. Curiosity overcame him. It was very early, and no one knew he was there ...

He opened the door, didn't move, eyes wide, limbs paralyzed. The golden Philadelphia sunshine spotlighted the two figures waiting anxiously on the landing of the fire escape. He knew them well—loved them deeply. But it had been so long! So much had happened. He couldn't believe what he was seeing, but he couldn't deny his senses. He was awake. This was reality. They were standing before him—his brother and his mother!

Few reunions could have been more jubilant. An aged, bent-over woman shivered in the cool breeze, trembling from joy and disbelief. Bedros embraced her, enveloping her tiny body with his muscular arms. Ara wrapped his arms around the two of them. Ara looked very much like an immigrant—shabby, awkwardly dressed, astonishingly handsome. Ara had grown taller than Bedros during the years of their separation. Yughaper, however, seemed to have shrunk, the years taking a tremendous toll on her body.

As the three tightly embraced, in the rousing wind and the blinding glare of the yellow morning sun, they appeared to be one mass—one being. Three shadows—a human holy trinity—cast one giant shadow on the wall of the stone row house. It was as though they could never let go—each of them having passed the last few years in the tormented fear that they would never partake of one another's company again. It was like a reunion in heaven—when the first departed at last welcomed the souls of the last departed, whom the former felt lingered far too long in the frivolous world of mortality.

Finally Bedros broke up the emotional huddle and pulled them excitedly into the apartment. "Come in; come in out of the cold!"

They looked around in interest, obviously thinking what a startling contrast this tiny apartment was to the posh mansion of the binbashi. Hirair appeared and scratched his head in confusion, wondering what was going on. Then, without an introduction, he immediately realized who the two visitors were. So the same jubilant, enraptured reunion took place all over again. This time—a foursome.

Hirair lit the potbelly stove and considerately began to prepare breakfast, allowing Bedros to delight in the arrival of his family. They were, after all, the only family he had left—a fact that made them especially endearing to him. As he gazed into their tired but appeased eyes, it was clear that Bedros would never again let them leave his sight. It was clear that if God had taken them this far through so much and granted them this reunion, then they would remain together until he chose to separate them again—for the last time.

They warmed their chilled hands by the stove, took off their torn-and-battered scarves and sweaters, and enjoyed coffee, fried eggs, fried potatoes, sliced cheese, and crisp strips of a breakfast meat called bacon. There was an hour or so of excited chatter. Everyone was trying to outtalk everyone else. The stories flew back and forth like ricocheting Ping-Pong balls. The laughter was uproarious. Arms flew wildly about. Heads bobbed up and down in agreement, disbelief, and astonishment. Through it all, Bedros occasionally glanced at his mother as she puffed away on an endless string of Turkish cigarettes. They had discolored her teeth, and her breathing was very heavy. He wanted to cry each time he looked at her. Yet she still smiled, still joked, still had the glimmer of her younger days in her eyes; and for that he had to be grateful.

A knock at the door abruptly interrupted the celebration, and to their surprise, Mrs. Azarian had come up the steps to offer her greetings. She suggested that since the apartment was so very small and somewhat inadequate, Digin Yughaper could stay downstairs with her and her husband until other living arrangements might be made. She was most emphatic in her offer.

Bedros was surprised but appreciative, and Yughaper quickly agreed that this would be a fine idea. She knew what it would be like living in the apartment with these three perpetrators of havoc. What she couldn't know was that a few months would become almost three years. For all that time, however, the Azarians would make her as welcome as the very first day.

The family spent much of that weekend sight-seeing around Philadelphia and purchasing what few items they needed or could afford to make themselves comfortable. During a two-hour spree, wandering up and down Broad Street, Yughaper became exhausted and asked if she could go back to the Azarians for some rest. Hirair was happy to take her back. He had wanted to allow Bedros and Ara a few secluded hours together. Hirair took his adopted mother's arm and valiantly led her away.

As Ara and Bedros passed the Philadelphia College of Art, Bedros professed that as soon as he had the money, he would like to enroll there. Becoming a great artist had long been his talent and desire. Throughout most of his twenty-three years, his trunks, drawers, and chests had been containers for his stashed-away papers of ornately sketched birds and flowers and intricately designed machines and inventions. Ara teased him, assured that becoming an artist would be no easy task for a foreigner, an unknown alien like his brother. It would be better, Ara suggested, if the two put their technical minds together and began some type of business.

"Well, to start," Bedros said, "you will come to work with me on Monday. You will hate the foreman there—Peterson—but it will be a good experience for you. I am sure he will take you on. He owes it to me for risking my life every day."

Ara was shocked. "What do you mean by that?"

"It is a surprise. You will see on Monday." Bedros's sharp tone quickly ended the subject.

They wrapped big arms around each other. Ara was fairer and more delicately featured than his shorter, more solidly built brother. As they walked along, it was like the old days. Only their physical bodies had changed. They were still the two frolicking little boys they had been in Malatia. They always would be.

"Say, by the way, I need to tell you." Ara stopped walking for a moment and directed his words toward Bedros. "Garabed will not be coming straight to Philadelphia."

Bedros's bright face became masked with an old, familiar look of contempt. Ara remembered it well from the days when they had been building the extension onto Garabed's home in Malatia.

"What? He gave me his word!" Bedros suddenly realized he had a hold of his brother's arms and was squeezing them in his fury. He quickly let go, apologizing.

"Now, wait a minute, little brother; you are reacting just as Garabed said you would!"

"Oh, he did, did he?" Bedros was livid.

"Listen to me now, please." Ara was firm, annoyed by the immature reaction of his brother. He was baffled, as he had always been, over Bedros's distain for so harmless a person as Garabed. "He still has your money and has promised to repay you as soon as he is settled. He has an aunt in Chelsea, Massachusetts. She has a good-sized house which is big enough for all of them. It was at the aunt's request that they went there instead of here."

"At the aunt's request?" Bedros made a fist and symbolically swung it toward a visualized but absent Garabed.

"Bedo, if it's your money you're worried about, I am sure you will get it back."

Now Bedros was glowering at his brother. "Money! Do you not know me better than that, Ara? No, it is more than my money that the old fool has!"

Ara took Bedros squarely by his bulging shoulders and looked compassionately into his angry eyes. "It is Syrvart, is it not? I think you care for her more than you let on"."

Bedros laughed mockingly. "Syrvart? She is child. What can she be—thirteen, maybe fourteen now? No, she is not for me but perhaps for someone else. There are so many of us young Armenians emerging in this country. Any of them would be better for her than ending up with Garabed. I just want them to be happy."

Ara felt suddenly sorry for his brother. Bedros usually had all aspects of his life under control. Syrvart and Mariam were so far away and circumstances put them far out of Bedros's control. He was sorry to have brought up the whole subject.

"I wish I had a picture of her so I could show it to the Armenian boys that are here. Then maybe we could get both of them married off quickly."

"I have a picture, Bedo," Ara acknowledged, not sure if it was wise to have said so, judging from his brother's present emotional state.

"Syrvart handed it to me the day before we left. She thought you might like to have it."

"I do not want to see it. You keep it!" Bedros began walking so fast that Ara had to practically sprint to keep up with him.

Bedros turned into a doorway and disappeared. Ara followed inquisitively, looking up at the words, Joe's Bar, printed over the door. He walked into the dimly lit room and sat across from Bedros, who was settled in a booth. They ordered scotch and water and two sandwiches, and they ate rapidly without speaking. Bedros ordered another drink for each of them. Ara decided to change the subject and began to talk about how overwhelmed he was with the automobiles he had seen. He wanted to find an old one and take it apart to learn of its workings.

"I think we could use the engine from one of these horseless carriages to motorize factory equipment. Do you agree, Bedo?"

"Let me see the picture!" It wasn't an answer to his question, but wisely Ara went into his wallet and turned over the photograph to Bedros.

Bedros grabbed the photograph rudely. His behavior annoyed Ara. He wanted to reprimand him, but in watching his brother's strangely engrossed eyes, he decided to let the matter pass. Bedros looked at the picture for a long while, at first saying nothing—seemingly unimpressed, just coldly perusing. He shouted out loudly to the bartender for two more drinks. He put down the picture, looked absent-mindedly around the room, and then suddenly he softened. He put his head down, holding his unruly black hair in his hand, carefully examining every detail of the photograph. Ara could never remember him, in all they had been through, acting so curiously sublime. His flashing eyes were besieged with raging thoughts.

"Have you lost your mind in these past few years, brother?" Ara spoke gently with deep concern.

Bedros at last looked up at his brother, and gradually, like a sweeping wind blowing away a sagging fog, his face lit up, displaying its normal exuberance. "No, Brother. In fact, I think I have just found it."

"Thank God for that," Ara sighed, taking a long swallow from his scotch, which, in mingling with the already absorbed first two, was creating a most remarkable feeling of sublimation inside of him.

"If you do not mind, Ara, I will hold onto this." Bedros gently pushed the photo into a pocket of his shirt.

"That is why Syrvart sent it, Bedo."

They smiled. Bedros rose like a piston, leaned clumsily across the table, took Ara's head into his two cupped hands, squeezed in his face comically, and then drew him closer, kissing him wetly on both cheeks. The comical actions evoked a spontaneous laugh from both of them. The bartender laughed as well. Bedros looked over at him with a beaming smile.

"That's okay, Joe. You are one of the few Irishmen I will let laugh at me!"

As the brothers stood and ready to leave, Bedros unexpectedly grabbed the surprised bartender by his collar, pulled his head across the bar, and bestowed him with a traditional Armenian kiss on both cheeks.

Bedros and Ara walked south on Broad Street toward Vine. They passed a newsstand, behind which stood a distorted-looking, old geezer with a patch over one eye. He was missing several teeth, and the remaining ones were nearly as black as the soon-to-settle November night. A few flutters of snowflakes began to fill the air—not really falling to the ground but dancing around in a sort of limbo. The two Armenian brothers were revived by the cool, tantalizing air. They were dizzy from the inebriating scotch. They were delirious in joy over their newfound possession of one another. It was no wonder they ignored the callous huckstering of the man behind the newsstand as he called out, "Here y'are. Get your evenin' paper here!" And the brothers walked on—fortunately not hearing him and not seeing the heartbreaking front-page picture of starving Armenians in their homeland. For at this moment, while the two Armenian men were trying to begin a new life, the rest of the world was soliciting help for their starving kinsmen.

Returning to the apartment, they found Hirair settled in a small armchair, reading a letter. He welcomed them home and bounded up in excitement, showing them the note from his sister Sonia. Along with the letter there was a picture—a blurry, black-and-white photograph—of young Armenian girls, all wearing dull, gray uniforms and white blouses, all appearing forlorn in their two-tiered array.

"Look, Sonia sent this picture of these girls. They are all orphans from Constantinople. They are all without family there or here. Sonia says they are waiting for Armenian men here to send for them, bring them to America, and marry them. Sonia says they will make good wives."

"So"—Bedros laughed cantankerously—"let us buy a few, like a pair of shoes. If they do not fit, well, who cares?"

"Forgive him," Ara apologized. "He is drunk."

"No, no, Hirair. I am not drunk, not drunk enough, not yet!" Bedros flopped down on the bed, looking pale—his eyes half closed, his nose a blazing red.

"All right, baby brother." Ara put his hands on his hips in anger. "I had a surprise I wanted to save for a very special time, but since you are in such a dismal state, I suppose I will have to get it now!" He disappeared to the bathroom, where his baggage was stored.

In seconds he emerged, grinning. He held high in one hand an old but flawlessly crafted violin and in the other, a satiny black-and-silver clarinet.

Bedros blinked in disbelief. He sat up like a corpse rising from the dead and gawked foolishly in delight. "Where in hell—?"

"Do not just sit there! Let us see if you still remember how to use this thing." Ara walked over to his brother, handing him the beautiful instrument.

"Me? What about you?" Bedros scowled while bursting with excitement. "I never knew you could play such a fancy gentleman's instrument yourself, Ara."

"Listen, little brother," Ara proclaimed proudly. "I have done more in the past few years than sit around watching people get killed."

For a moment the thick silence of remembering overcame them all. It would never quite go away; only through the grace of God, it might diminish slightly. Then in determined unity, the three cast away their dreary memories and settled around the table, squatting on backward chairs. Hirair sang as Ara and Bedros found themselves playing the long-lost instruments with authority and precision.

Ara held his violin like a beautiful woman—delicately and softly in his outstretched arms. His head fluttered back and forth; his eyebrows flipped up and down to his melodious medleys. Bedros, somewhat less delicately, grasped his horn, strangled it, and took from it all it had to give.

Hirair quickly set up a bar on the tiny table. Then he made his way to the icebox to get out some *meze*, light nibblings, which were necessary to accompany serious drinking. He decided he had better put out a good amount, because this particular night wouldn't end soon. He knew too well that if their bellies were not slightly full, the morning would bring violent illness rather than the usual catatonic delirium. It wasn't easy getting around the apartment now. Ara's makeshift bed rested on the floor taking up what little space was available. But Hirair didn't complain. They would all have to work together and endure a little discomfort for a while. It was in anticipation of the fruitful days they all knew would eventually come.

Within a few hours the jubilant threesome grew outrageously rowdy and undauntedly loud, bellowing out the old country songs as if defying all of Philadelphia to hear them, daring anyone to resist them. They stomped their worn shoes so hard on the floor that periodically a thumping could be heard from below. It was obviously Yughaper, embarrassed, using a broom stick or the like to beseech them to quiet down. It was to no avail and, of course, she knew it.

Finally there was a knock at the door. It took them nearly five minutes before Ara bothered to answer it. There, in his nightshirt, a wool sweater, a matching scarf, and a nightcap pulled comically down over the entire top of his head, stood Dikran Azarian. His teeth were chattering as he quickly entered the loud, vibrating room. He removed his scarf and sweater and seemed to be pretending a look of anger, though actually he was rather intrigued with the jubilant atmosphere.

"My wife asks you three to quiet down so we can get some sleep." He used expressionless words, like a child repeating a grocery order from his mother.

"Sorry," Ara said, bidding the man welcome and offering him the last seat in the place.

"Dikran, my friend." Bedros stood up as if about to deliver an eloquent speech. "We were just about to finish up for the night, but please, will you not join us for a nightcap?"

The simple, kindly man reluctantly agreed, and Bedros poured him nearly half a glass of bourbon. He domineeringly placed the drink in the grocer's hand, daring him with his flashing eyes to complain that it was too much. Of course, he didn't.

They drank in happiness, using Dikran's arrival as an excuse to begin the party anew. Conversation was thick and a bit slurred. The words fled through years, through childhoods, atrocities, romances, businesses. Hirair showed the picture again of the orphan Armenian girls waiting to be brides. Bedros scowled, wrinkling up his pronounced nose.

"Sure, that is the way it is going to be." Bedros retorted. "We are all to marry our wives—sight unseen—and accept them, even if they are hairy, fat, and ugly. That is the Armenian way. Is it not?"

Hirair grew serious. "It is the only way for us, Bedo, and you know it. Surely you cannot expect any of us to marry American women. They would not have us. Why we would be fools to even try!"

"And who wants to marry a skinny, sickly-looking American girl, anyway?" Bedros roared, becoming uneasy with the grim dialogue.

"It is not that, and we all know it," interjected Ara, looking pensive and forlorn. "It is that we cannot turn our backs on our pasts or who we are. We must continue our heritage. We must raise Armenian children so that our mothers and fathers will not have died in vain."

There was no rebuttal. Ara had said it all. Sullen sadness shrouded the room. This time it was Dikran who lifted the disheartening fog. Unnoticed, he had been slowly, deliberately, delightedly getting drunk.

"I will tell you all a story you will not believe about this marrying business!"

The three younger men sat quietly and politely in wonder that this normally reclusive man could have any anecdotes of interest in what appeared to be his rather dull existence.

Dikran began to laugh to himself. He gathered his thoughts and cleared his throat with one more ample gulp of his drink.

"You know, I have a much younger brother from my father's second marriage. We are from Arabkir, just like my wife. My wife, my brother, and I came here together, thank God, before the Turks destroyed our town. All our Armenian friends and relatives who stayed are dead. But anyway, this is a happy story." He drank again, enjoying the fact that he had stirred interest in the now attentive youth.

"So, my brother Karnig—he had a girlfriend over in Arabkir who he really loved. But he was sixteen at the time and she, only ten! When my wife, my brother, and I came to Philadelphia, Karnig thought he would never see this girl, Lucy, again. So it happened that Lucy's family fled here a few months later, and Karnig found out that they were living over in the West Philadelphia area. He went over to see her. But the parents—they didn't like my brother. They never liked him even in Arabkir, because...well, we were grocers, and they thought us not good enough for their daughter. When we left, they thought they had seen the last of us. So, you can imagine how they must have felt when he showed up at their front door in Philadelphia."

In agreement, they all mumbled and shared a fine laugh. Bedros interjected a teasing moment, saying it might have been that they didn't want their daughter to marry another *Arabkirsi*. The joke caught favor among them all, including Dikran. "Yes, Bedros," he said, "and the only thing worse than that is marrying a *Malatiasi*." It was great fun as it had been in the old days, comparing apples, pears, goats, and girls.

"Anyway, if I may go on..." Dikran's playful, suddenly very young eyes scanned the listeners, procuring their attention. Once again he was in vocal command.

"You see, my brother—he is very devilish, not like me." At that moment Ara and Hirair immediately turned their attentions toward Bedros with glittering acknowledgement in their tearing eyes.

"Lucy—she lived in one of those redbrick row houses and this one had a balcony leading around to a second-floor bedroom window, which was where her parents slept. Karnig took a trolley over there very late one night. He had a huge burlap potato sack with him from the grocery.

He snuck up to the house and climbed up to the balcony." His audience roared with delight.

"From the balcony, he opened the door which led into the parents' bedroom. I do not know if it was unlocked or if he broke the lock, but he got in. Believe this or not—he went right past the sleeping mother and father, through their bedroom, and down the hallway to Lucy's bedroom. She slept with her baby brother. Karnig—he grabbed her and stuffed her in the sack! He took her kicking and screaming from the bedroom, down the stairs, out into the street, back onto the trolley, and back to our home. Believe it—the parents slept through the whole thing!"

The young Armenians were collapsing in drunken laughter. Bedros was holding on to his aching side, and Ara slid down out of his chair and onto the floor. Tears flowed out of Hirair's eyes, and he shook from his giggling. Bedros spoke through choking laughter.

"And what about the girl? What did she have to say about all this?"

"Are you kidding? Lucy loved my brother! When she realized it was him who took her, she was delighted. They went to Worcester, Massachusetts, to the Armenian church, and they were married. She was only twelve."

"Now that is the way to get a wife," Ara added. "But the poor girl. She wasn't even a woman yet. And what about her parents? Could they not do anything?" Always the sensitive one, always the one who could feel so deeply for other people, Ara wondered how he would have felt if Lucy had been his own daughter.

"Well," Dikran continued in a more serious voice, "my wife and Lucy's mother talked, and her mother came to realize that Lucy loved Karnig. It was a rare thing for Armenians to feel for each other before marriage, they conceded. So agreement was reached. Karnig slept right here in this attic, and Lucy slept downstairs with us until a year later when she began her menstruation. Then they were permitted to sleep together. They already have two children, each less than a year apart."

"Wait a minute," Bedros interrupted. Now he was upset. "You said you have only been here a little over three years, did you not, Dikran?"

"Yes." The grocer shook his head, realizing that what had started out as an amusing story had taken a rather somber turn. But he had begun it, and he had to go on. "Yes, I know what you are thinking, Bedo. That makes her now only fifteen."

The joking drinkers desisted rather quickly after that. It was very late. Their stomachs were upside-down. Their heads were inside out. It was time to end the party. Time to go to sleep. The jubilant madness ended as spontaneously as it had begun.

The next day, Sunday, was not spent in church. Yughaper and Anahid rose early in the morning to begin the lengthy process of preparing *kufta*. They brought the dinner up to the unconscious men at around four in the afternoon. It was the only time during the entire day the men got up from their beds or bothered to open their eyes. But no one begrudged them. Fun was as essential to them as was food and sleep in these days. It would continue to be so long into their futures.

• • •

The next morning at the sugar factory, Peterson was in an exceptionally miserable mood—even for him. His pale, blue eyes were rimmed with a circle of red. Two miniature puffy bags fell like obese teardrops from his bottom lashes. His usually ruddy face was pale and languorous. It was no wonder then that the sight of not one but two Vartanians made him livid. When Bedros asked him for work for Ara, he became a madman.

"What's this supposed to be, greenhorn? You took it on yourself to bring somebody else in here to hang from my balls!"

Ara was aghast. He pulled his arm back, ready to haul off and punch the man. Even with his limited knowledge of English, he well understood the Irishman's connotation. Bedros reached out and calmed his brother with a tight squeeze. Ara looked at Bedros in amazement. He never would have believed Bedros could succumb to anyone in such a manner. They momentarily conversed in Armenian as Peterson's pale face began to puff up and swell in redness, nearing the point of explosion.

"Why do you let him talk to you like this, Bedo? I cannot believe it of you. Let us leave this place."

"Ara, you must understand. Peterson is just a means to an end. He needs us, both of us; and right now, we need him. Now, calm yourself. I will take care of this."

"Look, if you two are finished with your monkey talk, maybe you might like to try English with me. That's what we speak in this country, ya know." he said, throwing his arms high in exasperation. "I don't want to hear anything about hiring today. I have a broken centrifuge, and I'm outta business if it don't get fixed fast. Just take your brother and get outta here, greenhorn. I'm gonna end up shuttin' down this goddamned place today"

Bedros beamed, and Peterson looked murderous, wondering what this damned immigrant found so amusing. "Look here, boss. My brother, Ara—he is a very smart man, even smarter than me. He can fix anything. Machines and Ara—they grew up together."

Ara looked at his brother with horror on his face. Then he suddenly drew a long breath and grinned from ear to reddening ear. Bedros was as he had always been—bold, daring, and on top of everything. He should have known better than to doubt him. The only problem was, how did he fix a machine he had never seen before for a man he hated?

"That true, brother of Mr. Greenhorn? You think you can fix my machine, huh?" Peterson was at his wit's end, deciding that at this point anything was better than losing a day's work. Plus, his normal repairman was notoriously unavailable for days at a time. Besides, if the dumb immigrant botched up the job, he had the perfect reason to get rid of them both.

"Sure, Mr. Peterson. I can fix anything, like my brother said." Ara smiled at the contemptible employer, then turned around with a look of "Well, here goes" to Bedros.

Peterson led Ara up a precarious iron stairway to the second level of the sugar operation, where most of the observing and servicing was performed. The entire operation was halted for now since there was nowhere for the liquid sugar to go—not without the workings of the spinning centrifuge. Briefly Peterson explained to Ara the workings of the giant mechanism. Bedros watched pensively from below as the two talked—first bent down, then knelt down, their heads hanging, straining over the dead machine. Peterson finally came down from his perch, walked out of the plant, returning with an armful of various tools. He then stood like a drill sergeant—legs spread apart, hands on hips, watching Ara as he bent over and struggled with his task. Now and then Peterson would smile and shake his head at what he considered the fruitless efforts of this ignorant alien. Bedros felt a surge of hatred overcome him. He could have taken anything the man could dish out, but if the bastard dared to offend Ara, he might just have to kill him after all.

Bedros's lethal thoughts were suddenly curtailed with the sounds—at first of puttering, then smooth pinging, swishing, and spinning of the motor. The centrifuge was working perfectly!

Ara continued to tinker and then wandered around from one end of the long, black iron bridge to the other, looking knowledgeably down on the whirlwind operations below. Peterson stomped down the steps, coming toward Bedros with a look of triumph on his pink face as if he himself had fixed the machine.

"Well, at least one of you guys has some brains, greenhorn. I'm gonna let your brother stay up there and watch over operations for today. If he does okay, I'll let him stay on as a repairman."

Bedros didn't return the insincere smile painted on Peterson's face. "Thanks, boss. You won't be sorry."

"I don't know about that, greenhorn, but you better get on with your work. That dago'll be startin' up the crane any minute now. Come on. There's work to do around here."

When Ara saw what Bedros's daily job at the plant was, he became furious. He stood, looming on his bridge with concern and fury in his eyes. Bedros looked up at him, smiled, waved his hands, and without words told him to mind his business and leave him to his.

For two weeks Ara and Bedros continued their daily routines at the sugar company. They excelled, showing intelligence not only in their profound mastery of machines and their workings, but also of people and their workings. Peterson gradually developed a strange love-hate feeling for the two brothers. He loved them for their mechanical worth, for the progressive, profitable ideas they had brought with them. He hated them for what they were, because they knew more, perceived more, than he ever could.

It was the day before Thanksgiving. November began its mystical exit, and advent marked the world. It was then that another incident occurred—a showdown in which the immigrants emerged victorious.

Peterson greeted Ara and Bedros on the Wednesday before Thanksgiving with a sardonic gleam in his eyes. He sent Ara on up to the bridge but called Bedros aside. Ara looked back curiously, but Bedros waved him on. Peterson then told Bedros that he wouldn't have him guiding the crane for today but that he had something else in mind. He took Bedros outside.

They stood shivering in the cold morning. Bedros was holding his head up high, watching as Peterson pointed out to him the fading letters—once a bright black but now an illegibly chipped gray, which said Pennsylvania. Sugar Company. Underneath the sign, which was painted directly on the brick of the building, a scant platform had been set up. It was made of flimsy plywood, and it sagged and swayed precariously in the riverfront breezes. This makeshift, primitive scaffold hovered thirty-five feet above the concrete sidewalk below. Bedros stood listening in disbelief as Peterson told him to take a ladder up to the dangerous ledge and proceed to paint the letters. A gallon of black paint and a brush were resting on the ground at the foot of the ladder.

At first, Bedros couldn't speak. He just glared at the man, who dared to suggest this climb to an almost certain catastrophe. "Mr. Peterson, excuse me, sir. But that ledge is not strong enough to hold any man. It's made of thin wood, and it's too narrow. If you would let me build something stronger, I would be happy to do the job."

Peterson snarled, put his cold nose up against Bedros's, and spoke with steam coming from his mouth. "Oh, ya would, would ya?" he mocked. "Well, I want this job done before Thanksgiving, and if you refuse, I guess I'll just have ta let you and your brother go. That would sure be a shame just before Christmas, wouldn't it greenhorn?"

Peterson bounded away. Bedros stood frozen in hatred and murderous contempt. He knew he should walk off the job. He wanted to do so with all that was in him. It wasn't worth his life. But then there was Ara. He was doing so well. He didn't want to take this job away from his brother.

Bedros reconsidered. He looked up to heaven. The morning sky was alive with sparkling, pink clouds, blue vastness, and the golden rays of a beautiful sun. Tugboats tooted in the background. Mighty vessels moaned and bellowed as they made their way to and from Philadelphia's bustling harbor.

"Well, Father, you have taken me this far. I guess you will not let me down now." He threw his head back in laughter at the irony in his prayer. "You better not let me down!"

Bedros lifted the paint and brush in one hand and proceeded to climb up the ladder. It was already feeling lopsided from the weight of the paint and the stiff winds as he progressed higher. He looked down and nearly collapsed from the sight of the drop. Heights had never been one of his favorite things. He had always been more adept at taking on human enemies rather than environmental ones. He shook his head, not believing himself or what he was doing, and began to put a wary foot up onto the vibrating perch. He drew a deep breath and gazed out at the misty harbor, remembering Marseilles, Constantinople, and the heinous tribulations through which God had taken him. It would be a rather ludicrous anticlimax to die in such a pointless way, splattered like squashed tomatoes on a cold Philadelphia sidewalk. He started to mount the ledge, then looked down and caught sight of Ara. His brother was looking up, his arms stretched pleadingly high into the air.

"Bedo," he warned, "If you take one more step, you will have lost not only your mind but your brother as well!"

Bedros looked down at him with a smile, waited a moment, and then began to continue on.

"Bedo, I am not fooling with you! If you do this for our jobs, I tell you, I quit right now. I mean it! Get down from there!"

Bedros considered. If Ara was serious, the risk wasn't worth breaking his neck for a job his brother was going to quit anyway. He knew

Ara to be just as adamant as himself on matters of principle. Happily he climbed down.

When at last his brother reached the safety of the ground, Ara grabbed him, and the two hugged and kissed in relief. Their huge, powerful bodies wielded intense warmth in defiance of the wintry, cold weather. But the slamming of the factory door and the appearance of Mr. Peterson abruptly shattered the heartwarming scene.

"All right, what goes on here? I give ya a job to do, and you lazy bastards stand here kissing." Peterson had foolishly taken himself a step too far with these two indomitably fierce young men, and he realized it when Bedros turned toward him with a vicious look on his face. Peterson had never seen him like that before. He suddenly felt like a matador, about to be gorged. A lump rose in his throat. The goose pimples that appeared under his clothing were assuredly not from the cold.

Bedros lunged forward, his arms outstretched, his eyes furiously raging fires emitting sparks of vengeance. This time Ara became the astute one. He held his charging brother with all his might. Then he confronted Peterson chin to chin, nose to nose, eyes to eyes.

"Mr. Peterson, you think we are dumb immigrants, but I want to tell you this." With the last word, Ara poked a stiff finger into the ribs of the Peterson. "I know something about this country and the working man; we got rights! You can't make my brother do anything that is dangerous to him. You got laws here. And you know it."

Peterson was reduced to a cringing coward. It wasn't so much the law that he feared at the moment but the two powerful men who not only outnumbered him but also vehemently hated him.

"All right, you win this time. But you both better get back to work before I have reason to fire ya!" He sped away, pretending triumph but experiencing shameful weakness. He was determined to get even—and soon.

Ara and Bedros returned to work. As was their way, they forgot about the incident—not letting it interfere with the jobs they had to do. Thanksgiving, they decided, would be profoundly meaningful this year.

But the happiness of Thanksgiving would soon end—leaving the thrilling anticipation of Christmas in her wake. The days fled by as if trying to avoid the increasingly cold and darkening days. Philadelphia began to fill up with more and more Armenians. Before long, a strict social structure, a well-knit web, began to develop. Soon there were churches, organizations, and schools—all created through the expenditures of Armenian time and money, all necessary for the preservation of a nationality swirling about in the intensely boiling melting pot that was America. And if it all seemed like foreign bigotry or a failure to assimilate, it really wasn't so; it was merely a matter of survival to these relentless, life-loving people, who wouldn't die.

As Ara and Bedros continued to surpass all other employees at the sugar refinery, Peterson grew more quarrelsome and dissident. He never missed the chance to taunt them, tease them, or tempt them with some devious kick-back plot or scheme to glorify himself at their expense. However, the Vartanian brothers were undaunted. Their pockets were growing fuller by the week. Their bellies were too as the land of plenty was manifesting itself in their well-rounded arms, legs, and torsos. They bought clothes—inexpensive but fine enough for them to enjoy an occasional outing with friends. A feeling of belonging was beginning to manifest itself in them.

And as for women—at least for Ara, Bedros, and Hirair—there were none. Some of their friends had dared go off into unchartered depths, patronizing nightclubs and informal gatherings, which included samplings from all the different nationalities now so rapidly entering the country. Some even dared to seek out, date, even marry *odar*—non-Armenian girls. But to these three young men, doing that was not only unthinkable but also deplorable. Though no doubt their insides ached through many a cold night, there could be no diversions, no temptations—not until the time was right and the circumstances perfectly proper. Or perhaps it was the watchful eye of one over the other that prevented any of them from straying. Meanwhile, within the closely knit Armenian community, there were countless attempts at matchmaking. Letters were written. Photographs came. There was the sister from Beirut, the aunt from France, the niece from Malatia, the cousin from Crete. None had caught any of their fancies. The three friends were beginning to think they would take their chances with a sight-unseen import from one of the overseas orphanages. But through it all Bedros had that one recurring dream. It was a voice from his God. There was a persistent responsibility that wouldn't desist. And one day Bedros made a decision, which clearly hinted to his roommates what his amorous intentions were.

It was a few days before Christmas, and the young Armenians were having their usual weeknight dinner together. Normally it was only on the weekends that Yughaper would join them upstairs, bringing with her one of a hundred beautifully prepared epicurean delights. But the evenings without her presence were welcome too. Then they could eat with gusto, drop their ashes on the floor, kick off their shoes, and forget to wipe their mouths. This evening Ara prepared the meal. Hirair would clean the apartment, and Bedros would do the dishes. They had designated to each other these weekly household duties, to which they were most faithful. Every week the duties would alternate, giving each of them the chance to learn varying housekeeping techniques. This was the week Bedros deplored. He hated dirty dishes—a reminder of his restaurant days in France. With the exception of cooking, which he loved, he thought any other domestic chores were demeaning for a man.

Dinner progressed slowly. Ara had made pan-fried pork chops, cooked more than necessary. He had made pilaf, frugally substituting water for broth and using margarine instead of butter. Then he had mixed sliced cucumbers with *madzoon*, a homemade yogurt, and salt and garlic; it was the best part of the meal. After coffee and fresh fruit, Hirair disappeared to the bathroom. Ara retired to a comfortable chair and drew out a Pall Mall, putting his feet up on the nearby bed. And Bedros sat back, staring at the horrendous mess. His food didn't settle well. He was already tired of his after-dinner job. He despised it before starting it. He rose slowly, paced defiantly around the tiny table, laden with dirty dishes, cups, glasses, and leftover food. It all rested on a green-plaid tablecloth. Suddenly he reached over, took hold of a corner of the cloth, and with one defiant, tremendously strong pull he swept the cloth and all that was on it in crashing glory to the floor. With the same motion, he left out a howl, from which walls vibrated. Then he disappeared for several hours.

When he returned home, he found his mess completely cleaned up. Ara and Hirair were sitting on separate chairs at different ends of the room, both concentrating their disapproving glares on him.

"All right, Pete," Hirair asked kindly, though he was slightly disenchanted, "what is the problem with you now?"

"No problem, Harvey, not really. I am sorry for the childish way I acted. It is just that we cannot live this way much longer. We have men's work to do, and it is enough to take up all our time. Soon we will each have to find a woman and marry."

Ara shook his head. "Always the impatient one, little brother! What is your hurry? We are only in this country a few months. There is time, much time."

"True, Ara, there is. But like all great endeavors, we must begin laying the groundwork first. That is all I mean." Bedros hastily threw off his sweater and removed his shoes. He flopped down by the potbelly stove and rapidly rubbed his hands together.

"All right, enough of this conversation. What will we all be doing this Christmas?" Hirair asked lightheartedly.

Bedros looked up, suddenly beaming as if a fantastic idea had just occurred to him. "Well, I do not know about you, but I am getting on a train. I am going to take a little trip."

"A trip where?" Hirair laughed. "You do not even know anyone in America to go and see."

Ara agreed with him, teasing. But Bedros was quite serious and ignored their chiding. "On the contrary, I do. And all I need from you now, Ara, is the address."

"What address?" Ara asked, not really knowing what his brother had in mind.

But Bedros was already undressing, slipping under the covers into the cold bed. He looked up dreamily at the ceiling. "You know, boys, they say Massachusetts is beautiful this time of year."

• • •

Chelsea, Massachusetts, was a veritable picture postcard—a Christmas greeting with a colorfully embossed, glistening winter scene. It was the embodiment of simple, cordially comfortable America. There were lush hills—something foreign to the flat vastness of Philadelphia. There were white churches with tall, heavenly pointing steeples. There were small cottages encircled with vine-enveloped picket fences. Here and there, carriages tottered along, children frolicked in the gathering snowfall, and ladies in high-buttoned shoes and busty dresses bade good-day to neighbors along the winding, tree-embroidered streets. And as the virgin snow lay her white blanket all over the peacefully sequestered town, even the affluent owners of Model T Fords didn't dare to dishonor her purity with their sputtering, splattering innovations.

As the Chelsea suburbs slowly thickened into her city, some of the cleanliness and carefree crispness disappeared, although as small cities went, she was still unusually quiet and lacking in the rude, rushing inhabitants who flourished farther south. The Armenians had gained a heavily populated, though understated, gathering in the New England area. Already Armenian churches, though extremely modest, were in existence. It was this community that had drawn Mariam Hamparian's sister-in-law, now widowed for five years.

It was here in a small home where Garabed, Mariam, Syrvart, and Hagop Hamparian settled when they came to America. Mariam's aunt had gone to New York for the Christmas holidays to visit relatives, leaving Garabed and his adopted family to celebrate in their simple way. Since Garabed considered the American customs of Christmas trees and piles of presents frivolous and unimportant, they were resigned to long evenings by a roaring fire. They were thankful for their life in America, but still apprehensive about their futures. In the past year, Garabed had become particularly more ill-tempered toward Syrvart, and she spent much of her time trying to evade him in innocence and embarrassment. Mariam could only protest mildly. Like her daughter, she feared the moody man.

It was Christmas Eve, and appropriately a gentle snow fell continually over the Massachusetts town. Humanity was through with its money spending and wrapping and rushing and baking, grateful now for this placid, blessed night to enjoy some of the peace Christmas was intended to provide. The Hamparian house, with a wiggling puff of smoke rising from its chimney, was the only one on the street with no candles in the windows or tinseled trees or wreaths on the door. Inside, the family sat around a fire, dreaming of what it must be like to celebrate a real American Christmas in this wondrous new land.

Hagop wandered around the house, hugging a well-worn, stuffed teddy bear with one green eye and a half-torn-off, red felt mouth. It was his "welcome to America" gift from his aunt. He wore a snuggly pair of pajamas, which were made with snaps running up the front with a comical flap around the rear. He had turned into a little boy—no longer the whining infant he had been—and Mariam was going to start him in some sort of schooling very soon.

Mariam sat by the roaring fire, mesmerized by its hypnotic, flashing flames and sparkling warmth. She was at last comfortable and safe in her life. America was more than any woman from her part of the world could have ever dreamed of. If she was unhappy and uneasy with the two-sided Garabed, she was at least sure of him, as she might not be of any other Armenian man whose intricacies she didn't know. With the coming new year of 1916, she would be thirty-five years old. She had dearly tried to keep her small, trim body youthful and pleasing. Her dark hair was only slightly dotted with streaks of deep gray, and already she had learned the American way of good grooming and cosmetics, which helped to make the most of any woman. Garabed jeered at her meager attendance to herself, but she didn't care. She knew, in fact, that he liked to look at her.

It was evening. Mariam wore a red, polished cotton dress with tiny, round buttons running up its front, from the waist to the top ruffle of its high neckline. She looked down in childish delight at her intricately laced, high-buttoned, black leather shoes, and she swung her legs rhythmically as she worked with squinting eyes over a shawl she was crocheting for Syrvart.

Her daughter, now thirteen, looked very much like a young woman; she was mature in her stature and stern in her stare. The difficult years, the responsibilities, and the relentless scolding of Garabed had hardened her. Though she was still soft of voice and reticent by nature, her spirit was strong, her housekeeping skills on par with many older girls, and her morals above reproach. Her round, moon-shaped face bore a slight smile as she gazed into the burning fire, thinking to herself how the flames reminded her of the last look she had seen in Bedros Vartanian's eyes. She had been continually dwelling on the young man. She would tell no one, not even her mother, and was ashamed to admit it to herself. She was angry with herself for harboring such fanciful thoughts. He no doubt had forgotten her and was involved with some vivacious, magnificent-looking Armenian girl who was much closer to his own age and much more compatible with his outlandish personality. In her crisscross, laced, green velveteen dress and bone-colored, high-buttoned shoes, she was a lovely picture nestled by the fire. The flames illuminated her deep, hazel-brown eyes and her long, dark hair, which was parted in the middle and pulled meticulously back in a perfect chignon. She was resigned to projecting her stare toward the fire. For when she looked up, she would find Garabed staring at her. Now and again he would jump up and pace nervously around the room. In his way, Garabed had become a good-looking man. His build was acceptable. His face didn't really have one thing wrong with it. And indeed his fine, lacquered mustache and new American hairstyle—parted and combed to one side—enhanced his features. But there was always that frown, that disillusionment in his eyes, which only disappeared after a few drinks. Tonight he wore a fine, gray flannel suit with a stiffly starched, high-collared white shirt and a gold chain hanging from his middle.

Though he was an exasperating and often unpleasantly rude man, there was something about him that evoked pity. He looked like someone who should have been more, could have been more. And yet through the channels of time and torment, something had gone wrong. He worked days in a tannery in the downtown sector of Chelsea, and his pay was respectable. He was accumulating a meager nest egg; and if only one of the women in his household should have looked at him with something more than apathy or disdain, he might have married her. That would have made him a completely fulfilled man.

The scene was tranquil but dull, lacking the luster of Christmas Eve, which made it no more than any other winter's evening. Suddenly there was a thunderous knock on the door. It shook the rafters, brought Hagop stumbling into the parlor, his thumb hanging from his mouth, and made Mariam and Syrvart sit up, wide eyed, and wonder who could be visiting them on their first Christmas in America.

Garabed stomped toward the door, mumbling something about who would be so bold as to disturb them. And when he opened the door, he answered his own grumbling question. His face was aghast with a mixture of astonishment and fury. Hagop let out a gleeful yelp of delight. Mariam at first rose elegantly, then rushed over to the intruder in giggling excitement; and Syrvart stood there, staring in ecstatic disbelief, smiling more broadly than she had ever smiled before.

At the door stood Bedros Vartanian, his eyes shining like the star of Bethlehem; his thick, black lashes encrusted with wet, white snowflakes; his ample lips spread wide in a mischievous smile. His windblown mass of impudent, black hair was dotted with little piles of snow. He wore a thick, blue cardigan sweater, buttoned high; a red scarf wrapped around his neck; dark, navy trousers; and a blue felt cap cocked precariously on the side of his head. He held a bulging sack in one hand and supported a freshly cut fir tree on his broad shoulder.

"Merry Christmas to you all!" Bedros bounded in, dropping snow and tree needles all over. His scarf and sack fell on the floor at the feet of the dumbfounded Garabed.

"Welcome, Pete," responded Garabed with a cool hug and a very Americanized tone to his Armenian. "Come in, as if you have not already."

The two men laughed, and even in his distaste, Garabed showed a glimmer of happiness in seeing this integral part of his past once again.

Bedros lifted Hagop high into the air. He tickled his belly and brought him down to his face for a kiss.

"How is my little roommate?" he asked the giggling child, who responded in Armenian that he was fine. "And you, my dearest Digin

Mariam?" So saying, Bedros held out his muscular arms to the woman, who came to him in an overwhelmed, welcoming embrace.

"How can I be anything but wonderful at the sight of you, Bedros Vartanian? Why, the last I saw of you was a shawl and skirt floating through the water." She laughed. They all laughed, and Bedros gave an embarrassed smile.

"I know it wasn't a very gentlemanly exit, but as you can see, I am back to stay." He added the last two words for the express benefit of Garabed, who had now turned away to fetch some brandy for this shivering, sopping-wet, unlikely Santa Claus.

And then Bedros saw Syrvart. She was standing quietly by the fire, her delicate hands folded curtly in front of her. She had a gentle, pleased smile on her face and a determined coolness in her stare, which she hoped would conceal the thumping of her heart, the knocking of her knees, and the blushing of her cheeks. There came a sudden mystical silence as Mariam lifted her son into her arms and watched blissfully as the handsome man made his way over to the crackling fire and her enamored daughter. It seemed that with each step he took toward her, the young girl's eyes widened a measurement more, and her smile faded into a look of uncomfortable inadequacy as she realized she didn't know what to do or say.

"Little flower!" Bedros said, bending gently down to kiss her cheek. He knew she wouldn't make a move toward him. "Little? Listen to me! Why you are a young woman, are you not? Yes, indeed, a fine-looking young woman!"

Syrvart looked as if she would collapse. She shakily made her way back to her chair by the fire. Obligingly, Bedros turned away from her for a moment, giving her the chance to compose herself. He knew exactly what he was doing to the little girl and enjoyed every minute of it. He was assured of his affectionate prominence in her life.

"Yes, Mariam, I must compliment you. She is her mother's daughter—a perfect replica of your loveliness."

"And you, Bedros, are the perfect replica of a flatterer who tries to melt ladies' hearts." Mariam was trying to keep a very warm moment from catching into uncontrollable fire. "Sit down and take off those wet shoes, Bedo. Here, let me help you." She escorted him to the chair next to Syrvart and helped him to remove his soggy shoes and swampy socks. She placed them safely in front of the fire.

"Syrvart, see if Garabed has an extra pair of slippers in his closet; if not, just fetch a pair of socks from his top dresser drawer."

Syrvart was grateful for the chance to get away. She would also make sure to check in a mirror before returning to the parlor. She could feel Bedros's eyes following her out of the room and up the stairs—those beautiful eyes!

"Does Garabed have his own bedroom?" Bedros found himself foolishly inquiring with a look of mistrust on his troubled face.

Mariam smiled at him curiously. "Why, yes, of course he does, Bedo. He and Hagop share one bedroom, Syrvart and I another; and my sister-in-law has her own room. We are really quite comfortable here."

Bedros looked around in delight. It was a real home—reclusive, warm, and alluring-the kind he would one day like to call his own. A home he would fill up with a fine and energetic family— extensions of himself.

At simultaneously inopportune moments, Syrvart scurried in with a pair of slippers just as Garabed lumbered in with a brandy embraced in each hand. Bedros rose, uncomfortably taking the shoes and placing them on his still-frozen feet, then walked over to Garabed, who stood stiffly by the parlor entrance. Bedros pleasantly accepted the brandy from him.

"So," Bedros bellowed, trying to soften a most awkward moment, shattering the icy unfriendliness of Garabed's aura with his booming, grasping voice. "Come sit by the fire with me, old friend, and tell me what goes on up here."

Reluctantly Garabed took a chair across from Bedros next to the fire. Syrvart and her mother removed themselves to the kitchen, knowing instinctively when to get away from Garabed. Hagop was sitting excitedly next to the great, fallen tree, brushing his tiny hands along the bristly needles in childish wonder. His eyes were glowing in the joyous astonishment of Christmas, American style.

"It seems you keep turning up, Pete—like an old shoe." Garabed was smiling now—cautiously, almost musingly, at his visitor.

"I guess you better get used to it, Garabed. I am a part of your life, and you are a part of mine. Whether either of us wants it so is beyond question at this point." Bedros's tone was serious, his glare avid yet remorseful.

"That is rather presumptuous of you, is it not, old friend?" Garabed was as cold as the thickly accumulating snow out the front bay window but not nearly so soft or inviting.

"You well know, Garabed, that I shall never leave the thoughts or adorations of the women in this family. In fact, you should be grateful that I wish to include you in my plans at all."

Garabed jumped up from his seat. His eyes were afire with indignation and disbelief. "You! You are incredible! You pompous, self-righteous idiot!" His face was glowing red, his eyes filled with tears of fury. He took his brandy glass into his left hand and flung it violently into the fire. The liquor made an explosive *poof* sound when it joined the flames—like the lifelong encounters of these two men.

Bedros rose slowly, his eyes burning in disgust with the immature tantrums of this grown man. But then he mellowed and felt sorrow for the torment he knew Garabed must be inwardly experiencing. Bedros grabbed Garabed's shoulders and held them tightly. Though the man tried to untangle himself in twisting jerks and stomps, it was to no avail.

"All right now, just settle down!" Bedros was demanding, and the look in his eyes told Garabed he had better submit. "Sit down and listen to me before flying into another of your childish rages, old man!"

Garabed obediently settled back into his chair. He stared sullenly at Bedros, as if all fight had suddenly been drained from his body.

"Go ahead, Bedo. Let me hear the plans you have made for my life." His sarcasm didn't stir Bedros, who took a seat and carefully considered what he was about to propose.

"You have not fared poorly in listening to my plans, have you, Garabed?"

There was no answer to the well-placed question. Just a long, deep breath and a disinterested shrug of the shoulder.

"To continue," Bedros was undaunted, and he began to unravel his future plans to the dumbfounded Garabed. "I have come up here, as you well know, to make myself a permanent fixture in the lives of these women. Now, the question is what is the best way to approach this situation? There are two eligible women here and they would each fit well into our lives as attentive, loving wives."

Bedros got up a moment and paced around the room, looking out the window at the magnificent, magical mounds of white snow. He wandered matter-of-factly over to the archway leading into the parlor and peered down the hall toward the kitchen to make sure the women were still preoccupied with their preparations. He noticed Hagop squatting by the fire. He bent over the child and whispered something in his ear. The secret evoked a giggle, a wide-eyed stare, and an immediate exit from the room. Bedros returned to his seat and the morose Garabed.

"This is how I want it to be, my friend. There can be no argument. I shall propose marriage to Syrvart."

Garabed's hands grasped the arms of the chair and started to slowly rise, but Bedros got up quickly and gently pushed the rising man down into his former position. "You will not get up again while I am speaking, or indeed, you will not get up again!" he said as Garabed sat back, assured that Bedros meant every word.

"As I was saying, I will marry Syrvart. I must admit, even to you, that I have had a strong feeling of what the Americans might call love for the girl. I've felt it for many years, I suppose."

"And she for you, I will grant you that." Garabed's words were filled with remorse and envy.

"Well, that is understandable." Bedros chided and laughed, but didn't stir even a tiny grin from the dismal Garabed. "I must in turn accept Mariam and little Hagop as part of my family. I will bring all of them back to live with me in Philadelphia, where one day soon I hope to have my own business."

Garabed just glared. His eyes were tired and red from holding back tears of self-pity. "And that leaves me where you have always wanted me, does it not? Out in that blizzard, alone!" He pointed a quivering finger toward the window.

"No, Garabed, on the contrary. I feel an odd responsibility for you, though I will never understand why. You will come with us."

Garabed's face was suddenly overcome with an incongruous mixture of gratitude and contrived contempt. His mouth opened, but he couldn't speak.

"Of course, there is one condition, my friend," Bedros continued with a faint smile.

"Is there not always?" Garabed's face quickly returned to its caustic display of being stoic.

"Oh, but this is such a nice condition!" Bedros continued, now beaming like a scheming, little elf. "You must marry Mariam."

Garabed was frozen, his face paralyzed; only his eyes rolled about in incredulous astonishment. "You are mad!" He somehow forced the words out of his still mouth.

"No, not at all. It is only fitting and proper. I will not have you living under my roof as anything other than Mariam's husband. That will help you to understand your position as far as Syrvart is concerned, and you shall have a fine wife as well."

"What if I, or she, refuses?" Garabed glared at him defiantly.

"No one will refuse me." Bedros was now glowering—the poignant patriarch. "They cannot, because Bedros Vartanian will not have it any other way!"

Garabed sat for a long while without a word. He pondered the person seated across from him partly in hatred, partly in love, but mostly in envy for the self-reliant man he was. "Then, I suppose, so it will be." He shrugged.

"Right!" shouted Bedros, slapping his hands down on his thick thighs. "Now, let us get busy and put up this fine tree. It is Christmas Eve, you know; but it certainly does not look like it around here."

"But of course you will make it all perfect, will you not, my old friend?" Garabed was now standing, holding out a limp hand to Bedros. His soul had surrendered.

"Yes," Bedros answered, holding out his hand and grasping Garabed's tightly in a robust show of friendship found. "Everything is going to turn out fine!"

Shortly Mariam and Syrvart entered the parlor with Hagop at their heels. They were each holding a platter piled high with choeregg, cheese, *lahmajoon*—a tiny Armenian-style pizza—olives, *toorshi* of all varieties, and steaming, little lamb balls of *kufta*. The two women froze in the archway at the sight of Bedros and Garabed working together in what appeared to be happy spirits. The men were putting up the fir tree and decorating it with red-and-green glass ornaments from Bedros's sack.

Hagop screeched in glee and rushed over to take his part in the trimming festivities. He tore open a package of glimmering silver tinsel and began to carelessly toss it all over the tree. Garabed stopped his tinkering and kindly explained to the child that each strip should be placed on the branches individually. Mariam looked over at Syrvart, and the two stared in disbelief and joy at the sight. The food was placed on a table in front of the sofa. Garabed and Bedros enjoyed the food and several celebrant chalices of liquor.

In the next few hours, thanks to Bedros, it had aesthetically become Christmas Eve.

That evening they all slept secure in their dreams and sound in their exhaustion. The next morning, they enjoyed a filling breakfast, which barely found stomach space from the meal the night before. The new and unlikely family then retired to the parlor and sat around the shimmering Christmas tree, while Bedros, the self-appointed patriarch, passed out his modest gifts to the family.

For Hagop there was a small, handmade, wooden dog, whose hinged ears flapped up and down and whose tail moved comically from side to side. The child, in his unspoiled appreciation, was ecstatic. For Garabed there was a box of Antonio and Cleopatra cigars and a fifth of fine Kentucky Bourbon. For Mariam there was a silky, white bed jacket with adornments of frilly, pale, pink lace and tiny, embroidered, bright-pink rosebuds. Finally, to the shy Syrvart, he offered a small, unwrapped box. Still dumbfounded over the delights of the past few hours, she held it in her hands and silently beamed at the looming Bedros.

"Well, do not just sit there, my girl! Open up the gift." Mariam, still gazing in delight over her lovely bed jacket, gently drew her daughter out of her delirium with a soft nudge.

Syrvart shook her head. She was embarrassed receiving any gift at all but especially from this young man, whom she had loved for so long. Her small fingers trembled as she lifted the tiny lid and removed a square of flattened cotton. She looked down, her head unmoving as though she were asleep. Mariam rose, gasping. She held her hand over her mouth as she spied the glittering article in the box.

At last Syrvart lifted her head and stared into the fire, then at her mother, then out the window, anywhere she could to avoid Bedros's stare. Knowing there was no escaping him, she looked into his dancing eyes and nearly melted from their radiant intensity. Her tiny heart thumped inside her. Her whole body trembled. "It is a ring." It was all she could say.

"Bravo, my girl. You have guessed it!" They all laughed at Bedros's joking, and even Syrvart attempted a smile.

"It is so fine, so lovely. It is a diamond, is it not?"

Mariam was now nestled by her daughter's side. "Yes, my child, it is a diamond. The mother gazed up at Bedros with tears in her overjoyed eyes. She was well aware, more so than her daughter, what the gift meant.

"It is a *hoscab*," Mariam said, looking proudly at her future son-in-law. "It means that Bedo would like you to consider becoming his wife."

At the words Syrvart dropped the ring to the floor and threw her head down into her hands. She cried. It was a little girl's cry, slightly excited, slightly terrified. She held her hands tightly against her face for safety, for seclusion from this adult happening, with which she couldn't cope.

Bedros bent down and picked up the modest, silver ring with its tiny diamond sparkling in the reflection of the fire. He gently pulled Syrvart's right hand away from her face and put the ring on her finger. It slipped awkwardly around. The ring swung downward on her tiny finger, and the sight of it brought a shy giggle out of the little girl.

"Well, that is just the point, little flower. Of course we will wait until your finger grows into the ring. Until we are settled back in Philadelphia. I didn't intend to marry you this very night, you know!"

They laughed—all of them, even Garabed, at whom Syrvart glanced, wondering why he wasn't tearing the room apart.

"Of course," Syrvart said, looking over at her mother. "It is up to *Mayrig* and Garabed."

"We most happily agree to your marriage," Mariam insisted with a proud grin. "Do we not, Garabed?"

Obligingly, Garabed nodded in acceptance of the arrangement, over which he knew he had no control. He decided to attempt a few appropriate words, but as his mouth opened to speak, it was Bedros Vartanian who was talking.

"Of course, Garabed is delighted for you, Syrvart. And besides, he has something to be pleased about this night as well. Do you not, Garabed?"

Garabed was dangling helplessly from Bedros's hook. By the nose he was being led into the remainder of his life. In honesty he couldn't complain that it would be so awful. He smiled an astutely stiff smile and turned his cool, unromantic eyes toward Mariam. In an instant the wise woman realized all that was about to transpire—all that Bedros had contrived.

"Mariam," Garabed began in a businesslike voice, "I am sure you would agree that it is only fitting that you and I should once and for all be married."

Mariam looked at Garabed in touched sorrow. He was younger than she. He was oddly morose and unpredictable. Without marriage to Garabed, she could fare much worse. She wasn't a young girl anymore and Bedros would always be there, ever watchful of Garabed's behavior. With Bedros she would have no fears and as the new patriarch of her family, it was her responsibility to respectfully comply with Bedros's wishes At last, Mariam smiled.

"Of course, Garabed. If it is your wish."

"It is," he added emphatically and rose to fetch some more glasses for a toast.

So it was that in front of a shimmering Christmas tree perched proudly in the parlor of this small home in Massachusetts, a troth was set. The lives of five people were to be indelibly intertwined.

Bedros left the following day. His final look into Garabed's eyes was a fierce but friendly warning. He patted Hagop on the head, embraced Mariam in the comfort of his promise, and offered his betrothed a gentle kiss. Then he disappeared into the still-falling snowflakes.

• • •

Back in Philadelphia it was another Monday morning, and no one was particularly joyous to return to work, especially those at the Pennsylvania Sugar Company who had to give up the blessed tranquility of the yuletide for the glum glowering of Mr. Peterson. Bedros and Ara were in unusually gay moods, though. They were happy in the celebration of Bedros's engagement. At last there was something certain and bright in their futures. They both greeted the puffy-eyed, swollen-bellied foreman with a cheerful good-morning, to which he gave a groan in reply. Ara ran up to his perch atop the centrifuge machine, and Bedros went back to the shipping area. There he took the usual care of his inventory and then found his place underneath the squeaking crane, manned by the quiet Vincenzo.

The factory was running smoothly. Like a well-lubricated wheel, it spun and churned. Over and under and up and down flowed the sugar, speeding along its many different stages. Bedros stood—head held high, neck aching and hurting more than usual since he had been away from his work for a few days. Ara watched over his centrifuge faithfully, only now and then craning his neck to see whether his brother was all right. He despised Peterson for making Bedros perform such a perilous task. He continually begged his younger brother to complain, to take on other functions at the factory. Bedros refused, calling him silly. Despite Bedros's assurances, Ara was still uncomfortable with the whole situation.

The lunch whistle blew, and the noisy factory instantly turned into a silent graveyard. Most of the workers sat quietly in some remote corner with a lunch pail or brown paper bag in their laps. They couldn't afford to eat lunch in a restaurant, and the cold weather prohibited them from going outdoors.

Bedros and Ara squatted by the great shipping-and-receiving doors. Each brother sat on a large burlap sack filled solidly with sugar. Yughaper had prepared them cold turkey sandwiches. There was a thermos of hot coffee, some strips of carrots and celery, and two juicy, red apples. They were so perfectly flawless that biting into them seemed sinful. The brothers munched and gulped and chattered excitedly in their mother tongue, reliving the happenings from the holiday in Chelsea and contriving plans for the future.

"You will live with us, Ara. Remember that." Bedros didn't speak clearly; he was encumbered by a bulging mouth. "Do not get any ideas that you will be out of my life just because I marry."

"I see," laughed Ara. "Just like that you have planned my life?"

"No, just until you are married and settled. Then you can move out and find a place of your own. But not until you are ready, understand? That is the way. We have to stick together, brother." Bedros slapped him on the back.

"I know that, Bedo. I couldn't bear it any other way."

Ara looked lovingly at his precious brother. Bedros was and always would be the anchor of the family. He was the gladiator, the master, the heart of the machinery. Ara could fix the parts and make them run, but without Bedros there would be no family, no life at all. He thought how he would kill anyone who might jeopardize the future of his younger brother—this beautiful, unique human being who had borne so much and still wouldn't be quelled. The lunch whistle blew him out of his melancholia, and the two brothers hastened back to their jobs.

It was nearly four o'clock, and already the darkness of impending night was shadowing the windows of the factory. Ara was very tired. He stared down at the whirling machine, and his head spun hypnotically around with it.

Then he heard the screeching and the yelling and the crash.

Ara Vartanian looked down toward the sounds in terror. He saw Vincenzo running and screaming in Italian, his hands on his head. He saw an immense bag of sugar sprawled on the floor, split open and spilled all over the concrete. Just inches away—on his back, deadly still, his eyes closed, his legs and arms covered with sugar—was his brother. Ara flew down the iron stairway. He felt as if his heart had stopped and he couldn't breathe. He knew Bedros was dead. His mind began to plan what he would have to do—to whom he would turn. Ara's face was drained of color and with arms outstretched he ran over to Bedros's body. Many other workers were now gathering all about the scene and the multitude of various excited languages created a tumultuous, undistinguishable din. Ara fell down over his brother. He lifted his limp head up in his hands and cried out in tormented Armenian.

"Please, dearest brother, do not be dead. I beg of you, God, do not let him be dead!" Ara rocked his brother's head in his arms. He looked down into those great eyes, impeaching them to open.

At last, Bedros did open his eyes. He blinked, shook his head, and brought his hand up to his forehead. He looked up at Ara with a faint but reassuring smile.

"So, it happened again?" Bedros managed the words.

"Are you all right, Bedo? Can you move? Do you need a doctor?" Ara was near hysteria.

Bedros took a long breath, then assured Ara he was fine as he shakily rose to his feet. "I guess I just fainted from the fright."

"I guess you did." Ara replied, all the while his eyes were raging upward—toward the bridge where Peterson stood looking down silently on the scene. Bedros continued to talk, steadied himself, and brushed off the sugar, but when he turned to embrace Ara, his brother was gone. Bedros looked around as all the workers were frantically babbling and pointing up toward Peterson. He stood high up on the iron bridge, and Ara was sprinting toward him, bounding up the iron stairs, and making sounds like a snarling tiger.

In a dizzy fog Bedros started after him but was still wobbly on his feet. He grabbed a hold of a sturdy section of the crane and screamed at his brother, begging him to stop. But Ara continued on in furious frenzy, murder seething in his eyes. Peterson suddenly realized what was happening and started to run down the bridge. But Ara, like a svelte cat with his every ensuing move, leaped into the air, lunged forward, and landed squarely on top of Peterson's body. The two men fell in a rolling, jostling heap on the bridge, which reverberated with the vibrations of their struggling bodies.

Bedros was below, shouting, begging his brother to stop. The other factory workers were huddled at the base of the stairs, looking up and cheering for Ara. They were unified in their hatred for Peterson. Beneath the two fighting men the dangerous centrifuge steadily spun —casting off the molasses from the sugar. Ara hit Peterson with a hard right punch squarely against his jaw, and the man fell backward. His arms were hanging down over the railings like two limp rubber bands. His head hung directly over the centrifuge, which was only a few feet below and was suddenly transformed into an instrument of death. Ara held his hands tightly around Peterson's neck and tenaciously began to squeeze. Peterson's red face turned a deep purple, and his limp body began to slide farther down off the iron bridge. Ara wasn't sane. He didn't care. He wanted Peterson to fall and be torn to shredded sug-arcane in the centrifuge. His only thought was that this hateful man would hurt his brother no more. Peterson couldn't be forgiven for what he had almost done. Though the terrified foreman struggled, Ara began to push the man's body farther down until his hair actually rustled in the swooshing air stirring from the centrifuge. Just one hard shove and Peterson would be among the sugar crystals—spun and separated into oblivion.

Bedros felt as if he was running through a nightmare. His mind was willing, but his legs felt heavy and slow. He felt sure he would never reach the bridge in time - not to save Peterson but to save Ara. He forced his body to make one last effort up the black iron railing onto the bridge, and over to the two bodies. He grabbed Ara and, using all the might he could muster, he pulled his brother up and off Peterson. Bedros held Ara fast—not reneging, not lessening his grasp, until he was sure his brother's spasmodic muscles were relaxed and his madness finally allayed. He grabbed Ara's two shoulders and held them tightly in his hands, shook him furiously, then changed his grasp to an exasperated hug. The two brothers stood, enveloped in each other's arms on the shaking iron bridge.

"If you kill him, you kill yourself. You kill all of us, Ara."

Ara looked down at Peterson, who was as white as the past Christmas snow, his eyes wide as he looked down at what might have been his whirling deathtrap. He slowly rose, brushed himself off, and wandered down the iron walkway. His head dangled in dejection and shame. He was a crushed and beaten man. The factory workers watched in silence as the demeaned demagogue walked out of the factory, leaving behind some part of himself, which he would never regain. Ara calmed and understood that he had done enough to the pathetic man. Peterson could never rule with any authority again. Ara turned and smiled at his brother, wrapping his arms around Bedros's broad stretch of back.

"Let us get out of here, Bedo. Tomorrow we will get a new job. Tomorrow we will begin again."

With the continuing mechanical churnings in the background, the workers returned to their stations. Peterson was gone. Vincenzo had walked out, never to return. Ara and Bedros Vartanian, their arms still wrapped around one another, silently and assuredly made their way out the great metal door leading from the Pennsylvania Sugar Company and into the crisp riverside air of Philadelphia.

The next morning the two brothers walked the streets of Philadelphia in search of work. They couldn't be idle; life was running by too quickly. There was no time...no time to waste.

By the end of the day, they were both hired. Now they were where they belonged, not in a place of syrup, but in a place of strength—the Pennsylvania Steel Company. There they would acquire the priceless knowledge of the forging and stamping of metals, an education which would serve them well in the future.

The following month brought with it many warm afternoons, when Ara and Bedros would stroll, delving farther into the vastly transformed growth of Philadelphia. During one such stroll, Bedros spied a small, three-story, brick row house on Columbia Avenue with a For Rent sign handwritten and taped on the front door. He tapped Ara on the shoulder and pointed at the home.

"Ara, this is where I am going to live. You too after you get married, like a good Armenian man should." Bedros was aglow; his eyes shimmering like stars as they perused the structure.

"Bedo, you have not even seen the inside." Ara, as always, was overwhelmed with his brother's impulsiveness and blind self-assuredness.

"I do not have to see it! I know it will be the right house."

The following day Bedros returned to the modest row house. A toothless old man wearing a flannel shirt and gray pants greeted him. The shirt was too big; the pants were too small.

"What ya want?" the decrepit man asked.

"I want to see this house," Bedros proclaimed.

"You're a foreigner, ain't ya?" The man peered at him through half-closed eyes.

"No," Bedros answered, staring him down. "Are you?"

The suspicious old man showed him through the modestly furnished home. It was surprisingly clean and more than adequate. Though things would be tight with only three bedrooms and one bath, Bedros liked it. He looked astutely at the bent-over man and asked the rental fee.

"Fifty a month," the man splattered out, still spying Bedros with suspicion.

"Here is forty, cash. That is what it is worth. I don't know when I will be moving in, but I will pay you on the first of each month to hold it for me until I do." Bedros put the money into one limp hand of the speechless old man, shook hands with the other, and bounded out the door.

Now at last for Bedros, all things were in place. He returned to Chelsea, confident of his future and ready to begin it with Syrvart. On their wedding day, God watched them proudly. These children who, like Job, wouldn't be beaten, would shout at the devil and even their Father, and then would pick themselves up, moving on to even greater adventure. In His delight the Almighty took out His paint brush and dipped it in mortally unattainable hues of bright crimson, golden yellow, and burnt orange. Carefully, He painted the trees and the grass and the sky so that on one fine, crisp, dreamy September Sunday, Bedros Vartanian and Syrvart Hamparian could be married, surrounded by the colorful beauty they so deserved. It was a modest wedding, opulent in love and warmth, sparse in guests and fanfare.

Bedros and his new family returned to Philadelphia on a puffing, rumbling train. Hagop was in his glory, running up and down the aisles and taunting his mother whenever he could. Mariam kept a close eye on him as she sat next to Garabed, to whom she wasn't yet married. In Chelsea, without Bedros present, there was no one to question him. Now he was unsure of what the future would hold.

They all moved into the tiny rented home on Columbia Avenue, and family life of sorts was begun. Mariam and Syrvart prepared a delicious dinner for their first night in Philadelphia. It was after dinner that the sleeping arrangements proved to be a problem. Bedros and Syrvart took the main bedroom. Mariam and Hagop took another, and Garabed took the third. This wasn't how it was supposed to be. Garabed and Mariam should have been married before this. Restlessly Bedros tossed and turned through their first night in the house. Something would have to be done very quickly.

The next day Bedros returned home from the mill, changed, ate, and quickly rushed out. In an hour he came back, bringing with him a local Armenian priest, and that evening in the tiny, barren living room, Mariam and Garabed became man and wife. Bedros Vartanian slept quite well after that, because at last things were right.

Chapter 8

THE BUSINESS, 1919

In the ensuing years, Bedros's life took on tremendous, new twists and turns. Syrvart, a mere child herself, gave birth to their first baby—a daughter. They didn't know that the little, red-haired girl was to commence a parade of six more children thereafter. All of those children, too, would be born in the same bed in which they were conceived.

Ara finally chose his wife from a photograph, and within a year, she would be arriving from Syria. Ara and Yughaper lived on their own, but there was no question that when Ara married, they would all move in with Bedros. That would be the case until Ara was financially able to begin in a new home of his own. But he would never have to leave, as far as Bedros was concerned.

Finally, Hirair married his mail-order orphan girl. To his dismay, he discovered very quickly that she couldn't cook or sew and knew nothing of domestic matters. Furthermore, Hirair had not yet acquired the ownership of the Azarian grocery and found that his wages were far too meager to afford renting his own home. Bedros, after listening to his unhappy friend, offered that the two come to live with him until the young girl had acclimated herself. It was pitiful. The girl was so naïve that she didn't even know she was pregnant, and when her time came, the infant fell out into Syrvart's open apron.

The house on Columbia Avenue was crowded, but no one complained. They were hilarious times—hard times but good times. The struggling new families coexisted in the tiny row house and miraculously got along very well. There was no incompatibility, jealousy, or argument. Except for an occasional outburst from Garabed, their commune fared quite nicely. The women knew their places well, and the men were glorified in their sanctity.

Bedros, however, knew he would need a larger home soon, especially when Ara married. The brothers met often and spoke of their financial woes. After several years at the Pennsylvania Steel Company, the brothers had learned much and they felt the time had come for them to pull up their britches and buckle down to some good, old American ingenuity.

It was a fine, late October morning, and Philadelphia was aglow with autumn brilliance and a sparkling, clear blue sky. The city was preparing for Thanksgiving, and there were even a few hints of yuletide in the air. Ara and Bedros ate scant breakfasts and met at Bedros's house to discuss their quest, their lunge into some frightening but necessary new venture.

The plan was to rent a small, inexpensive building suitable for light manufacturing. Initially they would make chisels—a relatively simple tool and one which they felt was always in demand. The brothers determined they would go to their factory in the morning and manufacture the tools. Ara would continue working there the rest of the day while Bedros would cover the city, knocking on doors, stopping people on street corners, and selling their wares anyway and anywhere he could. Surely there was no finer salesman in the world!

As they combed the streets of Philadelphia, the Vartanian brothers found themselves on Vine Street, where they saw a house with a sign that read, BASEMENT FOR RENT. They looked at each other excitedly, shrugged, and smiled in agreement that they would take a look. It was a small, three-story house, very old, and quite a mess; but all they would be renting was the basement, which would probably be cheap.

The door to the basement was unlocked, and on it was tacked a handwritten note. "Come in and look. If interested, see proprietor upstairs." They opened the creaking door, which pushed along with it a scooping of loose dirt. They went down the five steep steps leading into the cold, empty room. Bedros and Ara were dumbfounded, their feet sinking into the sandy, muddy floor beneath them. That was it; that was the whole of it. It was a large, very cold, very dirty, empty basement. The walls were thick with sloppily swirled plaster. And, wonder of all wonders, above their heads, attached to one newly installed sagging wire, swayed a light bulb. They looked around at the bare walls. They looked down at their dirty, worn shoes, which sank into the muddy floor. They looked up at the swinging light bulb. They placed their hands on their hips. Then they looked at each other and broke into laughter.

Only foolhardy madmen would have even considered the place. Only two idiots who were so driven that they believed they could turn even this dingy basement into a working factory would have bothered to discuss it. Ara and Bedros were both. They went up to the owner of the building, signed a year's lease, and ran all the way to Joe's Bar for celebration and conversation.

For a long while they sat silently, looking down at their ham-and-cheese sandwiches, side orders of french fries, and frothy glasses of spring beer. Finally Ara confronted his brother, a slight frown encumbering his otherwise brightly smiling face.

"Okay, Bedo, and where do we go from here?"

"Well, you said once—I think it was in this very place—that you could rig up a Model T motor to turn a grinding machine. So, now is your chance." Bedros was serious. His eyes were darkly still and pensive yet still wondrously alive with determination.

"I did, did I not?" Ara mused. "Well, of course, surely I can."

"Fine." Bedros slapped his hands down on the table, and the white foam spilled down the sides of the glasses onto the red-checkered tablecloths. "Next, we purchase the grinder machine. We can go to the steel mill for the ingots. Surely they will give us a good price. Let me see; we will need a potbelly stove for heat, an old file cabinet to begin our records, and well, whatever else we will buy as we go along."

"As simple as that?" Ara laughed, worried inside.

"As simple as that, Brother," Bedros announced, self-assured and ready.

They washed down their lunches with a double scotch and water, and then set out to submit their resignations from the Steel Company. The resignations were accepted with much regret. Both Ara and

Bedros were offered considerable salary advancement and the promise of future foreman status as enticement to stay. But, as inviting as it all sounded, the thought of owning something of their very own, of being their own keepers and agitators, was far more appealing to both of them. They spent the rest of the day shopping. Ara acquired his grinder machine from an old machine shop with a GOING OUT OF BUSINESS sign in the window.

The two brothers lugged the huge machine over to Bedros's already overburdened house and dragged it into a detached garage in the rear yard. There, utilizing the power from an old Ford motor, Ara worked relentlessly to make the machine run. As winter set in, he dressed in heavy, bulky clothing and worked without gloves on his nearly frostbitten hands. Often in the mornings, the machine was frozen solid, and Ara would have to use a blowtorch to defrost the parts to make it work. At times it all seemed insane, that it would never work, but right before Christmas the grinder machine was ready.

During this tedious time, Ara received a letter from Malatia. It had been delayed several months. His bride-to-be, a fifteen-year-old girl, whom he knew only from a photograph, would be arriving at Ellis Island in January. Her superiors at the orphanage hoped that someone would be there to meet her and see to her needs.

"*Asdvadz,* help me, Bedo," Ara yelped while reading the letter. "I am not ready for this! Our factory will just be starting. I cannot leave you with all this." He was shaking all over.

Bedros took hold of his brother's arms and pulled them forward as if he were a robot. He held him tight and steady.

"Slow down, brother dear. It is only Christmas. You have some time before she arrives. We will be well settled and running by then."

"But, Bedo..." Ara was white and horror-struck with this added burden to his already confused life.

"Have I ever let you down, Ara?" Bedros interrupted.

The two looked deeply into each other's eyes. Ara calmed down, outwardly at least. "No, you never have, Bedo."

"And I will not now. Just as you have never let me down. So let us eat dinner and get some sleep. Tomorrow we begin our new business."

The next morning Ara and Bedros moved the grinder over to the rented basement. They were a comical sight, trudging their way on foot, hauling the large, clumsy machine. The room was now prepared with the tiny heater, a used filing cabinet filled with order forms imprinted with the words VARTANIAN BROTHERS, INC., some pens and pencils, and a few flasks of whiskey. Bedros stood, balancing the grinder against his body, as Ara opened the door and stepped down into the basement to help his brother lower the heavy machine into its place.

Suddenly Ara let out a forlorn moan and bounded up the steps to Bedros, who was aching from holding the slipping machine. Ara's face was pale and horrified.

"Bedo, Bedo, we are idiots! Now we have done it. Now we have really done it!" Ara was beside himself with confusion, and Bedros held fast to the grinder, which was now halfway down the steps.

"Well, while you are yelling, help me hold this damn thing, Ara. What in God's name is the matter with you?" Bedros couldn't understand his brother's ridiculous behavior. Everything had been so well planned, so well thought out—he was sure of it. Almost completely sure of it. And besides, the grinder was heavy.

"Bedo, do you not see? Look, look at this damn grinder. Jesus, it is nearly nine feet high."

"And...," Bedros began to argue but immediately stopped himself. A sick feeling overcame him, and he felt as if he would collapse. Ara needed to say no more. The grinder was nine feet tall. The basement ceiling came only to the tops of their heads. The machine wouldn't fit in the basement factory.

"We are finished! All this work! A year's lease. God, Bedo, we are fools!"

"Ara," Bedros mellowed. "Here, help me lean this monstrosity against the wall and let us go down and take a look. For every problem, there is a solution, Brother."

They stood for several minutes, looking about the room. Ara nervously paced, mumbling to himself in a frenzy. Bedros was silent. He kept lifting and lowering his head. At first his motions were very methodical and slow, then he gradually began to pick up speed, and the up-and-down motion of his head made him look as if he were ardently agreeing with someone, conversing with him from above. Then Bedros began to hum and his black eyes burst open with a solution.

"Bedo?" Ara looked at his brother, assuming Bedros had an idea. "Come now, Bedo. Let us face it. We cannot raise the ceiling."

"Ara," Bedros went on, his mind whizzing, his eyes afire with glory and inspiration. "Go quickly and get us some picks and shovels. I will stay here and guard the grinder."

Ara pondered his brother. He loved him as never before for his refusal to die, for his indefatigable quest for success, for his head-on rebuttal to any and all obstacles. He wouldn't dare question him.

"Brother dear," Bedros began, embracing Ara in the womb of his eyes, answering his unspoken inquiry, "You are perfectly correct. We cannot raise the ceiling. So there is only one thing to do." He began to laugh. "We have to lower the floor!"

Ara threw his arms around his brother. They embraced, kissing either cheek a second time, then a third time. Ara flew away, excited tears in his eyes. He was glad Bedros couldn't see him crying. Bedros stood in the middle of their basement factory, looking around at the grand venture, into which they had plunged. He was thankful that Ara wasn't there to see him cry.

Ara returned quickly with the picks and shovels. They proceeded immediately with the arduous task of digging out the basement floor. With aching muscles, pouring sweat, and twisted knots in their backs and groins, they worked until they thought their bodies could endure no more. Afternoon became evening. Their bellies growled. Their eyes burned from the dusty air kicking up all around them. The blisters on their hands had broken open, displaying red pockets of blood.

At last, they had dug out enough of the floor to sufficiently fit the grinder into its place.

In exhaustion, they left the dark basement and began their usual journey to Joe's Bar. Snowflakes began to gently fall and Christmas shoppers bustled obliviously around the two young men. They made their way wearily through the gently swirling, white flakes, their arms wrapped solidly around each other's shoulders as they had always walked back in the old country.

But it wasn't the old country. It was a new, hectic, impatiently growing country. A country with little time for its own let alone two immigrant brothers with big ideas but no money to back them. Ara and Bedros had handicaps beyond most men of their times. The wonderful thing was that neither realized it, or if they did, neither would admit to it.

The next morning the two lingered over coffee, as Syrvart briskly cleaned up the dishes and packed hefty lunches for the brothers. Secretly, she longed for the arrival of Ara's bride. Mariam was helpful, of course, but not as young as she used to be, and Hirair and his wife were now on their own. Syrvart Vartanian, nursing an infant and pregnant with her second child, was weary and worried. Her faith in God and her wonderful Bedros was in constant battle with her cynicism of America and its doubtful promises.

As Bedros sat sketching and mumbling to himself, Ara wrote what was to be his last letter to Aroushag, the skinny little girl who would soon be his wife.

"I am thinking," Bedros said, pounding down on the table with his usual exuberance. "We cannot just depend on one thing, like chisels. There are many people out there making chisels. We must think, Ara. Think of many different things, inventions, and new ideas. Special things from special minds like ours. Out of one of them, for sure, we will come up with something no one else has. Then we not only make it and sell it, but we will get patents. Lots of patents. They will be our backup. It is, after all, the American way."

Ara scribbled his letter and looked up happily at his brother in agreement. Certainly there were no two more ingenious minds in the world. They would do it, and they would do it well.

All morning they shopped, using up the last of their paychecks from the steel company. They bought a used kiln, which Ara would revamp to use for melting the steel. They bought conveyor belts, gasoline for the Model T motor, and a punch press. With the press they could form several different chisel-like shapes, allowing them to make such things as screwdrivers and scrapers.

After a quick lunch (which neither of them could eat from the excitement of getting on with the mini factory), they rushed to the basement of the old house. Ara ran a huge shaft of steel across the entire length of the ceiling, from which he connected several pulleys and conveyor belts. In effect, that one converted Ford engine was to become the single power source for a multitude of operations: the punch press forging out its tiny creations, the belts, and the grinder machine which would sharpen and refine the finished products.

By midnight the Vartanian brothers—sweating, backs breaking, hungry, and troubled—had created a wondrous, giant Tinkertoy of belts and fans and whirling motors in the tiny, dimly lit room. In exhaustion, they had fallen asleep on the floor. They awoke with difficulty to a frantic knock on the door. The room was bitterly cold since the fire in the stove had burned out during the night.

"Ara! Bedros! Are you in there?"

It was Hirair, sent by Syrvart to make sure the men were all right.

"Bedo! Ara! Will one of you please open this door? I am freezing out here!"

"All right. All right. Coming," a sleepy Bedros answered, his breath visible in the cold room.

"Well, good morning. Syrvart was worried, so I said I would check on you. Is everything all right?"

"Fine, fine, my friend," Ara answered from behind his brother. He got up and brushed off his dusty pants. "We were just too tired to go home; that is all."

"Well, what do you think?" Bedros said proudly. "Not bad for two dumb foreigners, eh?"

Hirair bent down and peered up, under, and around the conjured-up mechanisms. He shook his head, smiling in wonder. Ara and Bedros trailed behind him, nodding in unabashed pride.

"So," laughed Hirair teasingly, "it looks pretty good, but does it work?"

"Work!" Bedros howled. "You ask if my brother and me, the two best minds in all the world, would make something that doesn't work? Show him, Brother!"

Bedros bowed to Ara, allowing him to do the honors. Ara marched over to the engine and cranked it up. The three stood waiting, hands clasped tightly, like giggly, anxious little boys. But after a second and third effort, the machine wouldn't start.

"Oh, God damn!" shouted Ara. "Now what? Always something. Always!"

"Shit!" Bedros hollered out with pure American proficiency. "The goddamned thing is frozen. We forgot about that, did we not, Brother? The damn place has no heat!"

Hirair offered to run and get a blowtorch. They used the torch to defrost the engine, and in no time the magnificent machine was buzzing and humming like Bedros's heart. They knew there would be one hundred more cold mornings like this and a hundred more episodes of headaches and barriers, but compared to what they had seen on the other side, none of it could ever be as overwhelming. "The business"—as they would lovingly refer to it in the coming years—was born, and it would consume them evermore.

In the next few weeks, the tiny factory spit out all kinds of things: windshield wipers—to wash away the inequities of the past; chisels—tiny javelins the brothers thrust daily from their souls into the waves of the world; screwdrivers—to open up closed, prejudiced hearts; scrapers—to chip away the debris of language barriers and poverty. On and on the punches furiously pounded away like the brothers' hearts. Ara produced, and Bedros went out to do the selling.

The sales were meager; a tiny hardware store took a dozen screwdrivers; a mom-and-pop grocery took some windshield wipers; another variety store took a dozen of each. The sales helped to feed the children, but for Bedros that wasn't enough. Nothing would ever be enough for this business.

During his daily sales trips in and around the city, Bedros had noticed the Brothers Hardware Stores. They were big, he had decided, because there were ten of them, at least; and their stores were large, bright, and well maintained. He could see the salesmen coming in and going out, carrying their little black briefcases, and he longed to be among them. Here was growth. Not a few items to a few tiny stores but big, bulk orders to growing companies that could sell the hell out of his goods. So he tried again and again, knocking on the doors, only to be curtly turned away; peering through the windows, making comical faces, only to be threatened that the police would be called. Two months had gone by, and no one at Brothers Hardware would see him.

Then late one afternoon, Bedros hid around the corner from what he surmised was Brothers main store—a huge structure right on North Broad Street. He watched as the workers left, and then at last he spotted "the man."

He'd seen him making a showing at most every Brothers store he'd visited: a good dresser, astute, graying at the temples. He'd watched him and was sure this was the owner, the one he had to get to.

There wasn't much time. The man was leaving, heading for his car, no doubt. Bedros had to think and act fast...fast like the time he'd changed the bullets to nails in the crates...fast like the escape from the hospital in Constantinople...fast like his dive into the water, leaving Syrvart and her mother screaming in the background. In this life, you sometimes get only one chance, and you have to take it...fast.

He followed the man around to the back of the store through a tiny alleyway, which led to a dirt parking lot. He watched him as he got into his brand new, gleaming, white car. Quickly, Bedros Vartanian pulled out a sample scraper from the satchel he carried with him everywhere. Quicker yet, he bent down and scooped up a huge ball of thick, wet, brown mud, accumulated from the few days of early spring rain. How perfect! He ran to the car just as the man was starting it. He pulled back his mighty arm, and with a grin and a crazed howl, he threw the mud ball directly at the windshield of the gorgeous, new car.

From behind the filthy glass, Bedros could see the furiously bewildered face of "the man." He got out of his car slowly and started toward Bedros with venom in his eyes.

"You! You...!" He sputtered with his hands clenched and his mouth agape. "I'll kill you!" He lunged at him, but Bedros ducked and bowed like a wiry jester. He grabbed the flabbergasted man's arm, pulling him over to the car. The poor man was now too stunned to struggle.

"No, please, please sir. You cannot kill me, cause then you will not see the great scraper me and my brother made."

With that Bedros let go of the man's limp arm, whipped his scraper through the air like a triumphant sword, and cleanly, swiftly, and completely whisked away the globs of drippy, gooey mud from the windshield.

The Brothers man bought three dozen of everything the Vartanian brothers had to offer...for starters. He gave Bedros references to other heavyweight names in the hardware-and-tool business, and the names became more orders. In addition he became a devoted friend of Bedros Vartanian for life.

• • •

Ara's wife arrived, and the two moved in with Bedros for the first few years of their marriage. Together they would have four children, while Bedros and Syrvart would be as productive in children as the business was in orders.

Chapter 9
CHICAGO, 1945

It seemed that the merciless March wind had blown the square-block-sized Sears Building away from pulsating downtown Chicago and pushed it out toward the less formidable west side. It was a massive structure nevertheless—appropriately housing the offices of one of the largest department stores in America. The great company even boasted of its own bank, which adjoined this multileveled brick complex.

Mr. Whitticomb's office was on the third floor. They had all come there that blustering day—the salesmen with their wares, hoping for the big break—making the big sale to this hardware buyer for the mighty Sears chain.

They tapped their feet and shifted uncomfortably in their seats, waiting for a ten-minute turn with Mr. Whitticomb. In that short time they and their respective companies might be either made or broken. They all knew that having the finest hardware item in the world didn't guarantee Whitticomb's acceptance. What might have a bearing on their business futures could depend on what the illustrious buyer had had for breakfast or whether he'd had sex the night before. Sad criteria but a painful reality of the business world.

A pleasant-looking secretary with a blonde chignon sat behind her metal desk near the door, which led to Whitticomb. Now and then she would peer up from her work and look over the nervous men seated before her. In particular, she eyed the large man in the corner—keeping himself well at bay from the other men sardined on a long, red vinyl bench. He was handsome in a rough sort of way. His hair was an unruly black, splashed with bursts of gray. He didn't look like the others. He didn't act like the others. She guessed he was probably an uneducated foreigner. Still there was something magnetic about him, something captivating—sitting there pompously in his less-than-chic suit.

He sat with his charcoal felt hat nestled precariously on one knee. On the other knee rested a large tool resembling hedge shears. And on the floor, in between his two aged shoes, lay one ragged, laceless, man-sized sneaker.

Bedros was very early—by an hour or so. There was nothing else to do but sit and wait his turn. He perused the room, pondering the other men, who had been waiting there before him. How well dressed they all were. How sweet they smelled! They held their samples on their laps — samples of hammers and saws and various kinds of tools. Most of them had been through this type of presentation a thousand times before. For Bedros it would be the first time. Most of them were far more educated than he. He was sure they all spoke spiffy, polished English. He certainly didn't.

But he had something special about him, even in his poor suit and worn-out attire. He had confidence, a determination in him none of the others seemed to have. There was dogged indefatigability on his face and invincibility in his eyes. It was probably because, unlike them, he was desperate.

This was his last big chance to save their faltering business. They had been through bad times before. In the decades since their first days working out of their basement factory, they had been cheated and fooled into signing over their business to conniving competitors. They hadn't been able to properly comprehend the contracts, and they had trusted many unscrupulous lawyers. They had fallen prey to the Depression and lost everything. Their children had had to take to the city streets, selling candy apples and home-knitted afghans, and their wives had taken in laundry.

It was because of the war things began to go well for the business. At Joe's Bar, he'd met with a buyer for the government. Bedros had persuaded him that he and his brother could make the navy the finest, heaviest, most durable chains in the country. The purchasing agent believed him, and the lucrative order was given. It was an unbelievable dream come true. He felt he'd made it at last. All the past disappointments didn't matter. He and Ara had made it.

But it was now 1945, and it was no secret that the war would soon be over. Already the orders for chains had faltered, and all too soon there would be no more government business—at least not enough to sustain them in their present life.

He couldn't complain. He had many fine daughters, and—thank God—his strong sons had all come home from the war in perfect health. He and his wife also had a beautiful, four-year-old boy—a welcomed surprise. No, he couldn't lament the war's end, nor could he be so reckless as not to think of the future.

So they had made these magnificent hedge shears—he and his brother—and there wasn't anything close to them in the entire world. They had worked on the shears for two years, and now they were perfected. But that wasn't enough. Now he had to sell this man Whitticomb. He had to sell him as if his very life and that of his family depended on it—which they did.

A man came out of Whitticomb's office. The secretary called another name. In less than three minutes, the dejected man came out. For him it had been a wasted trip. The secretary called another name. The salesman strutted into the office. He grinned optimistically as if it would help. In six minutes he came out. His grin had turned upside down.

Bedros laid his hedge shears down on the floor next to the sneaker. He ran his thick, manly fingers through his hair as if to tame it in some simple way. It wouldn't be tamed. He brushed off his wide, gray lapels, and then bent over to tie the lace on one of his worn-out shoes. He heard Whitticomb's door open. The salesman came out with a glowing smile on his face.

The secretary ran her finger down a list on her desk. She peered up and gave a sterile smile to the man in the gray suit. There was no one else waiting. He guessed it must be lunchtime. Whitticomb would be hungry, rushed, and disinterested.

"Mr. Var...Var...Vart...?" the secretary stuttered in a nasal pitch.

"It is Vartanian!" he retorted as if chastising her for not being able to pronounce his beautiful and proud name.

She responded humbly. "I'm very sorry, Mr. Vartanian. Mr. Whitticomb will see you now."

"Thank you." He mellowed, grabbing his shears, his sneaker, and his hat. Dauntlessly, he bolted into the office.

Mr. Whitticomb was seated behind a large, mahogany desk with his head bent down over a pile of papers. His office was cold and pale. The floor was a black-and-white-checked asbestos tile. The walls were pale gray. The curtains, as if to excite the bleakness around them, were a deep burgundy. They didn't succeed.

"Mister Whitticomb, I am here!" the salesman announced.

The buyer lifted his head and stared at Bedros curiously as if he had no idea what he was doing in his office.

"Yes, I see you are," he finally said.

"Yes," the unaffected man answered, standing stoically, still clutching his hat, shears, and sneaker. "I see that you see!" He grinned through wide, gleaming, white teeth.

"Well, this conversation could go on all day, couldn't it?" Whitticomb said, showing a surprising glimmer of a smile. Whitticomb pondered the man before him with a new interest. This was a large man—nearly six feet tall. He had a rugged, ruddy complexion, which gave him the glow of tremendous health. His eyes were sparkling black, and they seemed to be dancing in their thick, black-fringed sockets. His eyebrows were bushy and rambling—perfect accompaniments for his wide and prominent nose. He was as creviced and corrugated as a rock and every bit as massive and powerful looking.

"It sure could!" the salesman agreed, laughing with exuberance.

"Let me see," Whitticomb began, checking his notes. "You are Peter Vartanian. Correct?"

"Oh, yes, sir. Very correct you are. That is me. I am Bedros. But you can call me Peter. Or you can call me Pete. Yes, I am happy to see you, Mr. Whitticomb."

He thrust out his large hand in a greeting. He had at least said the buyer's name properly. He had practiced it enough times.

Whitticomb couldn't help laughing a little at the unique charm of this man. His English was so bad as to be ludicrous. He sounded veritably ignorant. But Whitticomb could tell instinctively that he wasn't.

"Yes, well, please sit down, Peter. I see you are here to show me new hedge shears."

"Yes, sir, I am. Brand-new. The best in the world. No other shears like them."

"Well, before you go on, let me explain that we really cannot consider taking on another line. We have hedge shears coming out of our ears. And believe me, they are very, very good."

Peter Vartanian felt a pang in his heart as if Whitticomb had knifed him. His blood ran cold. He hadn't worked this long, come this far, endured all that he had to be rebuffed so neatly.

"Wait a minute!" he howled, jumping up out of his seat and swinging the heavy shears like a reed back and forth across Whitticomb's desk. "I come all this way, go to all this trouble. At least you have to give me a chance, Mr. Whitticomb! You have got to do at least that!"

The buyer sat back rigidly. He was half sympathetic toward the enraged salesman and half terrified of him.

"Hold on now, Pete. I didn't mean I wasn't going to listen to you. I simply wanted to make you understand what kind of competition you're up against."

"Understand? Me understand? I spent two years making this! I worked and worked, day and night. Me and my brother, we both worked. These shears are better than anything on the market today."

"That's easy to say, Pete. After all, it's your product. But we have to do our tests. Then it has to go to the board, then to the president. It could take months, and even then your chances would be slim for being taken on as a committed Sears line."

Peter Vartanian frowned; he didn't have that kind of time. His eyes were livid, and he grinned demonically. He bent down under his chair and scooped up the sneaker. Valiantly, with one hand he held the hedge shears up like a torch. He waved the sneaker in the other.

"You want proof? Okay, Mr. Whitticomb, you will get it! Call some-one right now and have them bring you the best of your hedge shears. Bring all you want!"

"Really, Pete, I simply don't have time—"

"So, this is it? They say this is a free country. This is the land of opportunity. Sure it is -if you were born here, and if you wear fancy pants, and if you speak the language real pretty!"

Peter Vartanian loomed over Whitticomb's desk with venom in his voice. He locked horns with him—eye to eye. He smothered him with his indomitable spirit. Whitticomb drew a tired breath and picked up the phone. Bedros sat down. He knew what was about to happen.

"Tony?" Whitticomb said breathlessly. "Bring me up the five best models of our heavy-duty hedge shears. Well, how the hell do I know? They're in the stock room somewhere! Look near the samples. Look all over! Just get 'em the hell up to me fast!"

"Thank you." Peter sighed.

"Care for a cognac while we wait, Pete?"

"Don't mind if I do. Thank you."

In a little more than ten minutes, the blonde secretary knocked on the door. Whitticomb called her in. She entered, holding two hedge shears, one under each of her delicate, silk-sleeved arms. Following behind her was Tony. He held the other three. Whitticomb motioned to them to plop their bounty down on the desk. They left, cautiously eye-ing the foreign man, who stared back at them with a grin.

"Well, here they are, Pete. So show me what you want to show me. I'm getting hungry."

"I'm not going to show you. You are going to do it yourself!"

"Your gall overwhelms me. Now you want me to do the work!"

"Look, all you got to do is take your big, fancy shears and cut this here gym shoe in half."

Whitticomb was aghast. The man was insane for sure.

"Christ, Vartanian, that's impossible, and you know it."

"Maybe it is for your crap but not for my baby here!"

"You're nuts!" Whitticomb shouted.

"You scared?" the salesman insisted back.

"All right, all right, goddammit. Let's get this magic show over with." Whitticomb stood up, surrendering reluctantly.

"Good! Now I'm going to hold this sneaker in the air and you are going to cut it in half with your shears. See if you can cut this shoe in half with any of them!" Whitticomb decided to start with the lesser-quality shears. Peter held the sneaker up by the heel, keeping his arm stretched out well clear of the shears' blades. Whitticomb took a good thrust, clamping down with gusto on the two handles, but the sneaker just bent over as if in anguish. And so it went with the second, third, fourth, and fifth hedge shear. None of them even made a split in the sneaker.

"Doesn't mean a thing, Peter, and you know it. You've just wasted my time, hoping to break me down. You know damned well no hedge shears can cut a gym shoe of this size and weight in half. You know it all right!"

He shook his finger wildly, but the cool salesman didn't falter. He gave Whitticomb a confident grin and captivated him with his tenacious, black-gem eyes.

"Now if you don't mind, Mr. Whitticomb, please hold this gym shoe up for me. Here, this same way by the heel. Don't be afraid, Mr. Whitticomb—I am a good shot." He laughed, opening up the well-oiled blades of his mighty shears like the jaws of a killer shark.

Whitticomb took a deep breath and held fast to the shoe. Bedros Vartanian opened his mouth widely in imitation of the shears. Then in perfect unison the salesman snapped his mouth shut; at the very same second, the handmade hedge shears sliced the sneaker in two like a piece of composition paper. Whitticomb stood, dumbfounded, and held the heel section of the shoe; his mouth foolishly held open in disbelief as the front part of the sneaker fell to the floor.

• • •

Peter Vartanian got on the elevated line and took a taxi to the center of Chicago. In his pocket he carried an order from one of the largest, most respected retailers in the world – an order for half a million hedge shears.

It was two o'clock and the luxurious Broadway Limited did not leave for Philadelphia until the dinner hour. He had plenty of time. His insides were heaving with excitement and unabashed joy. He wanted to shout at the disinterested passersby that he had gotten the Sears contract, that his troubles were over, that he and his family were going to be rich and that America had fulfilled her promise to him.

He strolled down Michigan Avenue and walked into the Conrad Hilton Hotel. He had a light lunch in the coffee shop. The food barely made it down his throat.

Wait until he got home! There would be a party the likes of which they had never seen before – and God knows there had been parties.

He left the hotel and walked a few yards to the nearby shore of Lake Michigan. It was a viciously cold day but he wasn't chilled. He had battled far worse enemies than Chicago's relentless March wind. He strolled along the shore. The lake roared and rolled in and out at him like a lioness from the sea. He sat down on the cold, damp sand and watched her rhythmic maneuverings in awe. She was like his life – dangerous, tumultuous, powerful and magnificent. He found a large silvery stone and examined it thoughtfully. With a burst of laughter he threw it into the water. It landed in the wake and was lost – consumed by the overpowering surf encircling it.

Some men were like that stone. Bedros Vartanian was not.

EPILOGUE

The last name of Vartanian used in this novel is, in actuality, Vosbikian.

The brother's fledgling Philadelphia company became Hardware and Industrial Tool, Inc. – a formidable competitor in its field. From this emerged Quickie Manufacturing Corporation, the largest manufacturer of home cleaning products in the country at the time.

Between them, the two brothers amassed over two hundred patents. Among these patents was the triangular blade paint scraper, compound action cutting tools and the world famous Quickie Automatic Sponge Mop.

In 1939, Peter Vosbikian fulfilled another of his dreams by buying a large home in Cheltenham, a suburb near Philadelphia. The home housed his entire family, their spouses and children for many years. It also was a refuge – a haven – for Armenians in need of help and a place for endless celebrations with food, fun and music.

Peter's sons formed the famous "Vosbikian Band" which performed throughout America for two decades.

The family became a legend in its time!

ACKNOWLEDGMENTS

My deepest gratitude to those who helped make this book possible:
Ardashes Megerdichian
Stepan Hovnanian
Henry Morgenthau, US ambassador to Armenia during the genocide
Samantha Testa, for her brilliant research
Pamela Sisolak, my devoted assistant.

Finally, Bedros Vosbikian, who captivated me with the retelling of his extraordinary life which compelled me to write this book.

Made in the USA
Middletown, DE
13 October 2014